Praise for *Will to Wild*

"Drawing on anecdotes from thrill seeke~~rs~~ summited Kilimanjaro, Stanger weaves a b experience, and nuts and bolts tips. . . . Tho~~ught~~ing to break in their hiking boots will want to pick this up."

—*Publishers Weekly*

"A rollicking operating manual for navigating modern malaise."

—James Nestor, author of
Breath: The New Science of a Lost Art

"Whether your 'call to the wild' is a solo hike, a new hobby, a career change, or a radical overhaul of your whole life, *Will to Wild* will help you spot the signs, show you what is possible, and give you the confidence to take the first step."

—Melissa Urban, *New York Times* bestselling author of
The Book of Boundaries and cofounder/CEO of Whole30

"A priestess of adventure for our times, Shelby Stanger inspires us by curation, example, and her generous good sense. This book may very well change your life."

—Florence Williams, author of
The Nature Fix and *Heartbreak: A Personal and Scientific Journey*

"Shelby Stanger's signature optimism, curiosity, and joy shine brightly in this inspiringly adventurous book—a great trail map for inviting more wild into your life, or just taking the first step."

—Mary Turner, deputy editor at *Outside* magazine

"True story: I've written more books (5) than blurbs (4). I almost always refuse because, c'mon, when's the last time you read a blurb you actually believed? You can tell it's mostly friends blowing smoke for friends. That's why I only blurb if I read the entire book and believe the writer has something special to say and the chops to say it—and it's why *Will to Wild* just evened the score at five all. Shelby Stanger isn't a motivational speaker; she's a motivational *listener*. She's interviewed scores of people over the years who've cracked the code for turning their dreams into their day jobs, and she lays out her discoveries in a book that's beyond inspirational: it's instructional. Stanger digs into the tough how-tos, first by sharing stories of all kinds of everyday folks who've broken free and 'gone wild,' and then detailing how you can follow in their footsteps. She tells you how to finance your wild dream; why it may radically change your personal life and even romances; and what to do 'when it all goes haywire,' as she puts it, and you hit that 'Oh f—moment.' This is the first book that ever made me stop reading, walk out the door, and try one of Stanger's tips (singing in the face of anxiety). And guess what? It works. Shelby Stanger knows her stuff."

—Christopher McDougall, bestselling author of
Born to Run and reluctant blurber

"*Will to Wild* is just as captivating as informative for anyone who has ever dreamed of taking that leap outside their comfort zone. An intimate memoir written in a candid, playful, and illuminating style, you will feel compelled to search your will to wild. Had I known of this book, it would have saved me years of doubt and research. I'm so grateful it is available for you all to read!"

—Silvia Vasquez-Lavado, explorer and author of
In the Shadow of the Mountain

"The outdoors has a transformative power that all of us can tap into. Shelby Stanger has shared that as creator and host of REI Co-op's *Wild Ideas Worth Living* podcast, reaching millions of listeners and REI members. In *Will to Wild*, Shelby blends her own uplifting, personal stories with some amazing guest voices to show how the best version of ourselves is right outside."

—Eric Artz, REI Co-op president and CEO

"Beautiful, profoundly inspiring, and laugh-out-loud funny, *Will to Wild* feels like being on an awesome outdoor adventure with your best friends. After every chapter, you find yourself planning a new adventure."

—Jaimal Yogis, author of
The Fear Project and *Saltwater Buddha*

"*Will to Wild* is the ultimate guide for anyone looking to try something new and have more nature in their lives. Shelby makes it fun and relatable—skillfully weaving practical tips, effective advice, hilarious stories, inspiring examples, and heartfelt encouragement into a clear step-by-step format that will make you feel supported as you take the leap into whatever endeavor is calling you."

—Captain Liz Clark, author of
Swell: A Sailing Surfer's Journey of Awakening

WILL TO WILD

Adventures Great *and* Small *to* Change Your Life

WILD

SHELBY STANGER

SIMON ELEMENT

NEW YORK   LONDON   TORONTO   SYDNEY   NEW DELHI

SIMON ELEMENT

An Imprint of Simon & Schuster, LLC
1230 Avenue of the Americas
New York, NY 10020

First Simon Element paperback edition June 2024

SIMON ELEMENT is a trademark of Simon & Schuster, LLC

For information about special discounts for bulk purchases, please contact Simon & Schuster Special Sales at 1-866-506-1949 or business@simonandschuster.com.

Simon and Schuster: Celebrating 100 Years of Publishing in 2024

The Simon & Schuster Speakers Bureau can bring authors to your live event. For more information or to book an event, contact the Simon & Schuster Speakers Bureau at 1-866-248-3049 or visit our website at www.simonspeakers.com.

Interior design by Laura Levatino

Manufactured in the United States of America

Hand drawn camping icons by Mike McDonald
Vector mountain with texture by Julia Korchevska

10 9 8 7 6 5 4 3 2 1

Library of Congress Cataloging-in-Publication Data has been applied for.

ISBN 978-1-9821-9430-7
ISBN 978-1-9821-9433-8 (pbk)
ISBN 978-1-9821-9432-1 (ebook)

To all the listeners and guests of REI Co-op's *Wild Ideas Worth Living* podcast. Thank you for sharing with me, showing me what is possible, and how to make some of the wildest ideas I've heard a reality. Also to my team at REI Co-op, Puddle Creative, and to everyone who has worked with and on *Wild Ideas Worth Living*. Thank you for giving me a platform to explore the topic I've been most passionate about since I was a kid. Thank you to my friends and family for always supporting my own wild ideas. And to you, dear reader, for diving in.

Books are wild ideas. In writing this book, I presented these stories as accurately as I could. In one story, I've changed someone's name, but everything else has been written as it happened to the best of my memory. Enjoy!

CONTENTS

CONTENTS

WILL
TO
WILD

INTRODUCTION

A little adventure is life's antidote.

A re you gonna go?
It's April 9, 2009, and I'm twenty-nine years old. I'm sitting in the Pacific Ocean, legs straddling a six-foot surfboard at a picturesque surfing break called Rockpile in Laguna Beach, California. I'm hemming and hawing about finally taking off at the peak, the highest part of the wave, where it generates the most speed and provides the best ride. *What if I fall? What if I break my surfboard? Or my body? Or just embarrass myself?*

Rockpile is named that for a reason. To surf it requires perfectly angling your body and board to slip between a giant boulder plunked in the middle of the break where the waves break and a smaller, sharper cluster of rocks with a shallow reef in front of the wave nicknamed the Cheesegrater. Time it incorrectly, go the wrong way, and well, your skin is more than exfoliated. But time it and angle right, and the thrill is incredible.

With Rockpile conveniently located across the street from my small studio apartment, I've paddled out there several times. The few times I tried to catch a wave at the peak, I barely missed a slicing at the Cheesegrater. Since then, I've only tried to catch waves on the shoulder or in the middle section, which is easier—never at the peak, where the wave is biggest and the most powerful.

Rockpile breaks in a stunning covelike setting with a cliff above, lined with a manicured walking path. On sunny days, tourists and locals alike walk dogs, go for jogs, have picnics, and create paintings outside on easels while taking in the majestic scene. It's a natural amphitheater, and in my mind I am center stage in the water.

The rocky reef is home to an abundance of sea life. At low tide, through the water, it's easy to see colonies of mussels attached to the rocks as well as schools of bright orange Garibaldi fish swimming through holes in the reef. It's a place where one can't help but experience a moment of complete awe—a feeling I will later learn is integral to being absolutely present in the here and now, to evoking the sense of childlike wonder, to catalyzing growth, and to inviting change, which are all key conditions before deciding to make a leap.

Today at 6:32 a.m., I am alone; the beach and the ocean is mostly deserted.

Are you gonna go?

I do want to go. I want to catch a real wave at Rockpile at the peak. I want to experience riding in the sweet spot.

The problem: I'm scared.

Are you gonna go?

THE QUESTION doesn't just refer to the wave. It's goes much deeper. I am going to tell you a little story about myself before we get to others', so you know where I was, and why this book pertains to you.

At the time I am not just scared, I'm stuck. I'm at a job I no longer love, in a relationship that's over, and I feel like I've been swimming through thick seaweed; it looks so easy to swim through from the surface, but it's impossible to cut through such viscous weeds.

Are you gonna go?

It's a question I've been wrestling with for months, and will be asked again and again, whenever I need to make a change, to leap, to explore the unknown. It's a question that will end up informing my own Will to Wild.

What exactly do I mean by "Will to Wild"? It's the way I have come to think about how to live, especially when I'm scared or stuck, like I was that day. It's about the decision to say yes to a change or path that may be uncertain on the outside but feels more authentic on the inside. It's about dropping into a wave that might be scary, or perhaps even scarier, about dropping into a more intentional way of living. The will is living with intention. And the "Wild" refers to being in connection to both Mother Nature and your own true inner nature.

Ever since I was a kid, I have been fascinated by adventure and mesmerized by its profound effects. As an adult, I was always blown away by people who had embarked on a life-changing adventure, even women I taught to surf who shortly afterward started new careers, left dead-end relationships, or moved across the country to a place with a better beach. A little time in nature, with moments of awe, could propel them to massive change in their lives.

When you set out on an adventure—big or small—you learn so much more about yourself and develop courage that you can bring with you to the rest of your everyday life. What do I mean by "adventure"? It's usually outdoors, but more important, it involves some risk and some unknown, from a short surf session to a multiday hike. Adventures physically take you somewhere else—into the trees, the trails, the mountains, wind, waves— and take your mind into a different state.

That combination of nature and adventure always seems to have a synergistic effect. The times I have hiked up to a waterfall, gotten away from traffic and looked up at the night sky, or seen a whale in the wild—those are times that have helped me to slow down, get out of my head, connect to the world and to others around me, get present, and to show me how much more capable I really am. My journeys into the wild have cracked me open every time, helping me shed a version of myself that no longer served me. They have also helped me to be more loving to others—and mostly more loving to myself.

Studies have shown that being in nature and embarking on an adventure can have powerful effects on our mental states, lowering stress hormones, boosting mood, decreasing ruminating thoughts, helping us make better decisions, and reframing our outlook. Even a walk in a park can lower cortisol levels and allow us to experience the perspective-changing feeling of awe. Adventure does this for me every time. It's the same way so many people I've interviewed for my podcast have told me that hiking something like the Pacific Crest Trail and looking back to see how far they've walked from their previous campsite couldn't help but make them feel more badass. Do that enough times, over and over, walk enough miles, surf enough waves that previously scared you, spend enough time in trees or looking up at the stars, and you'll change your way of thinking too.

For me, an adventure becomes a wild idea when it scares the crap out of you, makes butterflies churn in your stomach, but you still pursue it and it ultimately changes your life in a positive way, leading to so much more. Wild ideas are the ones with no certain outcome that sound fun and exciting but still make the hair on your neck stand up. And wild ideas are self-perpetuating. One wild idea will lead to another and another.

For the last two decades, I've written stories about outdoor trailblazers and explorers for magazines, brands, websites, and newspapers. In 2016, I launched a podcast all about adventure called *Wild Ideas Worth Living*, which is now owned by REI Co-op Studios and that I still host. On the podcast, I interview people who have taken a wild idea, one that usually involves adventure, and accomplished it. I interview people who have bucked the system, taken the road less traveled, and made their wildest ideas a reality. I love hearing stories of people who choose curiosity over fear and adventure over being stuck. We talk about how to start and how to succeed. About grit and hustle. About fear and failure, and taking time to have some fun and smell the pine trees along the way.

Over the years, I've come to learn that wild ideas can come in a lot of shapes and sizes. But they usually start with a question that often keeps us up at night: *I wonder if I could I do X?*

Could a couple in Oregon quit everything to start a small organic farm? Could a Canadian marketing executive break the record for most vertical feet skied in a year? Could a conservatory-trained musician and teacher become a sponsored ultramarathon runner, even though she weighed 250 pounds? Could a couple in their fifties ski unsupported to the South Pole, even as one of them experienced some of the most uncomfortable symptoms of menopause? Could twenty-two-year-old twins paddle from Alaska to Mexico on oversized surfboards? Could a middle-aged commercial artist dabbling in sidewalk art accidentally amass over 3 million followers on TikTok? Could a surfer and aspiring photographer and food writer trade surf lessons for bread-baking lessons and become one of the best food photographers in the industry? Could a self-proclaimed soccer mom start guiding groups of non-experienced women to climb frozen waterfalls?

These are the kind of wild ideas that inspire me. And the thing about wild ideas is they often spread like wildfire.

I bet you have a wild idea of your own, or have a few you've pursued or accomplished. Or maybe you'll develop one while reading this book. Or perhaps, like me back in 2009, you just need a little boost to get going.

AT ROCKPILE THAT DAY, I felt like there was no will and no wild in my life. I had no idea that finally tapping into my will and pursuing a wild idea with no certain outcome would lead to so much more. I would eventually answer yes to that *Are you gonna go?* moment. And I would eventually take off and ride that wave at Rockpile, leading to many more waves in my life.

Don't get me wrong, saying yes and surfing one wave wasn't a quick fix; it didn't cure the depression I was feeling overnight, or land me where I am today. But it did help me start untangling the seaweed I felt I was struggling to swim through. It did start a chain reaction that gave me the courage to change a lot of things at once. It did give me focus, direction, and a desire to wake up and embrace the next day again with a huge sense of purpose.

The day I finally took off on the peak at Rockpile, I walked away from the trappings of professional success and began a life that felt a lot more uncertain but a lot more authentic. I learned firsthand that wild ideas, even ones as simple as taking one wave that scares you, can start a chain reaction.

There have been other wild ideas, before and after, but since that day at Rockpile I've been on a mission to share the stories of others who've heeded the call to wild, and to help others do the same.

Yes, there's the obvious stuff: I ended up catching the wave, and quitting my job. Then, I gave a healthy two months' notice since my work had been so good to me, and because part of living wildly is being a good person. After, I began life as a journalist covering adventure sports for outdoor magazines. That would lead me to where I am today.

But that makes it all sound so easy. There is so much more to setting out on a new path than just dropping in on a wave or starting a new career. It's not all puppy dogs and ice cream. I have plenty of scars to prove it.

I DECIDED TO WRITE *Will to Wild* because there have been times in my life when I've felt stuck and scared: afraid of being broke, afraid of being alone, afraid of falling flat on my face, and mostly afraid of pursuing my own wild ideas, notions that were scary to me, but that I knew would make me a better person. I also know firsthand that hearing stories of other people going for it has given me courage to go for it too.

Every time I've felt stuck, I wished I'd had a trail map of how to get unstuck, to take a wild idea and actually make it a reality. Often, the place between where I felt stuck and a singular wild idea that I thought could change my life, felt like a giant wilderness.

This book is a map of trails to that wilderness, an atlas of how to live differently. It's how any of us can get from desk to open ocean, from commuting in gridlock traffic to admiring a pregnant cow along a dirt road in New Zealand. From wondering *if* to *actually* summiting a mountain. This book is for anyone for whom the call to leap is getting louder and more intense. Anyone looking for the answer to *What would happen if I could do X? What do I do now?* So the question is, are you (yes, you) going to actually do the thing you want to do?

Will to Wild is the book I wish I'd had when I was scared to switch careers at the height of the recession in 2009. It's the book I wish I had later in Indonesia, paddling overhead waves as the only woman among ten guys on a boat trip. It's the book I wish I'd had when deciding to move to New Zealand with a guy I'd met only a few months prior while in Costa Rica. (Over a decade later, we're still together.) It's the book I wish I had when wanting to start a podcast with no technical recording skills and zero social media following.

In the pages that follow, I'll share some of my journey, as well as those of many others I've interviewed over the years—some famous worldwide, some known in smaller circles, and some you've never heard of.

Each chapter focuses on the steps to finding a wild idea and seeing it through. I'll share how I was completely and deeply stuck and how I got out. I'll talk about using "real-life" trail signs to discover the wild ideas you want to pursue. I'll talk about what to do when you have doubters, including the biggest doubter of all, the one in your own head.

This guidebook of sorts will show you how to make the leap even if it seems overwhelming and daunting or doesn't add up on paper. I'll cover the nuts and bolts of educating yourself in your new endeavor, and mapping your own trail, with deadlines so you don't turn back before you get to the starting line. I'll show examples of people who completed extreme adventures along with those who planned smaller ones that had just as big of an effect on them.

I'll talk about what happens when something goes wrong, which it will inevitably on almost every adventure. Lastly, I'll talk about finding the joy on the journey even when we fail, and then what to do when that journey is over, exploring together how to bring that sense of adventure to your everyday life.

That's part of what the Will to Wild is about. It's about that peace you get when you consciously choose to pursue your dream. It's also about the choice to physically go outside to change your perspective and decide to change your internal circumstances as well.

Interspersed throughout the chapters are a few pro tips to serve as helpful reminders and points of orientation for folks who may be reading through for the second or third time. And at the end of every chapter, there are additional tips, stories, and inspirational bits from myself and other adventurers I've interviewed to help get you going. Like any grand adventure, you get to take what you like and leave the rest.

BEFORE I GET TOO DEEP in the proverbial woods, though, let's get clear on what this book is not. This is not a book about how to quit your job or empty your bank account to have an adventure. We all have different circumstances and duties in life. However, there are likely many things you can do within a few miles' radius of your home that will connect you with nature, and many adventures that don't cost more than a park pass or take more than an afternoon. There are those adventures, of course, that require more planning, time, and investment, though this book is about showing what's possible no matter where you start.

Will to Wild is not just for the hard core either. Everyone has a different call to the wild. Maybe it's a desperate need to change a habit, to get healthier, to take the family on a grand adventure, or even to make a commitment to watch the sunrise or sunset a few times a week. One person's swim across the English Channel is another's first swim in a small lake. Another's hike along the Pacific Crest Trail is someone else's first time going to a national park. Maybe you're not going to paddle to Alaska or climb Mount Everest. That's okay—I'm not either. This book is about heeding your own call to the wild, whatever it may be.

In the following pages, you'll read stories from people of all different backgrounds and walks of life. Every person's story and wild idea is important. As Dr. Edith Eger, a Holocaust survivor you'll meet in chapter 3, says, we should never compare ourselves to one another or compare our suffering. We are all beautiful. "God doesn't make junk," she says. We have to celebrate one another, as every human is part of one human family. Comparison, as the saying goes, is the biggest thief of joy.

All wild ideas, however, do have one thing in common. They will scare you, and on your way to pursuing them you may try to turn back. But if you follow where they lead, life will never be the same. I hope if this book does anything, it inspires you to go after your wild ideas, to connect deeper to nature, and to say yes to your own version of *Are you gonna go?*

CHAPTER 1

GET UNSTUCK

**If you want to live a life you've never lived,
you have to do things you've never done.**

—Jen Sincero, *You Are a Badass*

Over the years, I've interviewed hundreds of entrepreneurs, travelers, and explorers, and I've been struck by a common refrain: a lot of them have told me that being stuck is what catapulted them to action. That's not to say you need to be stuck to choose to live wildly. But I've come to realize, the opposite of stuck is adventure. Adventure excites and invigorates, with forward momentum and action. You aren't stuck if you're moving.

On that day in 2009 at Rockpile, I am epically stuck. But first a fair warning that, yes, telling this story makes me cringe a little. At the time, my job is pretty sweet. I work in marketing at Vans, the iconic shoe company. I love my coworkers and the brand. It's the height of the 2008–09 recession. Quitting makes zero financial sense, and the job is the envy of many friends. Something else is tugging at me, though. I want to be a writer. It's been a dream for the last few years, but I am afraid to quit my job and go for it. Fear has kept me stuck.

I'm also in a relationship with a guy I've been dating for five years—a guy I don't see a future with, but I am scared to fully end things for good. Most significantly, I don't fully understand, or am willing to accept, that mental health issues run deep in my family. At the time, I believe that, as an athlete, I am different. I can "will" my depression away.

At first, I attempt to cure myself by exercising. I run in the hills above my Laguna Beach rental until I injure my foot and can no longer run. I swim in the open ocean until I hurt my shoulder. I go to a Buddhist monastery and sit in silence for a weekend, which is positive. My friends call me a hippie.

Decisions as simple as whether or not I should order fish on my tacos become impossible. I start getting short with people, bitchy. It feels like PMS on steroids. I am moody, morose, and beginning to feel apathetic. I busy myself by working harder, and trying to work out harder, which just makes me more tired and more depressed. After a few months, not even surfing sounds fun. I've lost my sense of spunk and humor. Even my desire to date is gone.

I know what I want to do, but I can't seem to do it: I want to quit my job and end my relationship. I want to make a change. I just don't know how. I feel like a spoiled millennial (and technically I'm a GenXer). I beat myself up more for not having the answer. The cycle is vicious.

I see one therapist after another. Four different doctors suggest I take antidepressants. I tell them all without hesitation no way. Medication feels like a quick fix to my symptoms, not the problem. To me, my problem feels more like a situation I just need to change. While today I believe medications can be, for many people, a lifesaving treatment, things were not as clear for me over a dozen years ago.

My feeling then was more like I had deferred a dream for too long. I'd dreamed of being an adventure journalist ever since I was a kid. Writing is what turned me on, starting when I was fifteen. In 1995, I won an essay contest and published my first story in the *San Diego Union-Tribune*. I worked as a youth reporter for *360 Degree Magazine*, a national publication for, by, and about youth. When I wrote an article about a family member's battle with addiction, other kids wrote in saying the story affected them. My soccer teammate shared the story with her boyfriend, who decided to get sober. I learned at a young age that words can travel far and that stories can impact change.

Journalism, in fact, is what brought me to Vans. I studied journalism in college, writing a local newspaper column about surfing and adventure sports one summer called "Breaking News," and spent another summer covering sports for the Cape Argus, South Africa, newspaper. I interned at CNN and spent six weeks after graduation backpacking through Fiji, Australia, and New Zealand. When I came home, I landed a job as the first female journalist on the infamous Vans Warped Tour in 2002, leaving on a tour bus the day I turned twenty-two.

THE VANS WARPED TOUR is the longest-running punk-rock music festival in the world. When I started in 2002, it traveled to sixty cities in two months, featuring as many as one hundred bands a day, as well as skateboarders, BMX riders, and a motley crew of performers, punk-rock personalities, and activists at every stop. At the time, the tour had a mostly male crew and the guys doing the interviewing weren't sure a girl could "hang." So I beefed up my résumé in my interview, claiming I had a tattoo on my backside, and that my favorite band was blink-182. I know, I'm cringing too. But I was twenty-one. Even then, the truth is, I preferred Bob Dylan over the Dead Kennedys. And I don't have any ink. But I wanted the job, and the Vans crew—who knew I was joking—laughed and gave it to me on the spot.

My job consisted of taking one hundred photos a day with an early digital Canon ELPH and writing two daily stories.

In 2002, sending those stories meant using a dial-up Internet connection, which meant needing a phone line, which meant needing to find a phone line. Vans Warped Tour concerts were held in fairgrounds and stadium parking lots, and the few makeshift offices with phones were occupied by tour staff, some with thick Mohawks who intimidated me. (I would learn later the guys with the scariest-looking tattoos and Mohawks were often the nicest; many had been through a lot.) I resorted to wandering the venue or even getting in the mosh pit to find a fan of driving age who looked the least likely to be an axe murderer. I would trade them free Vans shoes or a T-shirt for a ride to a Kinko's or, in some smaller cities, their parents' house. Then I had to get back to the tour bus before it left that evening.

After that, I bop around for a few years, writing about action sports for various outlets, and even host a small action sports TV show in a mountain town in Colorado. I eventually land back at Vans, where I am placed on the small international marketing and sales team that oversees all of Latin America, Canada, Asia, Australia, and New Zealand. I spend that time flying business class, going to dream locations with an amazing boss, and learning things I could never have paid to learn in business school. Most of my meetings in Latin America are in Spanish, which I love to practice, but spending days in malls and meetings begins to wear on me. (I also realize I don't exactly love wearing shoes at all. To this day, I still prefer wearing sandals or being barefoot.) And throughout this time, my desire to tell stories grows stronger. Most important, I feel like something is missing.

I love the Vans brand and I love the people who I work with. But at this point in my life, I'm not cut out for the structure of a corporate job. To help cope, every day on my drive home I call a friend and hear about how he's surfing a remote point break at lunch with no one else in the water. I'm happy for him, but I want to surf at 10:00 a.m. too, and not only at dusk or dawn or on weekends when it's crowded.

I make endless lists of pros and cons about quitting, checking my bank statements, asking friends and family if I should quit. They all tell me I'm crazy. I convince myself I should just suck it up and be grateful for what I have rather than chase a dream. I need to follow the plan. A plan that had been ingrained since childhood—go to a good school, get a great job, get married, have kids, and be happy.

I'm not happy. I start feeling more depressed. I try my best to hide my sadness at work, and I'm mostly successful. My parents call me and are concerned. I'm short with them, especially with my mom, and she knows something isn't right. I lose my spunk and my energy. I start to become apathetic about everything.

THIS ALL COMES to a head when one day my mom and stepdad, John, drive an hour and a half to Laguna Beach from my hometown in San Diego to "talk." I am annoyed, especially with my mom, a former university professor who organizes interventions for families with loved ones addicted to alcohol, drugs, and other substances for a living. I'm not using drugs. I am not even drinking. All I am doing is going to a lot of yoga classes, sleeping a lot more, and generally acting pretty moody and indecisive. As I am the youngest of five combined siblings—with two older sisters and two older stepbrothers—this intervention makes it feel like I will never stop being the baby of the family. Depression and addiction run deep in my family history, and fearing this might be my future too makes me even more depressed.

But the evening after their visit, John sends me an article about how it's not uncommon for women in their thirties, especially ones going through a change in their relationship or career, to experience depression. He includes another link, for a supplement called SAM-e, which could help my depression without serious side effects, a note that he knows might get my attention. That evening, I go to the local health-food co-op, where the guy in the supplement aisle agrees SAM-e might help, and tells me the recommended dose to take.

I take the dose, go to bed, and fall into a deep sleep, the deepest I have slept in weeks. I dream about going surfing. In my dream, I put on my wetsuit in the parking lot and walk across the asphalt to the water's edge. The whole time, I have to pee. I hold it in as I enter the ocean, but as soon as the frigid salt water gets to waist level, I let it go. The release is blissful. The urine warms my frozen legs.

Midstream, I catch myself. I place my hand to my now-soaked sheets. I cannot believe it. I start laughing out loud, a reaction I realize later is masking unease. I know subconsciously I need more help. I know that maybe I should try a therapist for more than one session. I resolve to take my mental health more seriously. But neither the intervention nor wetting the bed is a big enough sign to take the leap and make a real change in my own life right away.

I do, however, start to do the footwork to see if I can write full-time. That's something my mom taught me. "You have to suit up and then show up if you want to play in the game," she always says. I want to play on a different field, so even though I've been freelancing on the side for small magazines the entire time I have been at Vans, I decide to pitch stories to bigger, more mainstream publications than the small surf lifestyle pubs I've mostly been writing for.

Writing at night, after work, and on weekends, I pitch stories to *Outside* magazine about everyday adventurers paddling across the Pacific, surfing unknown waves, or defying gender roles. I spend time with some serious characters: moms who hop fences to skateboard abandoned pools, and lifeguards who, "just for fun," paddle thirty-two miles from Los Angeles to Catalina Island, run a marathon around the island, and then paddle back the next day. Researching these pitches, I feel alive, my soul on fire. I get the electric ping you feel when you find that thing you really want to do, and start doing it. But I am doing this on top of a full-time job with lots of travel, and am quickly becoming exhausted.

One weekend, I am visiting my parents at their house in San Diego, researching and interviewing for these story ideas I craft into pitches. My stepfather, John, overhears me on the phone. "Shelby, you sound alive!" he tells me after I hang up. It's true—talking to these people lifts my spirits. Taking action also makes the depression lift a little.

Outside passes on my ideas twenty different times, but on the twenty-first pitch I land a 120-word assignment—slightly bigger than the size of an average paragraph. "You have more hustle than any freelancer I've met," the editor tells me. I love hearing this, and even though I've felt the zing, and started to receive the signs, it's still not enough for me to truly listen and make the leap.

I am still checking my bank account, still making pro/con lists, and still debating on getting back together with my ex. I'm not ready to leap just yet. A week or two after I wet the bed, I'm stuck in traffic after a work event. A semitruck has jackknifed across all five lanes of freeway in Los Angeles. It's too far ahead to see it. Twisting overpasses and bridges block my view. Sitting there and feeling sorry for myself about wasting more time in traffic, wondering what I am doing with my life, which is consumed of so much traffic, I decide to call my ex-boyfriend, the one I'd broken up with five times. We talk for a few minutes and it is comforting to hear his voice, even though I know we should have ended things years ago. Just as we are about to make plans to see each other, my cell phone dies, saving me (and mostly him) from our getting back together yet again.

I sit in traffic for two hours more, not moving an inch. I am unwillingly forced to sit with my feelings. I've had episodes of anxiety and depression before, but this one feels different. I begin to cry, a big, ugly cry. I look to my left and right and above, embarrassed at what all the truck drivers next to me must be thinking. We're all stuck together moving nowhere. Literally. That's the moment the sign hits me dead on.

I finally realize I am epically stuck. Stuck on this highway. Stuck in my head. Stuck in my job. Stuck in an on-again, off-again relationship. I need to find another route forward. I can no longer rely on brute force, willpower, or denial.

In Dante's *Inferno*, Limbo is the first circle of Hell. The place between action and inaction. Of hemming and hawing. I've been in Limbo for months now.

Well after midnight, I make it home, go inside, and pass out. I am so exhausted from being sad, I feel like I am plastered onto my sheets. But when I wake, I hear crashing waves. Rockpile, which breaks best on a south swell, is on. My eyes still puffy from a night of crying, I get myself out of bed, walk outside, and check the waves. I walk back to get my surfboard, throw on a fresh coat of wax, pull on my wetsuit, and paddle out.

It's about 6:30 a.m. and there's a glow in the sky. Since it's so early, there are only three guys in the water, including a grumpy older local who always complains about how the neighborhood used to be covered in orange groves and cows. I get it—trees and cows would be so much nicer to look at than multimillion-dollar homes.

Still, it's gorgeous out. I look up at the pink hue from the sun rising, and then below through the glassy water where dozens of orange Garibaldi fish swim. The site is such a contrast to the twisting overpasses where I spent my last evening.

A set of waves comes, and the old grumpy guy turns his rusty red longboard toward shore, taking the first wave with ease. I hear him drop to the bottom of the wave, turn to the right, and whistle for himself. The second wave of the set is bigger, and I am next in position.

A gorgeous glassy wall of water comes toward me. This one is much bigger than the one before. I am scared, but I am also tired of being scared.

I spin my board around and paddle my heart out. As the wave lifts me up and propels me forward, I pop quickly to my feet, doing everything I can not to look at the Cheesegrater ahead and the sharp rocks below. Instead, I look where my board needs to go and feel a rush of endorphins as I zoom over the reef toward the deeper water to the right.

Just then, I hear a, "*Yeeeoowwww!*" Mr. Grumpy has seen the whole thing, and his cheers echo along the cliffs. He's seen me out there several times, and I've never heard him say anything even close to kind before now. His words scream exactly what I feel: pure elation.

What happens next is totally wild. I feel a huge shift in my mind and my body. No longer in Limbo, I've finally decided to drop in not only on that wave but also back into my life. I feel like I'm capable of taking responsibility for my own fate. In doing so, I feel a huge weight lift off my back.

On my paddle back to the lineup, I feel different. I see the Garibaldi below, who have become more vivid orange in color. The sky above is even more magnificent. Everything looks even more 3-D. I cheer on the other two guys who catch beautiful waves and wait my turn to catch another one.

I repeat twice more, each ride thrilling and the salt water transforming my puffy eyes. After two more zooming waves, I walk up the steps, standing a lot taller on my way up the cliff to my place. I decide I am sick of being scared and waiting on the shoulder. I am ready to make the leap. I finally read the signs.

> *ProTip:* Plan mini-adventures. If you have a window in the middle of the day, go on a hike, even if it's just thirty minutes. Get into nature where you can. Watch the sunrise or the sunset. Plan the heck out of your time off. Go camping after work. Take lessons from experts so you can fully enjoy wild moments without the hassle of having to plan them yourself. Try things like surf lessons, stand-up paddling, snorkeling, kayaking, rock climbing, et cetera. They're exhilarating and often cost less than a concert or a fancy dinner.

ON THE WAY TO WORK the next morning, I schedule an appointment with a therapist in San Diego, a woman I'd seen as a kid after my dad passed, and whom I really liked. She knows my story and I don't have to explain my past to her. She says she can get me in the next day. At my office, I work hard to check everything off my to-do list. On my way home, I get a call from one of the many publicists I've worked with over the years. I'd let her know I was thinking of quitting to write full-time, and to think of me if she had any great stories. She's calling to tell me that a journalist has backed out of a trip to cover a group of guys surfing remote waves off Indonesia. The surf trip will take place over ten days to waves accessible only by boat. Right now, the only people invited are men. I use the old Vans Warped Tour story to let her know I can hang with a bunch of dudes on a boat. She says she'll check with them and get back to me. I can't believe my luck.

The next morning, I drive all the way to San Diego and tell my childhood therapist what's going on: that I plan to quit my job, and that I might also be going to Indonesia to cover a group of guys surfing great waves.

I expect her to tell me what everyone else has, that I should just therapy my way to being happier with my current situation. That I should try an antidepressant. Instead, she validates my persistent feeling that I just need to change my circumstance.

"Next week? You know, Friday is the best day to quit a job," she tells me, with wide eyes and a huge grin.

"Friday? That's today!" My eyes bug out. I'm equally overwhelmed and elated.

"Take this," she says. She hands me a marble plaque with a picture of a staircase leading to nowhere etched into the marble. On it is a quote by Martin Luther King Jr.: "Faith is knowing when to take the first step, even if you don't see the whole staircase."

I wasn't raised with much religion, but this idea of relying on something greater than myself strikes something within me that it never has before. Having faith will become an important ingredient in the Will to Wild. I call my boss from the car and make an appointment for later that day. I listen to Tom Petty's "Free Fallin'" on max volume.

That afternoon, April 10, 2009, I walk into my boss's office, give my notice, and thank him for being so kind to me and teaching me so much over the years. I thank everyone at Vans for letting me work at such an incredible company. I promise my boss to stay on to get us through a big sales meeting and then give him at least two months to help train my replacement. First, however, I'm going to Indonesia, for the opportunity of a lifetime.

ProTip: If you do decide to quit your job, be a cool employee. Don't leave your employer high and dry. Give them plenty of notice. Train your replacement. Even if your employer is a total jerk, take the high road and leave on amazing terms. I am serious buddies with my friends at previous jobs and they have helped me in countless ways get new gigs over the years.

SOMETIMES IT'S EASY TO SEE that we are stuck. Other times it's harder. Feeling stuck can manifest as irritability, bitchiness, or flipping off some poor dude in traffic because you wanted to get somewhere five seconds faster and he accidentally cut you off. It can feel like apathy or boredom. It can feel like the urge to have another glass of wine (or two) after dinner or the desire to start a fight that takes you out of having to deal with your own life. It can manifest as rage. Rage at the current state of affairs, at how life is unfair, at a certain politician or person. It can manifest in spending way too much time on social media or screens. Or yelling at some poor customer service agent.

When you are stuck, there is always a *but* and a *should*. You can easily make an excuse for everything when stuck. For me it was I really wanted to be a writer, *but* I already had an amazing job and writing doesn't pay much. I had a boyfriend, but I didn't see a future with him. I *should* be following the corporate path, but I really wanted to do something else. For you it might mean, I want to study something else, but that won't guarantee me a good job. Or, I want to go on an adventure, but I am scared of taking time off or traveling alone. I want to do X, but I don't have the right funds, body, job, or whatever it is that you think you're lacking. Or it could be a *should*. I should stay in this relationship because it's safe even though it no longer brings me joy.

Trying to figure out what to do and not having answers creates a lot of anxiety. For me, too much anxiety turns into depression.

I hope you don't wet your bed as an adult like I did, but if you do, or you get in a fight, get a speeding ticket, get fired, find yourself on social media for way too long, find yourself imbibing one too many glasses of wine or another substance, or yell at some innocent person, stop and start to pay attention to the signs. I promise when the signs get too loud, too big, too in your face and uncomfortable, you won't be able to ignore them. And something I can't emphasize enough: if you do need help for mental health, please get help. That's the bravest first step you can take.

Maybe you are not stuck at all. Maybe life is just fine, but you want to have a little more wild in your life. Either way, if you are wondering what to do next, do what all hikers do when they are lost.

Start by stopping. Then look for the trail signs.

GETTING UNSTUCK

First check in with yourself, and honestly answer:

- Are you easily annoyed?
- Are you opinion shopping? Meaning you don't trust your own advice so keep asking others for theirs?
- Are you more bored than usual?
- Are you getting angry at causes, people, or events?
- Are you picking fights?
- Are you spending too much time on social media or screens?
- Are you drinking more?
- Do you feel frozen?
- Do you feel apathetic?
- Are you spinning?

If this is you, that's okay! It's okay to *not* be okay all the time. You are perfectly human, so don't confuse a temporary feeling for a permanent one. Here are a few things to try:

1. Stop beating yourself up. You might not realize it, but often when we are stuck we can be pretty mean to ourselves. Instead, give yourself love and approval for no reason at all except that you are alive and human. Try your best to also give love to everyone else.

2. For a moment, stop trying to figure things out. Doing so is like looking into an empty file cabinet for a file that's not there. Instead, just stop and be kind to yourself.

3. Take action to break the inertia. Go outside. Look at a tree, a mountain, or a body of water. Move your body. Cook a healthy meal with fresh organic ingredients. Drink more water. Get enough sleep. This is the obvious easy stuff, but if you are not eating well, sleeping well, or getting any exercise, everything else is harder.

4. Write out your values. Focus on making more decisions that align with your values and start saying no to things that don't.

5. Call a friend for a fun activity. Often just a get-together with someone you care about will get you back into the right frame of mind.

6. Unplug. Lessen your amount of screen time, social media, and TV.

7. Replace alcohol or negative substances with healthy alternatives. No one ever says they are grateful for having had another glass of wine when feeling low. Most people don't regret drinking more water either.

8. Do ten minutes of focused breathwork. Start with inhaling slowly through the nose for five

seconds and out slowly for five seconds. You can also try the 4–7–8 method. Inhale four seconds. Hold for seven seconds. Exhale eight seconds.

9. Try ten minutes of meditation. If ten is too much, start with five. There are plenty of free apps and videos to get you started. You can use a simple mantra. I usually say something I learned from Thích Nhat Hanh like, "Breathing in, I calm my body. Breathing out, I calm my mind." Or "Breathing in, I calm my body. Breathing out, I smile." Then I spend the rest of the time sending love to things, people, or situations that are bugging me.

10. Do ten or more minutes of body movement like yoga or Qigong or Tai Chi. Moving the body helps invigorate the mind.

11. Try an ice bath or a cold shower. I've interviewed Wim Hof, also known as the Iceman, who holds records for submerging himself under ice for long periods of time. I've taken plenty of cold showers and ice baths, and it's impossible for me to cry in freezing-cold water. Check it out yourself and try it (obviously do so safely).

12. Write down one hundred things you love about yourself and your life. This exercise is incredibly hard if you are epically stuck, but it will start shifting your mindset. If one hundred seems too daunting, start with twenty and add on throughout the week.

13. Start a gratitude jar. Even better, start dishing out appreciation to everyone around you. It will make them and you feel good and get you in a better frame of mind.

14. If you think you may be more than deeply stuck and might have a mental health problem, get help. Doing so is one of the bravest things you can do. You can start by finding a local therapist or mental health professional.

SHOULD I QUIT MY JOB?

Living wildly is awesome, but today you no longer have to quit your job to do so. Where there is Wi-Fi, there's a way. I meet plenty of people working remotely in the most exotic locations. Sometimes quitting can cause more stress than staying somewhere and starting your wild idea while you have stability. I tell people this: If you are so miserable in your job that your mental health is in jeopardy, then take appropriate action. However, if quitting puts your mental health in more jeopardy, then figure out a way to have more wild in your life until you are a little more ready to leap.

That being said, ask yourself this:

- Is my job making me miserable, and seriously affecting my mental health?
- Have I talked to my boss and HR about improving my situation but still do not see a solution?
- Do I have some savings, a plan, and have I started doing the footwork to find something else?
- Do I know or have some idea of what else I want to do? Am I prepared to do the work, or ask for help to do so?
- If I decide to go out on my own, am I okay potentially working harder than I ever did at my previous job, and taking responsibility for my own success and failures? There is no one else to blame when you work for yourself. You will likely work harder at first.

CHAPTER 2

LOOK FOR THE TRAIL SIGNS

When the path reveals itself, follow it.

—Cheryl Strayed, *Wild*

Skier Steph Jagger's sign was quite literal. She was on the chairlift at Whistler Mountain in British Columbia in 2009 when she saw it. Riding up to one of her final runs of the day, talking with her friends about how they used to ski so much more than they did now, Steph thought, *What if I could quit my job and ski every day, and not just on weekends, maybe even ski around the world?*

Steph then said it out loud. Her friends laughed—so she started laughing too—it was a joke, a story she told herself every time she went skiing, her absolute favorite pastime. A big day skiing left her exhausted yet euphoric. It connected her to herself and to nature. It was the activity that made her feel most alive.

At twenty-eight, Steph had a great career in public relations. She'd just bought a new condo in Vancouver. She couldn't just take off and go skiing around the globe. How irresponsible.

That's when she saw it. She was still on the chairlift. The sign stared her dead in the face:

RAISE RESTRAINING DEVICE.

The metal sign faced everyone on the chairlift, but that day Steph felt like she was the only one who really saw it. The sign pictured the device you have to lift up to get off the chairlift before you ski back down the mountain. It's the same device that prevents you from falling off the lift from a dangerous height. Today the words struck a chord. They burned into the back of Steph's head with a vengeance. RAISE RESTRAINING DEVICE. It went deeper than the illustrated stick figure reaching to lift a safety bar.

Steph loved skiing, she loved traveling, and she thought the whole experience could change her life—she was just afraid of making it happen. The message embedded within that sign went home with Steph. It followed her to work. And back home and to work again:

RESTRAINING DEVICE

Steph thought about all the restraining devices in her life. Some were a result of circumstance, like having to pay a mortgage. Some she imposed on herself, like rules she thought she *should* follow. First, there was her job, one she'd worked her entire twenties to attain. There was the condo she'd just bought. Then there were the stories she'd learned over time and decided were hers to keep: she was supposed to get a job, get married, buy a house, have babies, and, in short, be an adult. She was well on that path—why leave for another with zero guardrails?

The sign continued to burn in her mind over the next few days. And then it morphed. What would she do if she were to raise the restraining device on her entire life path? What if she decided to ski around the world, accumulating as many vertical feet as she could? The wild idea gave her the same euphoric feeling carving down a slope did.

And yes, there were other restraining devices that she thought of almost immediately. As a single woman, how could she travel safely? How could her legs handle that much elevation over that many days? How could she get the funds, the energy, the courage? Was she even that good at skiing? What if she left everything she'd worked so hard for behind, and then totally failed?

Steph wasn't a huge believer in mystical occurrences at the time. She wasn't religious or that spiritual. But over the next few weeks, she decided that her sign wasn't going anywhere. The feeling of pursuing her wild idea was so much more exciting than staying where she was.

If she were to listen to the sign and raise her own restraining device, it would mean leaving a solid career for the complete unknown. It would mean risking financial uncertainty, tapping into her savings, possibly refinancing her condo or selling it altogether. It would mean facing self-doubt, fear, and some of the most challenging vertical mountains across five continents. She'd have to leave a life of plans and controls for one without either.

It took some serious internal wrestling, but Steph eventually decided to listen to the sign. And when she did, she moved quickly. Over the next few months, Steph unraveled her well-laid plans and made new ones. She set a specific goal: she would ski 4 million vertical feet in a year, the equivalent of descending from the summit of Mount Everest to sea level about 137 times.

This wasn't the least expensive of dreams, but Steph felt euphoric just thinking about it, so she was willing to do whatever it took to make it happen. To finance it, she began pitching ski brands, asking for sponsorship money. Most said no. Rather than give up, she took out a line of credit against her mortgage and worked catering gigs and PR side hustles late at night until she'd saved enough.

In July of 2010, seventeen months after she'd seen her sign, Steph set off for the Andes Mountains in Chile. Over the next year, Steph skied just shy of 4.2 million vertical feet, unofficially breaking the world record for the most vertical feet skied in one year. Along the way, she encountered the most intense moments of joy and some serious roadblocks, like losing a ski in Japan in a whiteout at the top of a mountain she had to get down. It's pretty hard to ski down a mountain with one ski! Over the course of her journey, she slept in sixty-five beds, skied in forty-five resorts, took thirty-one flights, but miraculously only went through one pair of ski boots.

In the end, Guinness didn't recognize her accomplishment. (Apparently, there is a lot of paperwork and many tracking devices needed to get a mug shot next to the dude with the longest fingernails.) But so much else happened on that journey. More than could ever be awarded by Guinness. Steph's courage grew with every mountain, even the ones she had to suffer through with freezing whiteout conditions. The worst days ended up being some of the best for growth. Her quads also grew, and while she had been worried about her fitness, by the end of her adventure Steph was in the best shape of her life. She learned how to navigate last-minute cancellations and re-bookings and days when she wanted to give up. She grew in ways she never knew were possible, many of which she would not realize until years later.

In May 2011, when she finished the trip, Steph wasn't a totally different person. But she says the trip did make her a juicier version of who she already was. She learned not to underestimate herself. She also let go of expectations others had about her and began to live what felt like a life totally unrestrained by anyone's expectations but her own.

Having tasted that power of her own unrestrained life, Steph became a coach, helping people get out from under their own restraining devices. Because she no longer had to make herself fit into any certain box, her wild ideas kept expanding. The story of her journey was something she kept close for many years. She kept a journal, but the lessons from that trip took many years to fully form.

About six years after she set off for Chile, Steph went back to that journal and then worked for two years to craft her memoir *Unbound: A Story of Snow and Self-Discovery*, which was published in 2017. There were so many signs pointing her to write that book, and Steph said she finally listened. The biggest sign was that she couldn't stop wondering if she could do it. She poured her heart into her book and has become a huge believer in the magic of trail signs. And mostly of the magic that happens when you listen to them, and then when you pursue them, even if you are scared out of your mind.

"Signs are whispers from the universe," Steph says. "And they often come to you in a language that only you speak."

SIGNS ARE UNDENIABLY PERSONAL.

David Zinn's sign was just for him. On the surface, David is a fifty-something shy commercial artist with speckled gray hair and round glasses from Ann Arbor, Michigan. Although he now gives talks to giant crowds, and has lots of friends and followers, he considers himself an introvert. But over twenty years ago, David started making street art after following a sign that completely changed his career.

In 1985, when David was sixteen, he was walking home from high school, the same way he walked home every day in Ann Arbor, Michigan, when he noticed an image of Mickey Mouse painted onto the sidewalk. The Mickey looked like every Mickey Mouse in those days, except one thing: Mickey had no ears. Plenty of other folks would have just walked by and forgotten about it, but the earless Mickey struck a nerve with David that day.

That's odd, he wondered. *Who draws Mickey Mouse without mouse ears?* He couldn't shake it. A few nights later, David, who loved to draw, walked back to the same spot and noticed a streetlamp positioned behind the parking meter—casting a shadow of two perfect ears on either side of Mickey's face. "Genius!" The clever illustration seemed created for David's eyes only. He felt like he'd been let it on a secret, and was part of a special club. Its effects stayed with him.

Now, David wasn't the most sporty kid, but he loved the outdoors and he loved to draw. That's part of what made earless Mickey so alluring. As kids, David and his brother had "Doodle Battles." Each would take a blank piece of paper and scribble one line across it. Then they'd swap and the other would have to make a drawing of something from the one scribble line—a monster, a robot, an animal. The game kept David and his brother occupied for hours, no matter where they were. It was also helpful for David's creativity, as he was intimidated by entire sheets of blank paper. A blank canvas left him with way too many options of what to draw. A line gave him a starting point.

Flash forward many years later, David became a commercial artist, making drawings and signs for theater groups, nonprofits, and brands. It wasn't the most exciting job, but it paid the bills and he could still do what he was passionate about, which was to make art. In his thirties, David was still living in Michigan, where the weather is known for being erratic. One June day, he saw the sun poke its head out, and he thought it was such a shame to sit inside and work. He couldn't carry his drafting table outside, so he took some chalk instead, justifying it as practice for his profession.

That's when he saw another sign that tipped off everything: the sidewalk. Despite first appearances, it was not a blank canvas, but instead filled with cracks and crevices that created amazing shapes and textures in each square. For example, a certain set of weeds looked like the perfect moustache for a face. He took the chalk and drew around the moustache and made a face. Grates could make barbeques. An uneven line could be a tail for a flying pig. Manholes could become giant tables for imaginary monsters to dine on or even an oversized cookie. He felt a jolt of excitement run through him. When he broke his chalk, David realized he'd doubled his chalk supply. Even better!

David came back to his first chalk drawing two days later. A rainstorm had washed the whole thing away. Most people would be upset about having their artwork destroyed, but David chuckled to himself. He could create art, without too much pressure, for those who looked down to enjoy, just as he'd enjoyed that earless Mickey Mouse. Sometimes his work would wash away hours after its creation. That ephemeral quality freed David to create the kind of art he wanted.

David pursued his hobby every chance he could. For many years, drawing in chalk was just a side passion, one that turned into a side hustle without the hustle part, which is a great way to approach a wild idea. You get to test out the idea while keeping your day job.

David kept making sidewalk art. And people started noticing. Even though some people literally stepped on his art, completely oblivious to it, the people who did see it absolutely loved it. Companies and even cities from Laguna Beach to Taiwan commissioned him to create art on their streets. Then he started taking images with his cell phone and made short before-and-after videos of the creation of each piece of sidewalk art, and added them onto TikTok and other social media sites. In 2022, David released his first widely published book: *Chance Encounters*, which featured illustrations of David's temporary street art. The same year he amassed over 3 million followers on TikTok alone. Yeah, David is kind of like everyone's favorite uncle, but he's also a big deal! (Seriously, go check him out for yourself.)

It didn't happen overnight. But over about twenty-five years of practicing his wild idea—inspired simply by the joy of being outside and making whimsical art on sidewalks with chalk—he was able to turn his side hobby into his full-time career.

The best part for him? David gets people to look around, pay attention, and smile at outdoor art that one day will wash away. For all he knows, a David Zinn drawing may be a sign for someone else's wild idea one day, just as the earless Mickey led to his.

> ✴ *ProTip:* If you want to find a wild idea that also can turn into a job, take an online strengths finder test. You can use these as a starting-off point to find out activities you might like to do, and possibly get paid for. Taking one of these led me much later to starting the *Wild Ideas Worth Living* podcast in 2016.

SOMETIMES SIGNS can present themselves early in our lives, but we don't actually see them until we are ready.

In the early 2000s, twentysomethings Andrea and Taylor Bemis were living in Oregon. Andrea was working at a running store, and Taylor was working at Mount Bachelor as a ski coach and bartending at night. They loved being able to ski and run as much as they liked, but they were living paycheck to paycheck. They were happy, but not fulfilled.

Taylor had grown up on a sixty-acre organic farm in Massachusetts and had never thought he'd want to work on one himself. But the idea of farming began to percolate in his head. Every year, Taylor's dad over-nighted the couple a box of fresh organic blueberries from the farm. In 2008, the day after receiving a box, they busted out the blueberries on a hike. It's almost universally acknowledged by outdoorspeople that food just tastes better outside in nature after a long hike. These berries, hand-grown by Taylor's family, tasted extra special.

Andrea bit into the blueberries. She savored the sweet bursting taste and admired the smallness of the seeds. She looked out onto the beautiful vista, an endless array of pine trees, and then she looked at Taylor. "Maybe we should start a farm?" she said out loud. It was something she'd never wanted before, but like a burst of electricity it came bolting through her. Suddenly, the idea of working with their hands, growing something that could feed others, seemed like the perfect solution not only to living life on their own terms but also to being part of something bigger.

Taylor was shocked by the suggestion. Andrea had said exactly what he'd been thinking for some time. They packed up and temporarily relocated to his family farm on the East Coast, spending three years doing grueling hands-on labor to learn the trade for minimum wage. Farming was so much harder than they'd ever imagined. So many times, Andrea wanted to give up and go back to her old life in Bend. But farming was also so much more fulfilling than they ever could have dreamed.

The signs to keep going were pretty obvious: the feeling of contentment after a hard day's work; the incredible dinners Andrea cobbled together with all that fresh produce; the response from customers who were so appreciative of organic, nourishing food.

Three years later, they went back west, where in 2011 they leased a six-acre farm in Parkdale, Oregon. It was a financial stretch to even do that, but when it became possible to completely buy the farm outright the signs to keep going were pretty clear. The path ahead opened. Now that the farm was their own, the days were even longer and more labor-intensive. Nasty weather and pesky animals often destroyed crops, which was hard and sometimes heartbreaking. Imagine all that time spent planting, watering, nurturing, and cultivating vegetables only to have some deer run through or eat and trample them.

Andrea waitressed at night while Taylor bartended to pay the bills. It wasn't easy. Many times, the two could not believe they'd chosen this path. Farming was exhausting work, but they persevered. Every day, they woke up before the sun and tended to their land. They learned how to deal with freezes and wild weather. Surrounded by so many fresh ingredients, Andrea became an incredible chef and even better at taking photos of her dishes and teaching those farm recipes to others. Her work got noticed when she was contacted by a publisher and made a beautiful cookbook called *Dishing Up the Dirt*, inspired by the vegetables she and Taylor grew.

One of the biggest rewards from the farm was the sense of purpose they got from having to get out of bed before the sun rose, even though they knew the day ahead would be hard. Knowing they were feeding people with quality, wholesome ingredients was incredibly fulfilling. To celebrate each day, whoever woke first made sure to always brew a fresh pot of strong coffee for both to enjoy, and they would always celebrate with a beer when the day's work was done.

Over the years, Taylor and Andrea expanded their efforts. They grew the farm and cultivated a 130-person CSA community of fresh-food lovers who receive regular farm boxes from them. They also released a film about eating locally. Recently, they became parents to two adorable kids, which of course has only made them more exhausted but more fulfilled.

As the Bemises learned, signs for wild ideas come when the season is right. Sometimes those signs stay seeds until they germinate, grow, and burst with flavor, hitting you at the right time. Sometimes they come in the form of an event that happens sooner than we expect or a roadblock detouring us in a different direction. Sometimes a sign is a feeling that hits you like a jolt, and won't go away. Sometimes signs can even come from something we read or even something we dream.

> ✦ *ProTip:* Signs that show you what you don't want to pursue, as in the case of jobs or relationships, are often as important as signs that point you toward what you do want to pursue. Trust your gut!

PETE KOSTELNICK saw his sign in 2012. He was reading a book about a man who ran across America on his own two feet, and it made him so excited he thought he might throw up. If you ever have that kind of feeling, pay attention.

The book was *Running on Empty*, which told the story of Marshall Ulrich, an ultrarunner who ran from San Francisco to New York in 2008. Pete couldn't put it down; he kept rereading it, and every time he got the same serious butterflies.

Pete had only started running in 2009. He was a senior at Iowa State College, and one of his roommates, who happened to be very cute, was a runner. To get her attention, Pete laced up an old pair of running shoes and followed her out the door. It was hard at first, especially because Pete's college diet had consisted mainly of pizza and beer, but he kept going, because love can be a powerful motivator to do hard things. (Trust me, I once followed a guy to surf at 6:00 every morning. When he gave me a high five after I tried to hug him, I realized he wasn't that into me, but my surfing improved!)

Every day Pete ran, he also got better, and he loved the way he felt afterward.

Pete eventually married his crush, Nikki, and settled in Nebraska, where Pete worked as a financial analyst and Nikki as an engineer. Pete started running marathons, placing high in his age group. But he suffered a few injuries on the road.

Sometimes getting hurt can serve as a sign to help us change directions. A friend suggested Pete try ultrarunning, where races were longer but often on trails and more varied terrain—potentially easier on the joints than hard asphalt.

Pete fell in love with this niche sport and its community of those crazy and quirky enough to run such long distances. And he kept rereading *Running on Empty*. Every time, something new hit him like a dart.

Sometimes signs are emotions. Sometimes they are things we physically read or see. Pete's were both. The seed of an idea took hold: he felt a pull to run across the country, just like Marshall Ulrich, and maybe even break the longtime record for running across America, set by runner Frank Giannino Jr. in 1980. Even Ulrich, who had tried to break his record, came short.

Pete started with a small test. In 2013, a year after first reading about running across the country, Pete ran across his home state of Iowa. Those four hundred miles were tough, but Pete's friends crewed for him, and it felt like a road trip, with running, so it was also really fun. Experiencing success and joy while running across Iowa made running 3,067 miles across the USA seem even more possible.

It also gained him some recognition. Pete was virtually unknown in the running community, but the next year he was invited to participate in the infamous Badwater Ultramarathon. The race is epic. It begins in Badwater Basin, 282 feet below sea level in Death Valley, where temperatures can reach up to 130 degrees. The race finishes 135 miles later at the trailhead to Mount Whitney at 8,360 feet. The last stretch is entirely uphill, about 13 miles at altitude, which after running 122 miles is physically and psychologically demanding, and bordering on insane! Very few people even qualify, and fewer finish. To win it is almost impossible. But Marshall Ulrich, the author of Pete's favorite book, had won that race four times.

Pete was just twenty-six, a total newbie to ultramarathons. That year, race organizers had to skip Death Valley for permitting reasons, meaning the race was more mountainous. Pete had trained, and handled the hilly course, but had not mastered one of the most important skills of ultrarunning: training your stomach and body to handle eating while running such long distances. Pete fueled himself with bars and gels, but his stomach revolted and he started puking at mile sixty-five. He thought switching to real food, like a bowl of chili, might bring him back to life, but it didn't. Although nowhere near his peak, he still ended up in a respectable fourteenth place out of eighty-two finishers.

He was determined to do better. All through the next year, Pete ran about 150 miles a week, often doing 10 to 15 miles on a treadmill before and after work, 30 miles a day. Episodes of *Law & Order* got him through the longest treadmill runs. He focused a lot of his effort on also just trying to eat while he ran.

In 2015, Pete returned to Badwater. Temperatures soared to 120 degrees, and with pure grit and determination he took first place. Not only did he manage to hold his food down, but he also gave himself a heaping dose of courage to fully commit right then to running across America. He knew if he could win the hardest footrace in the United States he could probably run across the country. Ideally, Pete planned to train for a few years, save up money, and take a leave of absence from work before actually setting off on his wild idea.

But sometimes circumstances can propel our wild ideas faster. Sometimes we just need to say yes before we get scared and turn back. Shortly after Pete's first Badwater win, Nikki got a job offer in Missouri. So Pete decided to push up the start date for his wild idea to the next fall of 2016. "At the time, we didn't have kids," Pete told me. He figured it was as good of a time as ever to go for it. He could quit his job, run across the country, and then find a new job in Missouri.

In the summer of 2016, he entered the Badwater race and took first place again. That gave him an even bigger boost of confidence before setting out for his big cross-country run.

For Pete, listening to the signs came more easily because he never tried to hide or to resist them. He developed more courage every time he pursued one. He stayed open, and he kept his wild ideas at the forefront of his mind. And he listened to that inner feeling that made him light up.

Pete also got lucky. When he did tell his boss he was planning on quitting to run across the country, and that he was moving to a new state, Pete's boss thought it was such a cool thing to do, that he let Pete take seven weeks off and then work remotely at the same company after he finished.

That fall, Pete ran across America from San Francisco to New York in forty-two days, six hours, and thirty minutes, averaging about seventy-three miles a day and smashing Frank Giannino's thirty-six-year record by four days. In New York, at the end of Pete's run, Frank Giannino himself was there to greet Pete in person. The media had been calling Pete the Real-Life Forrest Gump. Pete went along with it, naming his support RV Jenny, after Forrest Gump's crush. Even Giannino wore a T-shirt when he greeted Pete that read: "Forrest Gump is Fiction."

The journey was, of course, really fun, but also grueling. Just a few days in, shin splints almost forced Pete to quit. His legs healed, and he kept going. He got lost more than once, ran the wrong way a few times, got rained on countless times, had nightmares that he lost his GPS trackers, which he needed to prove the distances he ran, and he had to find a way to eat 10,000 to 15,000 calories a day. He also met incredible people and learned so much about himself and what he could do. The experience changed his life.

Mostly, it proved to him, just as Steph proved to herself when she skied around the world, that he could do hard things, even when he wanted to give up. That he could plan complicated routes and deal with getting lost. That he could persevere, push through, and problem solve daily hiccups. And that he could break a long-standing world record.

Pete went back to work after his big run, but as wild ideas tend to do, his run across America sparked another wild idea. In the summer of 2018, Pete ran from Kenai, Alaska, to Key West, Florida, a journey of 5,384 miles. This time he ran unsupported, pushing all of his gear in a baby stroller. It was 2,000 miles longer than his run across America and much more complicated because he had to plan every day—from where to get food to where to sleep, while carrying all his gear and supplies.

It was a wild idea nobody had done before, but Pete wanted another adventure, something that would take him far outside his comfort zone. He also wanted to enjoy the scenery at a slower pace, especially since he wasn't trying to break a record. It took ninety-eight days to complete the 5,384 miles. The experience taught him it was okay to go slower to see more, and to appreciate the little things along the way. And also that wild ideas, ones that push you out of your comfort zone, always lead to growth.

As someone who has done so many wild ideas himself, Pete always encourages other people to pursue their own wild ideas as soon as they can. Sure, things come up, like pandemics or new jobs. But Pete says, "When we have wild ideas, they don't go away. We will try to put invisible walls on ourselves to get out of them, but it's better to do them as soon as you can. If you listen and follow the signs, there will always be a way."

Another thing Pete told me is that the more you let go of any limiting beliefs that say your wild ideas are impossible, the more obvious the signs to go after those wild ideas become. Once you have confidence in your wild ideas, the paths to pursue them tend to open up more easily.

SIGNS CAN BE IN YOUR FACE, as they were for Steph and David, or more subtle, as with the Bemises and Pete. They can start small and grow stronger as we lean into them. Or they can be awfully hard to find. We may feel constrained by our circumstances or by our own resistance. Usually this happens when the consequences of following the signs seem too hard, too daunting, and too uncomfortable—as they were for me when I ignored the signs to quit my job.

Resistance can show itself in ways unique to each of us. But one of those is the inability to see the obvious or making ourselves so distracted with drama that we ignore signs. Sometimes we are young and dumb and just say yes to signs and our ignorance leads us to a good decision. But when we are afraid of what might lie on the other side of our wild idea, we sometimes push the signs away. Other times, it takes someone or something else to force us to listen. There is a Buddhist saying: "When the student is ready, the teacher will appear."

That's how it often is with wild ideas. Sometimes a sign will appear as a person, an actual teacher, a book, a podcast episode, or even in a dream. But you only begin to see them when you are ready. This is why it's crucial to pay attention. Something may be speaking to you in a way that others don't get. The most important step is to put it out there, pay attention, and keep your eyes open.

It also helps to put down your devices, open the door, and get outside.

HOW TO FIND YOUR TRAIL SIGNS

We're frequently our own biggest obstacle when it comes to embracing and starting our Will to Wild. Sometimes you have to step back, get out of your own head, and give in to what the universe is showing you. Here are some tips to do that:

1. Recall the times you've had a surge of electricity shoot through your veins. Something that made you feel good, maybe scared, but at the same time made your heart sing. Now write that down.

2. If none of this resonates, then try asking the universe out loud for a trail sign to appear. Try to be specific as to how you want your sign to appear, but be open to the fact that it may come in a different form. For example, when I was debating working at Vans, I asked the universe to give me a sign. I was at a restaurant, and I looked down and saw the famous Vans side stripe on the waiter's shoes. I started seeing the side stripes everywhere after that, and I realized I should say yes to working there.

3. Be patient. Signs can take a while to appear. Start paying attention to things you see and hear, and also pay attention to roadblocks that come up. Is there anything that keeps repeating itself or

makes you feel a certain way? Is there anything that is really challenging and maybe suggesting you change direction? Is there anything suggesting you give up a bad habit or try a new path? (Like feeling moody, morose, or apathetic repeatedly?)

4. Read books. Listen to podcasts. Watch movies. Go to an art museum, or even better a park, and see if any of those activities start generating signs for you. When I first listened to Tim Ferriss's podcast, I was hooked. Not only were the conversations interesting, but I discovered that I loved the medium of podcasting. After listening to more shows, I wished Tim Ferriss interviewed more adventurers and more women, which helped give me the idea to start *Wild Ideas Worth Living*.

5. When you do see the sign, tune into how you feel. Even though it might seem like overkill, I recommend journaling your feelings if and when you can. Writing things down can really help bring clarity.

6. If you know following the sign will propel your life in a positive direction—even if you're scared—make the decision to follow it anyway.

CAN TRAIL SIGNS COME IN DREAMS?

from Davis Smith, founder and CEO of Cotopaxi

Davis Smith is an outdoor adventurer and mission-driven entrepreneur who founded Cotopaxi in 2014. Best known for their bright colors on backpacks and jackets, Cotopaxi is committed to minimizing their impact on the planet and maximizing the benefit for the people who live here. Davis spent his childhood in Latin America and, prior to starting the brand, launched several businesses, including an online marketplace for baby products in Brazil. That's where he came up with the idea to start Cotopaxi and the idea to use llamas as the mascot for the brand:

> When I was living in Brazil, I had a moment of inspiration one night as I was lying in bed. I had made a New Year's resolution in 2013 that I wanted to find a way to change somebody's life. It was May, and I was feeling a little discouraged that I hadn't found a way to use my life in a way to help others yet, which had been my dream since childhood. I had spent ten years of my life building businesses, but I hadn't figured out a way to merge my profession with my desire to help others. I was frustrated that I wasn't doing something more meaningful. As I was starting to fall asleep, I started having some ideas come to mind about how I might be able to blend my passion for entrepreneurship with my passion for doing good. I rolled over and started writing down the ideas in my phone, hoping that I could go back to sleep and come back to the ideas in the morning. The ideas kept coming,

and I eventually got out of bed and sat on my couch with my computer putting together this string of ideas! I sat out on the couch all night, the following day, and the next night. Over those thirty-six hours, a fully baked idea for Cotopaxi came together.

When that first idea came into my head, I was half-asleep, half-awake. While I had been feeling frustrated that my life hadn't been as fulfilling as I had hoped, I began to realize that my thirty-four years of experiences living in Latin America and building businesses were all needed for me to accomplish this ambitious new idea.

I'm a religious person, so I feel it was an inspired spiritual moment. I longed for, hoped for, and prayed for a way for me to know how I could help others throughout my life, and it all come together over a thirty-six-hour period. I took a very detailed journal those first few days, and it had incredible detail. I go back to those writings, and it's amazing how specific it was, and how in line what we're doing today is with that original vision. I knew the name of the brand; I knew I wanted a llama in the logo. Even our slogan, Gear for Good, was identified in those thirty-six hours.

SIGNS CAN BE SUBTLE

from Corina Newsome,
Co-organizer of Black Birders Week

Corina Newsome is a leading ornithologist and a co-organizer of the inaugural Black Birders Week, a series of events to increase and highlight the visibility of Black nature enthusiasts. It was seeing an everyday bird in a new light that led her to her dream career.

In my undergrad degree for zoo and wildlife biology at Malone University in Northeast Ohio, one of the required classes is ornithology. I had heard from older students that you had to memorize almost two hundred birds by sight and about seventy birds by sound. I didn't even know that there were two hundred birds in North America to learn, and I assumed they all looked and sounded the same.

So I get to the class just already expecting the worst, and before my professor even started talking about anything, there was just an energy from him about birds. It was weird to me. I was like, "Why are you so excited?" Because I'd had him for other classes, and he was never like this. Ornithology was his specialty, though. He gets to talking about birds, and he's introducing us to some of the more common species. He throws a blue jay up on the screen, and I yelled, "What is that?" And everybody looked at me in confusion. "A blue jay."

"That bird can't be out here," I responded.

Immediately after that class, I went outside and they were everywhere. And that's when I realized that simply not being taught about birds and not knowing they existed had shielded me from seeing all of this incredible diversity. I have been chasing birds ever since.

CHAPTER 3

HAVE A WHY

**Those who have a "why" to live,
can bear with almost any "how."**

—Viktor E. Frankl, *Man's Search for Meaning*

When you have a wild idea, it helps to go outside to clear your head, slow down, find creativity, experience awe, and get into flow. Being immersed in nature, away from screens and other distractions, will be good for clearing your mind. But no matter what the idea is, you are also going to have to go inside yourself to find your why. And this part can be a lot harder.

When I was debating quitting my job at Vans, I was full of fear and self-doubt. The whole losing my health insurance thing freaked me out the most. How would I pay for it? (Health insurance is still challenging for many of us.) I also wasn't sure if I could hack freelancing. What if I sucked at writing, or it just didn't pay? The bigger question was, what if I failed?

When I am scared, I tend to opinion shop; meaning that when I doubt my own opinion, I ask everyone around for theirs.

"Shelby, you have the dream job," my co-workers and friends told me.

I asked my sister, Felicia, who is four years older than I am, a total planner, and whom I have always looked up to, what she thought.

"You better not move home and live with Mom," was her first reaction. Felicia loves me immensely, but she thought I should do some adulting, which is fair. Plus, I valued her opinion. But I was finally realizing that I had been valuing other people's opinions above my own.

Other people are not always going to tell you what you want to hear. My family, co-workers, and friends just wanted me to be safe and secure. Felicia just wanted me not to go backward in life. She wanted me to continue on an upwards path. Wild ideas are not linear, though. Many times, we will go backwards to go forward. Sometimes trails zig and zag to get to the most epic vista.

When other people doubt you—which they likely will to keep you safe, or because they are scared themselves, or because they know you are doubting yourself, or for a host of reasons that in the end are none of your business—you have to tune out the doubters. Most of all, you have to tune out doubter number one: the one inside your head.

One of the best ways to do this is to have a why.

I wanted to quit because I wanted to try my own thing. I wanted to be able to say yes to gigs that kept coming up, like going to Indonesia on a surf trip. I wanted to tell stories of other people going for it, because doing so gave me a serious zing, and because, maybe selfishly, interviewing others who were going for it themselves pushed me to go after my own dreams. I also wanted to work on my own time schedule, even though I knew it meant working more hours and harder than I would ever work in my life. I wanted more time to work on my mental health. And I just really didn't want to commute in traffic to north Orange County ever again.

Finding my why took some time, and the crazy thing is, I figured out even more reasons behind my why *after* I jumped. As soon as I made the leap, I realized that I wanted to see what was on the other side of the life I had imagined. I was never going to be satisfied if I didn't test out my own *I wonder if I could* . . . feelings myself. After I figured out my why, a lot fewer people doubted me, mostly because I had stopped doubting myself. When things got hard, I would go back to my why over and over again. That's what's kept me going.

VIKTOR FRANKL was one of the first modern psychologists and philosophers to emphasize our need to find a powerful why—to develop meaning and purpose to keep going, especially when things get tough. The person who taught me this lesson was also a Holocaust survivor.

At ninety-one, Dr. Edith "Edie" Eger was the oldest guest and the biggest badass I'd had on my podcast. A psychologist for over fifty years, she wrote her first book, *The Choice*, at age ninety. During the pandemic, at ninety-three years old, she followed that up with *The Gift*. While the first book is more of a memoir, both books speak to the power to choose our thoughts and to transform negative events in our lives. Pain, Edie believes, can be transformed into purpose.

Edie's wild idea wasn't summiting a mountain or running across the country. It was at once a lot simpler and a lot harder than that. Her wild idea was to openly share her story of survival, how she endured the suffering of Auschwitz and the loss of her parents. Her why is that by telling her own story she can help others free themselves from what she calls the concentration camps in our own minds. The key to doing so, she says, is always in our pockets.

I first encountered Edie in 1993 when I was in eighth grade and she spoke at my school. Her energy was and still is infectious. Less than five feet tall and weighing less than one hundred pounds, she packs a powerful story. As a teen growing up in Hungary, Edie was a gifted dancer and gymnast. She always felt most alive while dancing. It's why she does a high kick at the end of every public speaking engagement.

In 1944, when she was sixteen, Edie was training to make the Hungarian Olympic gymnastics team. Those dreams were cut short, however, when she, her parents, and her sister Magda were forcefully taken in a wagon to Auschwitz. An estimated 1.1 million people died there, including Edie's parents, who were murdered in the gas chamber upon arrival. Edith and Magda survived. Their other sister, Klara, escaped the camps; she had been away at a music conservatory in Budapest and was hidden away by one of her teachers.

At Auschwitz, Edie witnessed countless horrors. At one point, she was forced to dance for Josef Mengele, the notorious Nazi SS physician known as the Angel of Death. He rewarded her with a loaf of bread that she shared with her fellow prisoners—an act of generosity that would later save her life when she herself grew too weak to walk and her fellow inmates helped her in return. Another time, she was placed in a line opposite her sister, a line that might have led to death. When the guard looked away, Edith quickly cartwheeled back into Magda's line. That act may have saved her then as well.

In Auschwitz, Edith found several whys to keep her going. One was that she simply wanted to be reunited with her boyfriend. She was a teenager, and first loves are always powerful. She also wanted to stay alive for Magda. And she wanted to find Klara again when they got out. Every day, even in those horrific circumstances, Edie tried to make the choice to be as positive as possible. Even in the worst possible scenario, she kept her biggest why in mind. She wanted to live.

Edie and Magda were rescued on May 4, 1945. A young American soldier noticed Edie's hand moving in a pile of dead bodies and miraculously pulled her out. Edie weighed about eighty pounds and had typhoid fever and a broken back.

Her journey back to health, then to the United States, and then back to school in her forties to earn a doctorate in psychology and become a therapist were all driven by a powerful why. Edie believes our minds are powerful and that we have to choose our thoughts carefully. "You have to want it bad," she says. And if you do, the how will be much easier.

Sometimes it's hard to find our why. Our motivations may seem trivial next to those of someone who survived Auschwitz. Other times, we may be blocking ourselves, caught up in our own stories and limiting beliefs. Sometimes we don't know why we're blocked, and other times we have to deal with trauma. And that in and of itself can take some time to process.

Edie told me a story about a wealthy client who was upset about the custom car she'd ordered. It had arrived in a different color yellow than she wanted. The woman was embarrassed to tell Dr. Eger the story. How could she be so vain as to care about the color of her car when Edie had dealt with so much more?

Edie knew the root of her patient's suffering was likely not about the color of the car. The woman had other issues going on at the time. "The difference," Edie told her patient, "is that I could see my enemy."

A lot of us have an invisible enemy that keeps us from experiencing joy or going after what we want. Many times, it's self-doubt. Sometimes it's fear. Sometimes it's imposter syndrome—the belief that no matter what you have accomplished, you are not worthy enough. Sometimes it's something you may have to work out with a therapist, a friend, or a lot of walks in nature.

The best way to break free is to have a why that's so strong, you find motivation for another day, even the days that are hard or mundane or just plain scary. Purpose is powerful. Your why is your purpose.

Edie lived through the most tragic and horrible events of our time, but in her nineties she has leaned into life's joys and humor. In fact, when we were together for the podcast, she shared another piece of wisdom with me—about the power of self-care and self-love. (Edie became a certified sexologist in 1992. Through all that, she learned so much about the beneficial qualities of sex. When we talked, she passed on the prescription that a good orgasm is the key to life and prevention of disease, making me blush in front of my partner.)

Her larger message was simply this: "Self-love is not self-ish."

Before you get all weird and wonder why I just went from talking about one of the worst events in world history to talking about orgasms in an adventure book, hear me out. Maybe your why right now is just that your wild idea will bring you joy. And maybe you think that's a selfish reason to pursue it. I'd argue that joy is a good enough why. Fun fuels action. If you want to do something just because it brings you joy, that is totally okay. That's not selfish. It's self-love! Get clear on your why, and then own it.

The desire to do something just because it feels good is a powerful motivator. Think about how motivated you are to do something for someone you love. Chances are you're pretty motivated.

Like Edie said, self-care is not selfish. Self-care, joy, and love are big enough whys to pursue your wild idea.

IN 2016, when I started the *Wild Ideas Worth Living* podcast, I'd been working as a business journalist in the outdoor industry. I wanted to own my own business, but I didn't want to start another clothing or shoe brand. I knew the media world well.

I also *love* interviewing people. I generally love people and hearing stories of how they created the life they have. I can talk to anyone. I have to thank my mom for passing on this trait. She talks to everyone: people at the gym, in checkout lines, you name it. The guys who bagged our groceries at the local supermarket used to come to my childhood birthday parties because we made friends with them. I genuinely love other people and tend to think everyone I meet has the most amazing story. The interviewing process of journalism is also the part I loved most.

But the tech aspect of podcasting admittedly intimidated me. I was nervous to host my first interview, and even more scared to release the first show. What would people think? What if they hated it? The thing that kept me from quitting was having a why. Then another why. Then an even more powerful why.

My first why was entirely for me. I wanted to make money on my terms, and I wanted to interview people who made me feel alive. I had met so many cool people through my own adventures and through journalism. I wanted to tell their stories. As I thought about who I wanted to reach, I came up with another why.

In my initial planning, there was one person I had in mind as my ideal listener: my friend Heather. We taught surfing together in 2011 in Costa Rica, when Heather was teaching at the University of California San Diego. At the time, she wanted to move to Costa Rica full-time. But with a master's degree and parents who worked as a doctor and a nurse, she thought it was irresponsible. The whole *what am I going to do about money?* thing was the trickiest. I saw a lot of myself in Heather, and it pained me to see her feel so stuck. I remember quitting my job at Vans and then getting offered the chance to go to Costa Rica to teach surfing, and thinking about how irresponsible and trite that sounded. I imagined my mother wondering why she helped support me through Emory only for me to go off and teach surf lessons. But doing something like that was part of why I quit my job in the first place. I would end up teaching fascinating people to surf, including an executive at NPR who told me that my idea for an adventure radio show was a great idea. (That's possibly the first time I got the idea for a podcast, even though I'd never heard the word "podcast" then.)

When I actually started *Wild Ideas Worth Living* in 2016, I thought of Heather sitting next to me in my recording studio, listening along as I interviewed guests. She messaged me after every show. She started to do some research on her own, and after a few months she landed a job in Costa Rica with an educational travel company. She now gets to work with teens (sharing the stoke with the next generation) and surf warm water waves all year long. The money part was indeed the hardest, but Heather says her paycheck goes three times as far in Costa Rica. She has paid back every single credit card bill and saved enough to buy a small patch of land.

My podcast likely had little to do with Heather's decision. She had her own why, but maybe listening in was a trail sign. She definitely influenced me, though. Thinking about her kept me going every time I got frustrated trying to find a sponsor, editing a long show, or figuring out how to use all the equipment. I was so pumped the day she told me she had found a gig in Costa Rica. Hearing the news only motivated me to try harder at podcasting and keep growing the show to reach more people.

Whys are powerful. They will get you to do the thing you want to do, no matter what. They will tune out the doubters outside. Most of all, they will shut down the naysayers inside your head. The ones telling you that you have no business surfing this break, taking up this sport, writing this book, starting this business, taking on this new hobby, running this trail, moving to a different place, or standing up for what you believe in.

> ⊀ *ProTip:* Keep yourself accountable and write down your why. Keep it on a piece of paper on your fridge or in the background of your phone so that you can look at it daily. If you can't ignore it, your why will start to become ingrained in your head and will keep you going when you want to quit.

IN THE MIDDLE of the COVID lockdown, I received an email from a random listener. Like all of us, Dave Sanderson had built up some serious wanderlust under the strain of the pandemic. He emailed me to tell me he had just hiked the Colorado Trail, a 486-mile backcountry trek from Denver to Durango, with his ten-year-old son. His email was so genuine and he sounded so excited, I had to email him back and find out more about their adventure.

What I learned is that sometimes a why can come from a crisis, like the pandemic. After two years of staring at our screens or being indoors, being lonely, or just working all the time from home, a lot of people, like Dave, have been motivated to do something wilder with their lives—to switch careers, move locations, take up new activities like baking, sewing, breathing, yoga, hiking, or in the case of Dave and his ten-year-old son, Porter, to set out on a grand adventure like the entire 486 miles of the Colorado Trail.

The idea didn't start so wild. Dave was a rowing coach at a university in South Florida. For all of 2020, his rowing meets and practices kept getting canceled and rearranged and Porter was spending all day indoors learning virtually in front of a screen. *This isn't a way to live*, Dave thought. Dave had been a Boy Scout growing up, but he hadn't been on a real backpacking trip in almost two decades, and Dave wanted to show Porter some serious mountains. Dave started Googling videos about the Colorado Trail. And take it from me, if you read or watch any story about anyone thru-hiking almost any trail, you are bound to get inspired. The Colorado Trail is exceptionally stunning, with wildflowers, stunning views, and thirteen-thousand-foot peaks. The idea to take Porter to Colorado for just a few days of hiking started to grow.

What if, Dave wondered, *Porter and I could hike the whole 486.4 miles of it?* His wife, Taber, was skeptical at first. That was a long time to be away. And they'd have to average 13.6 miles a day, which is no joke for anyone, let alone a ten-year-old.

They didn't actually all agree to the idea until almost a year later in February of 2021. But once they did, Dave says it was "game on!" Dave took Porter to the local parking garage, where they ran stairs regularly, and completed longer hikes near home. When the weather wasn't great, they trained in parking garages and in stairwells after work and school, racking up over five hundred miles before they even drove to Colorado. Dave's wife, Taber, also joined in. For Porter, the training was extra fun, because he would have done anything to have some time away from virtual school. His why was pretty easy. All that training also made him that much more focused while he was doing online learning, and he aced e-learning. When they were not physically training, Dave and Porter also tested shoes, socks, shorts, and food. They planned and packed food resupply boxes and sent them ahead to stations where they could collect them on the trail.

Dave cashed in all his vacation days and told work they probably wouldn't be able to reach him. Taber hugged her son and husband, and on June 16, 2021, they left for Colorado.

They spent a few weeks acclimating to altitude, and then hit the actual trail on July 3 in Waterton Canyon, just southwest of Denver. They averaged about 13 miles a day, with a few rest days in between. Forty-two days later, on August 13, they finished in Durango, in the southwest corner of the state. Dave said the experience changed their lives. For one, it redirected their attention away from the pandemic. "When the idea was cemented and the training began, we very simply had something to look forward to and to work towards, not just waiting around for the pandemic to end," he said. He also said the adventure far overshadows the days stuck at home, inside, in front of screens all day. "We remember the training, the planning, the anticipation, and of course the doing. We talk about this trip a million times more than virtual school or Zoom meetings." Dave also ended up changing careers, deciding to work closer to home as a dockmaster for the water program at his son's school where his wife already worked. He could now have more time with family still doing what he loved.

Dave specifically learned on the trail that things in life can be simple, really simple. "An extremely rewarding and satisfying existence consisted of walking, eating, sleeping, and literally living in the moment with very little stuff," he said. "Of course 'real' life isn't quite *that* simple, but it shows you can simplify and edit life and be pretty darn happy." He also realized he could do hard things, which gave him a newfound sense of confidence and made the doing part sweeter than even finishing.

Taber, who'd never spent that much time alone without her husband and son, said she learned most of all to trust them both, and that she could let go. "On trips with the three of us, I tended to coddle Porter," Taber said. "I loved the idea of Porter testing his boundaries and not hearing me warn 'be careful!' or 'watch out!' (Though this was an extreme exercise!) I also learned to never underestimate the determination of a ten-year-old and gained respect for Dave's mad camping and planning skills."

Porter went back to fifth grade with a heap of confidence and the best *How I spent my summer* story for his classmates. But most of all, Porter said, "I can do something hard. And when you do enough hard things they start not to be as hard anymore." He could see himself get stronger in real time day after day, and he also learned to be resilient and persistent, even if he couldn't totally define that for himself yet. He learned a vital lesson that he can take with him through life as he grows.

"I'm proud of my son and myself," Dave says. "I've had to be an 'embrace and enjoy the process' person most of my life in athletics, but this was the sweetest process ever. While crossing the finish line, it was immediately evident this adventure was entirely about what it took from both of us to get to the line, not actually crossing it."

Not wanting life to suck is a huge motivator. Kids and family are also massive motivators. But one of the biggest motivators and whys I've seen that keeps people pursuing and succeeding at wild ideas is the desire to help other people. At its heart, Dave was motivated by his care for another person, for his son, Porter. Taber was too. When you expand that care and take it out into the world on a wider level, it makes for one of the most powerful whys of all: altruism.

ALTRUISM IS A POWERFUL motivator to do something you thought you could never do before. Think about all the people who run marathons or bike long distances to raise money for disease research or to help others in need.

Singer-songwriter Ryan Kinder, whose first album, *Room to Dream*, came out in 2021, was motivated in a similar fashion. Ryan would have never considered entering a 444-mile bike ride, especially having never ridden with clip-in pedals, worn padded bike shorts, or really biked at all if not for his friend Kyle Wagley.

Kyle met Ryan because their wives were both cheerleaders for the Nashville Titans, and they became good friends through the women. Kyle was an active-duty US Army Chief Warrant Officer and loved cycling. He was always telling Ryan about his crazy-long bike rides, including the Tour de Natchez Trace—a 444-mile ride over four days along the historic route from Nashville, Tennessee, to Natchez, Mississippi. The ride helped raise money for military veterans and their families. A cancer survivor, Kyle was an incredible cyclist who completed the ride every year, but then his cancer came back in 2016 and Kyle became too sick to even enter. When visiting Kyle in the hospital, Ryan told his good friend Kyle right there, "I'm gonna do it for you. You're going to beat this [cancer], but I'm going to do the ride this year for you."

Kyle was well enough to laugh at Ryan. He knew Ryan was a good-looking, smooth-talking musician who had never ridden a bike for even a quarter of the time he'd have to ride for one day of this four-day trek.

Unfortunately, Kyle passed away about two months after that conversation. Ryan had not trained and had no knowledge about technique or nutrition when it came to endurance cycling, but he entered the race that year with Kyle's wife, Stormi. They would honor the man they loved and also raise money for veterans and cancer.

The ride hurt. Ryan took Advil to mitigate the pain. But along the way he had great conversations with Kyle's buddies, who had also joined in to support and honor their friend. One of those buddies had a weird-looking bike used for triathlons, a time trial bike, and Ryan started asking him about it. That conversation propelled Ryan to try his first half IRONMAN Triathlon only six months later, the Haines City 70.3. It took Ryan forever to complete it, but he realized something important along the way that would change his life. Ryan learned he actually liked all that training and especially all that time being outside. He also loved being motivated for something greater: honoring his friend and helping others fighting a life-threatening illness.

A year after that, Ryan connected with the IRONMAN Foundation. He learned he could not only keep doing longer distances and eventually complete a full IRONMAN, but he could also raise money for many causes by competing. This included raising money for a nonprofit he had started with his wife, Heather, in 2014 called Kinder's Kids, which benefits families affected by natural disasters. The non-profit was inspired by Ryan's own experience, when a tornado hit Tuscaloosa in 2011, where he and Heather were attending the University of Alabama. Once the tornado passed, Ryan ran out and started helping others. He remembers seeing a family standing on the slab of what used to be their house. It was just a foundation. But one image stuck out. A child was clutching a teddy bear. Everything else around had been destroyed. That stuck with Ryan. He couldn't imagine himself in the same kid's situation or in his father's shoes.

"It took a few years to figure out why I wanted to do what we're doing now, but that image stays with me to this day," says Ryan.

IRONMAN has completely changed Ryan's life. He used to wake up at 7:30 a.m. and write songs; now he gets up at 4:00 a.m. to train before the day starts. He still hates waking up early, but, he says, "that's what it takes to do something you really love. There's got to be a why. And once you have that why, you'll find the how. The how for that portion of it for me was getting up at four a.m." The why is doing it for other people. During every training run, swim, or bike, especially one that's extra difficult, Ryan thinks of Kyle, and of everyone else battling cancer, and of kids affected by natural disasters. He knows that pushing through pain is helping raise money for others. It keeps him going even when he wants to quit. These two whys keep him moving when the going gets tough.

"If there's no reason, then there's no drive, there's no discipline, there's no heart in it," he says. "There's got to be a purpose for everything you do. I mean, you do what you do because you love doing it. For the why of IRONMAN, the beginning of it was Kyle. Then, while still keeping the memory of Kyle alive and honoring him, my why became because IRONMAN bettered my life and time management and most of all my ability to understand that I'm getting so much more out of this than I thought I ever would. There's a sense of accomplishment; there's a sense of giving back. It's a bigger purpose that helped me get to the finish line in more ways than one."

Ryan completed his first full IRONMAN in November of 2019 in Panama City, and raced in Kona a year later. For Ryan, IRONMAN began as a way to honor his friend, and this greater purpose gave him the motivation to learn the sport. Once he realized that IRONMAN was going to be an ongoing part of his life, he decided to build on this purpose and do good for his community, just as Kyle had.

While we may have one why when we start new projects, we often find other whys to keep going. I think this is true with so many things that we grow to love. IRONMAN has opened up a lot of opportunities for Ryan personally. It's changed his lifestyle, but it's also created an avenue for him to give back to so many causes. As I finished typing this sentence, Ryan emailed to share that someone had made a short movie about him and his efforts.

Many guests on *Wild Ideas Worth Living*, never mind in the greater community, have started movements or nonprofits for what they believe in, whether it's climate change awareness, ocean protection, or greater representation for people who belong to LGBTQ+ and BIPOC communities. Doing something for a cause greater than ourselves is a great way to get us to do something we didn't think possible. Helping others also feels damn good. And it's true: you always get more from giving than you ever get from getting.

PERHAPS ONE OF the most powerful whys of all is the knowledge that life is short. Edie Eger, my friend Heather, Ryan Kinder, Dave Sanderson—all of their whys come back to that one basic truth. When I think about it now, that was the root of my own whys—both for quitting my job and for starting the podcast that would turn into a career. I learned that life is short at a very young age.

In 1992, I was eleven years old and my dad was forty-seven. We'd spent a beautiful Easter weekend together. That Monday, Dad complained of a stomachache. For some reason, I didn't do my homework; I hung out with him instead. We hooked up an early surround sound system to the TV and watched the Freddie Mercury Tribute Concert, a star-packed benefit for AIDS, which had killed Mercury the year before. To this day, when I hear any Queen song I think of my father.

My dad was never sick. He was a dentist, and he rode his bike miles on the weekends. A New Yorker by birth and culture, he did not understand surfing. But that Monday, he agreed to take me boogie boarding that next weekend at the local beach in Cardiff-by-the-Sea. That Monday evening, my mom was teaching a late class at San Diego State University. My father tucked me in.

"Good night. I love you," he said, and kissed my forehead. He went to my sister Felicia's room and told her he was picking up a prescription for his stomachache at the hospital. He'd be right back.

When my mom came home, she had a feeling something wasn't

right. Instinct forced her to get in her car at 10:30 p.m. and drive after him. She saw my father's car on the side of I-5, crashed into the center divider in Encinitas a few miles from our house. The police drove her to the hospital.

My sister shook me to wake me up. "Dad's been in a car accident. Get dressed! We gotta go to the hospital." I remember crying the whole time in the car on the way to the hospital, feeling terribly sorry for myself that I'd lost my dad at age eleven. But I also felt that I was just preparing for the worst but that the worst would never happen. That when I arrived, my dad would still be alive.

"Is he dead? Is he dead?" I screamed when we finally pulled up to the emergency room. I was still posturing. I imagined Dad in a cast, his leg pulled up by ropes, like in the movies. He'd be eating Jell-O in a Coogi sweater, his uniform when not in a dental coat, and charming the nurses.

My mom's face was ghostly white. She looked at us and nodded her head vertically, grabbing us into a giant sobbing hug. I never saw my father again. He had died of a heart attack in his car. He loved cars, and he crashed when his heart stopped pumping blood.

For me, the shock was sudden. My dad was here one day, gone the next, and now we had to have a funeral and bury him. It all seemed like a mean joke. He had so much more to see and do—watch me graduate from sixth grade, see my middle sister graduate from high school. All of us would go on to fall in love, get married or find significant others, have kids, and start businesses. He missed all of it.

This hit without a warning. My dad had no will, no life insurance. Nothing. Things changed dramatically at home, as he had been our family's main source of income. My mom was a teacher. And the three years before she met my stepdad, John, were beyond difficult for her, and all of us.

But the suddenness of my dad's death ingrained something new in me. I always tried to fit as much as possible into a day. I was that annoying kid in junior high egging on my friends to ask out the kid they liked, because life was short. "What if you die tomorrow?" I used to tell them. For much of my life, I never experienced being bored—which, looking back, was a bit of a fault. I was so scared I was going to die, I wanted to do as much as possible every day, and joined enough activities and played on enough sports teams to fill my entire days. I loved being busy and having a full life, but it would have benefited me to learn to use an off switch. I definitely needed to learn to chill, something I finally started to learn years later through surfing, yoga, and just spending more time in nature.

But even still, an older mentor told me in my twenties that if he had to do life over he would have played more in his twenties and thirties. When you retire, he said, you can't always do as much as you did when you were young. So you should retire when you are young and work when you are old. I am not sure that's the greatest advice for today's economic climate, but I do believe you have to take advantage of the juice you have in you, at whatever age you are.

KNOWING LIFE WAS SHORT helped me change when I was twenty-nine. I wasn't doing what I wanted to do. I was also super privileged and lucky, with money in my savings account, a healthy body and mind, no kids, and no real duties except to look after myself. But I wanted to become someone I was proud of. I wanted to experience things that filled my soul. And I wanted to be able to help others in a bigger way.

Yes, eventually I would have to learn to also enjoy stillness and not being busy. That would come much later. But the knowledge that life is uncertain is still a huge motivator. As I am writing this, I have just lost two friends in their forties to cancer in a two-week span. You never know what life will bring.

That uncertainty inherent in life might be your why. Your why may also change over time, which is healthy. My why in hosting a podcast now is because it brings me so much joy, I can't imagine doing anything else. For you, maybe you just want to do something because it brings you joy too. Maybe you have an illness, maybe you have something hindering you, and you just want to do what you can with what you have now, because you want to live as much as possible.

We all have our own whys to find our Will to Wild. Sometimes they will be motivated by joy, by our health, by the knowledge that life is short, or by something else entirely. Wild ideas may not make sense on paper.

And if you pursue them, you will not be guaranteed success. But you will be guaranteed an adventure. And sometimes in the middle of that adventure, something else great will happen, even if you fail.

One thing to remember is that you always have a choice. Like Edie says, the prison is often in our minds and the key is in our pockets.

HOW TO FIND YOUR WHY

My best childhood friend, Lisa Shields, an executive life coach, says our why is our "soul fuel," the thing that will get us to climb mountains, survive tradgedies, and complete our wildest ideas. Our why is also our compass that will bring us home when we get lost and keep us going when we come up against obstacles. Sometimes we get caught up in other people's whys (unsaid expectations, advice, opinions, rules) and that stops us from doing what we want to do. But when we connect with our own whys, we can focus, let go of the stuff that doesn't matter, and can pursue our wildest ideas with joy. Here are a few questions I've used, and many that Lisa uses with clients and friends who are looking to find their own why:

- What are things that make you scared but excited at the same time?
- What makes you forget to eat?
- What is it that brings you immense joy, that makes you forget about time and gets you into flow, that you can keep doing for hours?
- What type of advice do people come to you for?
- What is something you can do to help someone else?
- What is something you would like to teach?
- What is the legacy you want to leave behind?
- What difference do you want to make in other people's lives?

- Where is there pain that you can ease?
- What is something you have an innate talent for or knowledge in?
- What is something you would do even if you didn't get paid to do it?
- What would you do if you won the lottery and had one year to spend the money?
- If you could give a TED Talk on anything, what would it be?
- If you were a guest on *Wild Ideas Worth Living*, what would be your wild idea?

MORE JOMO, LESS FOMO

Your why is your why—own it. It's easy to look at other people's whys and be influenced by them. We all see people online whose lives look incredible, but we also know that, as Edith showed us, comparison is the biggest thief of joy.

Early on, when I started the *Wild Ideas Worth Living* podcast, I had a listener write me and share that every podcast he listened to made him feel crappy about his life. Then, one day listening to an episode about ultramarathon runner Scott Jurek running the Appalachian Trail, the listener went for a six-mile run and decided to extend his run to fifteen miles, the longest distance he'd run in his life by nine miles. He wrote me afterward and said he used to think wild ideas were about listening to your every whim and desire. Then he realized they were about living with intention and choosing consciously to adventure in a way that made you feel more alive. This book's goal is to help you bring your own Will to Wild alive and to let go of FOMO. Instead, have more JOMO (joy of missing out) and commit to doing more things that bring you joy.

CHAPTER 4

FIND COURAGE, FLOW & AWE WHEN YOU GET OUTSIDE

Look deep into nature, and then you will understand everything better.

—Albert Einstein

When I first fell in love with adventure, I wasn't looking for a trail sign. But I remember the moment vividly. I was twelve years old, at my first overnight camping experience at an old Boy Scout camp on the beach in Coronado, San Diego County. When we arrived, the sun was setting, and we surfed into the dark, skipping a shower. It left me with a salty body and crusty hair. We snacked on some pizza straight out of the box, and then roasted marshmallows over a fire to make s'mores. I can still taste the gooeyness of the chocolate and the burnt crisp of marshmallows in my mouth. To this day, I will eat s'mores anytime someone makes them.

I slept inside my sleeping bag on the sand, without a tent, underneath the stars, and fell asleep to the sound of crashing waves. It wasn't that wild in retrospect, but it felt wild to me. My family wasn't outdoorsy, so we had never gone camping, and here I was, staying outside overnight while at a water sports camp with other kids my age. Our instructors were college students from nearby universities, more like cool older siblings than babysitters. I remember waking up with sand in my hair and excitement in my bones, feeling sheer contentment. Sleeping on a soft sandy beach is like sleeping on a plush mattress. There was something so soothing about being lulled to sleep by crashing waves. Looking up at the stars, I felt small, but at the same time, connected to all the other kids and counselors around me. When I woke, the nice kid who'd been sleeping next to me told me that I smiled the whole time I slept. He thought that was so "weird and cool."

Camping on that beach was a different feeling than I'd experienced indoors or even on soccer fields, where I'd been a competitive player from a young age and where everything is organized with rules and lines. Sleeping outside on the beach, I felt excited and a little scared, but also invigorated and content, like I was meant to be doing exactly what I was doing. I've hung on to that feeling ever since.

Looking back, that feeling was a sign to go outside as often as possible. I love the unpredictability of nature, but also how welcoming and good nature feels. Over the years, nature has not only helped me process emotions and taken me out of my head but also taught me lessons and given me more courage than I have ever found indoors. Nature has also given me the best, wildest ideas.

CHANCES ARE, if you are reading this book, you know nature is good for you. Nature is incredibly healing. It's where most of our actual medicines originate. It's great for our bodies, and it's great for our brains.

Physically, I have never been in better shape than while living in the rain forests in Latin America, eating coconuts off trees and indulging in all the fresh produce that grows everywhere. A fresh mango from the store never tastes as good as one handpicked off a tree in the wild. Whenever I am in Costa Rica for a few weeks, I can see and smell better, and my taste buds always seem to be more distinct. Being on the constant lookout for birds and sloths in trees helps hone my distance vision. Being surrounded by monkey howls tunes up my hearing.

Mentally, nature heals because it is so grounding—taking us away from the things that cause us stress. More and more studies are proving that nature can help us stop being such Negative Nellies. One study showed that being in nature for as little as twenty minutes a day helped lower stress hormone levels.[1]

Another 2015 Stanford study demonstrated that people who walked for ninety minutes in a natural area, as opposed to participants who walked in a high-traffic urban setting, showed a decrease in rumination and negative thinking.[2] Using nature as a tool for healing has been, in fact, one of the fastest-growing areas for research and therapy in the outdoor world, with groups using nature to help with everything from addiction and ADHD to trauma and so much more. Writer Florence Williams, author of *The Nature Fix*, is one of the foremost journalists exploring how science backs up nature's super healing powers. She told me how, in nature, our blood pressure and stress hormone levels decrease, our nervous systems relax, and our immune function is boosted. Nature enhances our self-esteem, reduces anxiety, improves our moods, and helps us make better decisions. Bottle that up and give me some now, please!

Florence also told me how nature moves our brains into a state of "soft fascination," an idea developed in the 1970s by University of Michigan psychology professors Stephen and Rachel Kaplan. Most of the time, as the Kaplans found in their research, our brains are in a state of "hard fascination," engaged in highly stimulating activities that require us to fully stop and react. Like hearing your cell phone ring and having to answer it or seeing a stoplight turn red and stopping your car. In contrast, soft fascination is where our minds can move between objects that come into view

---

1   MaryCarol R. Hunter, Brenda W. Gillespie, and Sophie Yu-Pu Chen, "Urban Nature Experiences Reduce Stress in the Context of Daily Life Based on Salivary Biomarkers," *Frontiers in Psychology*, April 4, 2019, https://www.frontiersin.org/articles/10.3389/fpsyg.2019.00722/full.

2   Gregory N. Bratman, J. Paul Hamilton, Kevin S. Hahn, Gretchen C. Daily, and James J. Gross, "Nature Experience Reduces Rumination and Subgenual Prefrontal Cortex Activation," *Proceedings of the National Academy of Sciences* 112, no. 28 (June 29, 2015): 8567–72, https://doi.org/10.1073/pnas.1510459112.

more naturally. For example, when we're walking in a forest, our minds wander between trees and maybe to birds and butterflies. That sort of wandering allows for more introspection and reflection.

Nature helps us slow down. You can't rush while hiking near a ledge or crossing a river. It's also visually stunning, forcing us to pause and stare, and it's all perfectly organized. You do not have to KonMari or feng shui nature—it's already perfect, even in its imperfections, and it all sparks joy. Look at a tree, a root system, a leaf, or the petals of a flower. It's wild how nature designs things that fit perfectly and look amazing. Even a tree branch that is dead still looks cool.

I find that having a difficult conversation with someone is always so much easier while hiking on a trail or walking on the beach. We tend to be more vulnerable outside. One, because we are physically more vulnerable—we're exposed to the elements and therefore we tend to open up. Do you know how many deep conversations can be had around a campfire? How many introspective conversations have you also had with yourself outside?

Nature is also a great place to find metaphors that you can apply to your life. This can be helpful. I learned this while I was living in New Zealand. I'd been feeling isolated, and a little lonely. Winter afternoons provided a lot of rain, but also—rainbows. I realized right then: sometimes you have to put up with the rain if you want to see the rainbow. I took that lesson with me into the rest of my life.

So how does nature specifically help our Will to Wild? I've found that there are three primary sensations nature brings out in us that help us chart a wild new path: courage, flow, and awe. First, courage, which we're going to need when we are setting out to try anything new. Second, flow, that state of mental immersion that makes doing hard things easier and more enjoyable. And finally, awe, a feeling of respect and wonder that can transport your whole consciousness to a new level.

When you put courage, flow, and awe together, one wild idea can lead to another. Lots of time in nature doing an activity can produce a flow state, letting our imaginations run wild. Time outside our comfort zone builds courage and helps us realize how much more capable we are than we thought. Awe and the power of nature opens us up to curiosity and vulnerability, igniting ideas that transform our psyches.

I WANT TO START with courage. During of the summer of 1996, when I was sixteen, I spent four weeks in a small, rustic village in Costa Rica building a fence for a kindergarten alongside other teenagers. It was one of the most adventurous experiences I'd had. Every day, we slept inside the kindergarten classroom, on a half-inch-thin mattress pad on the cement floor. Cockroaches the size of notecards often came crawling in our sleeping bags, and I once woke up to a scorpion staring me in the face. We showered with a hose duct-taped to the wall outside. It only worked when the town had running water, which was probably about half the time. Lunch was held at a nearby house where a beautiful Costa Rican *abuela* cooked rice and beans with a side of pineapple for every meal. A few times when we heard a pig or chicken squeal, lunch was *arroz con pollo* or *arroz con puerco*.

To build the fence, first we used a machete to cut the grass. (How I did not slice my foot off is still a total wonder.) Then we poured fresh cement. Today the whole thing could be done in nanoseconds with machines. I remember seeing the most majestic birds, getting eaten alive by bugs, and only having to worry about my most primal needs. On the weekends, we visited surfing beaches, a butterfly farm, and even hiked to a waterfall and a volcano.

My sophomore year of high school had been challenging. Like so many teenagers, I felt a little lost. I was playing on three soccer teams, and was always exhausted, while some of my friends were experimenting with drugs and alcohol. A few times, I ate lunch alone. My sense of confidence waned.

But after a month in the jungle, eating mangoes off a tree and fresh pineapple harvested from the backyard, doing hard manual labor, playing soccer with the locals on jungle grass fields, hiking up roads and trails with no certain path, my jaw dropping after seeing the largest insects of my life and beautiful waterfalls, I changed. Nature had altered me in some unspeakable, but very real, way.

I came back to my junior year of high school brimming with confidence. I stopped eating lunch alone. I know it sounds overly simple, but a month outdoors doing something I didn't think I could do before changed me. I had to take the time to sit with my feelings and I developed courage knowing I could cut grass with a machete (and do so without losing a finger), teach English to locals, and survive giant bugs.

Over twenty years later, I had started my podcast about adventure, things were going smoothly, but I was experiencing some angst about what to do next and scared about speaking in public, which I wanted to start doing. I was also spending too much time inside, which was ironic because I was hosting a podcast all about getting outdoors.

Needing to break my rut, I signed up for an overnight survival course with Joel Van Der Loon, a survivalist who would go on to star in *Alone*, the hit reality show on the History Channel. The course was held on the Los Coyotes Reservation, east of San Diego, home to the Los Coyotes Band of Cahuilla and Cupeño people.

Joel had received permission from the Los Coyotes Band to access the reservation. Having been raised on tribal land in South Africa, he was privy to a lot of indigenous knowledge. Plus, he's the kind of guy who could get stuck on an island for twenty days and find a way to not only build a house, but also build his own surfboard.

For the trip, Joel allowed every participant to bring only one bottle of water, one freeze-dried meal, a pot, our clothes, a knife, and a sleeping bag. The goal was to learn to forage for our own food, filter our own water, make fire from sticks and a string, and sleep without a tent under the stars. It was survival lite. Still, I was a little nervous. I had not camped in years, especially without a tent. I also didn't want to get eaten by a mountain lion.

Joel laughed when I said so. A cougar would want nothing to do with our group. After all, there were seven of us. We would never even see a cat, he proclaimed. I wasn't sure I believed him. Why else would it be called Cougar Canyon? Surely, we were far from any town with older women on the prowl. The Native Americans are intentional about how they name places.

After a terrible dinner of instant ramen I failed to season, we went on a night hike. Thirty minutes in, about ten yards from the place where we'd sleep, one of the guys shined his headlamp into the mountains above. The light passed across a set of eyes. They were red, squinty, and stared right back at us. Joel assumed at first it could only be a bobcat. Just then, it bolted about forty feet forward.

"Yep, that's a cougar." Joel changed his mind.

Of course it is, I thought, rolling my eyes at Joel but also raising my eyebrows. How was I going to get any sleep that night? I didn't. When daylight arrived, I was incredibly relieved. One, I'd made it through the night. Two, now that there were no cougars around, I realized it was pretty special to have seen one in the wild. (Many things that happen during an adventure are better in retrospect.)

It may seem small, but knowing I had just slept near a cougar gave me a healthy dose of bravery that continued for the next few weeks. I realized again that I could sleep outside, without much gear, near a wild animal, and not die. I also forgot how amazing it was to only have to worry about my most primal needs—instead of things like social media posts, interview bookings, household chores, or even speaking in public, which, after sleeping outside for a night, suddenly seemed a lot less daunting.

Just two weeks later, I gave a keynote speech to six hundred people, the biggest audience I'd ever addressed. Because I was in nature and not on my computer, I also got a lot of ideas and a catchy story (about the cougar) to open my talk.

NATURE IS ALSO HELPFUL in getting us out of our own heads, and helping us get into the flow. That's why writers go to the mountains (or, like me, to the beach or jungle). When we engage our full senses and feel more relaxed, ideas can literally flow out of us. If you don't know what your wild idea is, or you don't know how you are going to pull it off, start by going outside and trying an activity like rock climbing, yoga, or surfing— one you can do outdoors but that also demands Zen-like concentration.

I learned a lot about flow from many of my podcast guests, including Steven Kotler, who founded the Flow Research Collective, and has written extensively on the subject. Psychologist Mihaly Csikszentmihayi was one of the first to really study the mental state of flow. In the 1970s, interviewing athletes, musicians, and artists who performed at the highest level, he defined the common ingredients at the very heart of flow: the feeling where time transforms, either speeding up or slowing down. The feeling where you are totally in control and focused on what you are doing. The feeling where whatever you're doing feels effortless. The state where your actions and awareness merge and you are without judgment, ego, or rumination. Where you are doing something simply for the joy of doing it, and it's intrinsically rewarding. When there is a balance between the challenge and the task. And when you are clear on your goals and the reward, and get immediate feedback.

Think about the times you may have felt those states yourself. Sure, you can experience them while creating art, making music, holding a baby, making love, maybe even doing laundry (as sometimes happens for me). But Kotler, who has been studying flow more recently, says that doing activities like yoga, rock climbing, hiking, snowboarding, skiing, and surfing—the things we do when we adventure outside in nature—help us drop into a state of flow almost immediately.

Surfing was my path to flow. I grew up in a household with a lot of being busy and a healthy dose of worrying. Surfing helped me be more flexible even when off the board. First, you just get looser in the water, and that attitude translated into my life back on land. Second, when you're in the water riding waves you have to focus, or you'll fall off. You get immediate feedback riding waves, and even though it's sometimes hard, you always feel good and have fun for hours without realizing the time.

For me, flow has also been great for hatching wild ideas. Every time I was stuck writing this book, I took a break and went for a run, a walk, to a yoga class, or for a surf. And every time, whatever I was stuck on seemed to get resolved almost immediately after. It doesn't always happen like magic. But when I'm surfing, running, walking outside, or doing yoga I'm almost always in flow. I'm present. I'm focused. I am not worrying. I'm often having a lot of fun and I forget about even the repetitive motion of whatever I'm doing. In flow states, I can relax and focus at the same time, and it makes getting stuff done a lot easier and more joyful.

IF FLOW IS ESSENTIAL for putting yourself in the headspace to receive and carry out wild ideas, then, in my experience, awe is the best thing to supercharge flow and also take you to a space where you are without judgment. You can lose your ego in flow, but you also lose your ego with awe. This is helpful because when you get caught up in your ego or start judging your wild idea you'll second-guess yourself and not follow through.

This is why awe, which *The Oxford English Dictionary* defines as "a feeling of reverential respect mixed with fear or wonder," makes you more humble and better connected to the world around you, which is helpful when it comes to your wild ideas.

Awe happens when we look up at a redwood tree so big that we can't help but imagine how something that full of life can keep existing for so many years. It happens when we see a monkey eating a banana in a tree, a bird in the sky we've never seen, a certain plant with such vibrant colors we can't help but feel like we're Alice in Wonderland. It happens every time I go snowboarding and see fresh snowflakes fall, and it happened when I recently hiked down the Grand Canyon and looked at the incredible geology everywhere. You get the point. When you experience awe, something shifts. Awe will stop you in your tracks and force you to gain a new perspective. It's hard to feel sorry for yourself or be mad at anyone when you see something that is so beautiful, it makes your jaw drop to the ground.

The week that I was writing this chapter, I was both on deadline and overwhelmed. The combination of stressors made me irritated. There happened to be a south swell that caused the waves to get beautifully big but also playful. The water was a turquoise blue, and a refreshing 68 degrees. I immediately felt better just getting in the salt water. It was midafternoon, an off time for surfing, and the wind picked up. The ocean was relatively deserted.

Someone had seen a shark earlier in the day and my partner, Johnny, and I asked the only other surfer out if he'd seen it. Just then a dark fin popped up.

I gasped.

A second later, I realized it was a giant dolphin, one of the biggest I'd ever seen. Next to it was another big dolphin and a baby. There were about fifteen other dolphins behind and I can only imagine how many more below us, all swimming directly toward us. Just then, a set of waves came and I took the first one toward shore. I kicked out before the wave fully ended, and as I paddled back out three giant dolphins were catching the next wave in the set behind me, headed directly toward me.

Dolphins are incredibly graceful, but they are pretty large animals, so I was a little scared. They were coming right at my face. There was nowhere to go but forward, so I just kept paddling toward them, hoping for the best, and as I ducked under the wave two of the dolphins parted on each side of me. Then they went right back outside and swam right next to us, before swimming away. Johnny had a similar experience, riding the third wave with other dolphins. We sat back on the outside with our mouths wide open. I surf almost every day, but I'd never been so close to dolphins that I could reach out and touch them like I did that day.

Adam Skolnick, the ghostwriter of *Can't Hurt Me*, retired Navy SEAL David Goggins's best-selling memoir, loves to free dive in the open ocean. He gets a lot of ideas swimming (which is not always convenient, because who carries pen and paper underwater?). Adam told me something that resonated with me. "I feel most joyful when I feel small and the rest of the world feels big," he said.

Right then, I felt really small. But also so much more connected to the vast world. It seems clichéd, but my deadline and stress seemed so trivial in that moment. That feeling of awe completely altered my mood. More and more scientists are studying this emotion, likely because awe goes hand in hand with humility and healing. It can provide perspective in times of stress.

While I was growing up, surfing was not only my answer to finding flow but it also provided me with a lot of awe. In return, I learned many lessons in the ocean, mostly patience, respect, and humility. If I could be accepting of the ocean conditions, I realized I could be accepting of whatever situation life threw at me.

As I got older, the ocean also humbled me. The ocean doesn't care who you are, how old you are, where you're from, what you studied in college, if you even went to college, or what you look like. Yes, people might judge, but when a big wave comes in and you are in the wrong place, the ocean will smack you down as equally as someone with a bigger or smaller bank account.

Stars do this for me too. Anytime something small bothers me, if I go outside and look up, I realize I am just a small dot in the universe. I am truly in awe of Mother Nature.

Nature is so much bigger and so much older than any of us, so it also teaches us perspective. It was here before us, it will be here after us, and it can totally destroy us. When you think about the fact the earth is 93.91 million miles from the sun, 238,900 miles from the moon, and about 36 million miles from the next planet, you can relax a bit about your current deadline or the fact that someone didn't return your call. My friend paleontologist Todd Wirths once found a whale bone that was 6 million years old at a construction site. Six million years is a long time, especially when you remember that we humans have only been here for about three hundred thousand years. We are total blips on this wild existence.

TO SEE HOW nature works its magic on a wild idea, take climbing-gym entrepreneur Dave Sacher. In 2009, when he was twenty-one, Dave decided to bike the Pan-American Highway, about nineteen thousand miles from the top of North America to the bottom of South America. Along the way, he was confronted with awe-inspiring landscapes, serious struggles, and a lot of time to think. That's when he came up with his biggest wild idea: to open VITAL, a unique twenty-four-hour climbing gym that runs on trust and community and has become his life's work.

Dave was not always so adventurous. He was the kind of kid who didn't even like getting wet at a swimming pool! But something changed when he and his older brother started surfing before school when Dave was fourteen. They'd get up before the sun, Dave's older brother riding a GoPed, using a jump rope to tow Dave behind him on a skateboard. (Maybe ask your parents first, kids!)

San Diego winter ocean temps are not as warm as most people imagine, especially if you are a kid with a crappy hand-me-down wetsuit with holes, like Dave had. He froze most days, but seeing the sunrise and watching the seagulls and pelicans feed while his classmates were still sleeping, then trying to zip off his wetsuit while his hands felt icy, evoked awe and made him realize that he could do hard and beautiful things. It sparked a curiosity to do more.

While in college, Dave saw his trail sign. During his sophomore year studying business at Cal Poly in San Luis Obispo, Dave met a friend of a friend, Emmanuel Gentinetta, who had biked the Pan-American Highway from Alaska to Patagonia at age eighteen and is a Guinness record holder for being the youngest and fastest kid to ever complete the route in 261 days on a mountain bike. Emmanuel was a legend, and when Dave finally met him at a party, Dave was inspired to undertake a similar adventure.

After thinking about it for weeks, Dave decided he didn't need to concoct a new scheme; he would simply undertake the same challenge— biking from the top of the world to the bottom of it.

After graduating in 2009, Dave, who studied business, had no idea what he wanted to do for a career. But he knew that after graduation he would make the time to have a grand adventure—something that would push his mind and body.

There were many things that could have stopped him from actually deciding to bike from Alaska to Patagonia. For one, he had never ridden the mileage he'd need to ride for seven months to get there in less than a year. Two, he'd never even owned a decent bike. Three, he did not have that much money. And four, a few weeks before the trip he had knee surgery to fix an old injury. "It's not like you're gonna go out and ride one hundred miles," his doctor joked. Dave just smiled. He did not tell his doctor about the plan to ride almost 100 miles a day for almost the entire next year.

Four weeks after surgery, Dave flew to Alaska with his bike. He had way too much gear. (Protip: You don't need camp chairs when doing a multiday adventure like this, as they take up too much space and weight.) He unloaded and learned as he went along. He started in Prudhoe, in the northernmost part of Alaska, riding and freedom camping from Anchorage to the Mexican border.

Dave pedaled down the Pan-American Highway, through Central America, and down the length of South America, mostly camping on the side of the road or in open fields. In Alaska, the sun never fully set and large trucks moved cargo all night. Through Oregon, he was pretty much a wild man, freedom camping alongside the highway. In California, he slept at friends' houses and even in his own bed. In Mexico, he camped or found five-dollar rooms where he could at least find a shower or hose to rinse off diesel soot and sweat. Through South America, there was more open land and Dave camped mostly in fields alongside the open road.

Dave learned so much along the way. He got really good at listening for the sound of vehicles and could tell just by hearing if a semitruck or sedan was behind him. He became skilled at finding food, water, and places to sleep on the side of the road. He understood that most people are naturally helpful and kind. Sure, he had a few random bad encounters but he learned to trust his gut to avoid any sticky situations. Most important, he realized he wasn't a quitter. He could keep pedaling ninety miles a day, figuring out logistics as he went.

Prior to his adventure, Dave had camped only a handful of times, and barely traveled. After weeks on the road, packing up his tent and riding his bike ninety miles every day to a new place, he now felt confident traveling by himself—whether it was a patch of grass on the side of a road or a makeshift room with a bucket of water outside, he could get by. He also learned that he could handle almost any situation by himself. When you do something over and over—like camping, reading maps, finding food and places to stay, and fixing things for yourself—over seven months, you start getting proficient at it.

He also became a skilled cyclist and his legs grew stronger from all that pedaling. Dave thought it was especially amazing that on month three of his trip, in Guatemala, the pain in his knee disappeared altogether. Perhaps it was the care package of orthotics he'd received from his parents, which changed the angle of his knee when he rode. Perhaps it was just time, or all that amazing healing energy from fresh air and trees. Most of all, Dave marveled that, while his bicycle cables could break and his tires could wear through, his knees and legs only grew stronger.

Six and a half months and 18,300 miles into his journey, the one thing he hadn't figured out—and by now it was really gnawing at him—was his next step. *What am I doing with my life?* is a question most people will ask themselves a few times in their lives. Not knowing the answer can create real distress. *What should my career be? Where will I live?*

Dave was almost to the end in Patagonia, and by this point he was pretty much out of money. Even though he was doing the trip as cheaply as possible, Dave needed to figure out what he was going to do next. He was going to have to support himself somehow.

He was riding through the expansive grasslands of southern Argentina when things finally became clear. He was in the land of guanacos and bright pink flamingos, giant armadillos, and majestic wild horses. There was so much awe. He was also in the flow.

But seven hundred miles from the finish, the ride started to totally suck. It had been tough going before, of course. Some people take three years or more to do this ride. Dave was doing it in rapid speed to finish in less than a year. With the wind in his face, Dave was only going about 4 miles per hour. It felt like the equivalent of pedaling through mud. Sure, he could have laid his bike down, called it a day, and found a place to camp, but he didn't. He was so close to the end.

On that day, pedaling in place against the wind, Dave was in the pain locker. He knew that negative thoughts were not helpful. And yes, he had plenty of them. But he decided to change his focus, away from the suck and toward the things that brought him joy.

As Dave's mind wandered, he imagined his closest friends rock climbing and hanging out. There was a grill in the background and great music playing. He thought back to college, where he and his roommate and best friend, Nam Phan, had gone to a local twenty-four-hour gym to squeeze in workouts at weird hours. He also thought of his favorite climbing gym, a little hole in the wall where like-minded adventurous souls gathered and where there was no front desk to check in. People could come and go using an honor code. He loved that about the climbing gym.

The thoughts downloaded fast. And then like a lightning bolt, it struck him: What about creating a climbing gym as a business? It would be similar to the one he went to in college, but taken to another level. Like many regular gyms, it would be open twenty-four hours a day. And like the climbing gym, the community would be inclusive. There would be an honor code, instead of a front desk, so guests would just be given the numbers to a keypad on the front door to let themselves in. There would be yummy coffee and kombucha and energy bars in the fridge if you got hungry—also to pay for with an honor code, leaving money in a box with a note of what you ate.

For months, Dave had agonized over his next step, but it had never become clear to him until that day, suffering through the wind and cold with the climbing mecca of Patagonia in the distance. How would he do it? He was out of money; he would make it happen anyway.

Dave told me that on that trip "I was forming a diamond in my soul. I know that sounds cheesy, but incredible heat and pressure is so intense and forms something so precious and untarnishable that you carry it forever." Like a diamond, it's a memory, precious to him, that he carries with him every day. It's something that many people don't even notice, but it's always there, waiting to be unearthed.

The rest of the trip flew by. Dave got back to San Diego and borrowed $2,000 from his brother. He found a space to lease, and also found investors to fund the wild idea that would become his life's work. One thing that surprised him was just how willing people were to help him after he told them about having finished his grand adventure. Because David was a person who said he was going to do something big, and then actually did it, it gave him credibility with investors who realized he was a person who would keep his word.

Dave Sacher and Nam Phan opened the first VITAL Climbing Gym in 2010. They slept on pieces of plywood ten feet off the ground, hidden behind the first rock wall in the gym, almost every night for a whole year to make sure it ran smoothly. Every morning when they woke, they did their best to not to freak out the customers who were already there climbing. VITAL now has three locations in Southern California, one in Washington State, and three in New York.

Dave said he never would have come up with the idea for VITAL if it hadn't been for that miserable, fortuitous day on his bike, after countless hours outside to think and contemplate, and after some serious time outside his comfort zone. He could have never accomplished his goals without that courage he built from doing something hard every day for seven months, all that flow riding his bike, and all that awe from looking around. Pursuing that wild idea led him to where he is today.

OF COURSE, face it—we're not all going to pedal to Patagonia. And certainly not everyone would want to! But we also don't all have the same access to get into nature. Not all of us have the means, time, or opportunities to immerse ourselves in the outdoors. In many places around the globe, people don't have the access or the time off to enjoy getting out in nature much at all.

Plus, the outdoors hasn't always been the most welcoming place for lots of people. But when anyone does get outside, nature can offer not only a trail map but sometimes even a path to a different lifestyle or situation.

I volunteer with an organization called Outdoor Outreach in San Diego that takes at-risk kids on excursions like surfing, snorkeling, snowboarding, rock climbing, camping, and hiking. I've seen how getting introduced to the power of the outdoors can create big shifts within a person. It did for me, and for most of the people I've interviewed, which is why I love introducing others to the outdoors too.

Of all the kids I've met through this program, one participant in particular stands out. Ryan Hudson came to Outdoor Outreach in 2004 when he was about fifteen, through the Toussaint Teen Center, which was a live-in shelter and school for homeless youth in downtown San Diego.

During Ryan's first year at the center, Outdoor Outreach took several Toussaint kids snowboarding. Ryan hadn't spent that much time in nature, at least not in the mountains and definitely not snowboarding. Sure, he'd seen parks as a kid, but he didn't always think of them as positive places. He was the youngest of five, raised by a single mom, and the family had been on and off the streets and in and out of shelters since he could remember. His family had slept in the park a few times. "We did what we had to do," he said.

By his freshman year of high school, Ryan was on his own at the teen center. When Outdoor Outreach picked him up to go snowboarding two and a half hours northeast of San Diego at Snow Valley Mountain Resort, he said, the experience changed his life.

Ryan had never seen snow before. It felt like what he would have imagined, but the whole combined experience was pretty eye-opening. From loading up the bus to driving to the mountains, seeing all that greenery, then putting on boots, strapping into a snowboard, riding the chairlift up, and trying to glide down a hill sideways with the most majestic vistas all around, and doing it with kids his own age all trying at the same time, the experience changed Ryan's world. And it sparked a fire within him.

Snowboarding felt different to him from any other activity. Even though he was moving his body, it was emotional. All those open spaces and green trees contrasting with the white snow was a totally different view from the one he saw in the heart of downtown San Diego on a daily basis. He loved the lines his board made down the mountain. It looked like art.

"I'll never forget that feeling," Ryan said. "I just wanted to keep doing it."

And he did. He went on every snowboard trip Outdoor Outreach offered. Ryan told me that snowboarding motivated him to try harder at everything. He recently found an old report card that charted his grades during the time before and after finding snowboarding. They improved after Ryan got on a board.

Ryan was a decent student and a good athlete; he had deep convictions and would have ended up on a positive path no matter what. But snowboarding cracked open a door that he didn't know existed. When it opened, he was ready to run right through it. The combined effects of riding down a mountain, making turns that felt like using a paintbrush on a canvas, and having to choose new lines every time brought him so much joy. "It's one of the most freeing, graceful, visually explosive, and peaceful things you can do," Ryan told me about snowboarding.

It also had the power to alter his entire life's trajectory as an adult. After graduating from high school, Ryan didn't have the opportunity to go to college. There was no financial cushion. No place to live. No substantial support. The founder of Outdoor Outreach, Chris Rutgers, suggested Ryan move to the town of Alta, Utah. It's where Chris had gone after graduating from high school and, under different circumstances, experienced a new path in the mountains and became a ridiculously good skier.

In Alta, Ryan worked a seasonal job that provided housing, food, and a snowboard pass to Snowbird Resort, also nearby, where he would spend 130 days snowboarding that first winter. With that much practice and so much love, Ryan became really good at snowboarding. He also found some time to process emotions.

It wasn't easy being a person of color in a mostly white sport. Even though there were a lot of people around, Ryan often felt alone. At first, he didn't think other snowboarders understood him, and he didn't understand their culture. It was weird. He said he thought a lot about who he was, where he was from, what that meant, how people saw him, how he saw other people, and what that all meant collectively. These are big questions, ones that being out in nature helped Ryan work through.

Snowboarding didn't lay out all the answers on a scroll, but it gave him an outlet—a place to sit with the questions, to express himself, to find peace, a lot of joy, and, of course, courage, flow, and lots of awe. It was also a place that ended up leading to other opportunities.

In 2013, when Ryan was twenty-four, he was invited on a heli snowboard trip to Thompson Pass, part of the Chugach Mountains northeast of Valdez, Alaska, to ride the biggest mountains he'd ever ridden in his life, ones that were only accessible by helicopter. The trip pushed him. It was definitely scary at times, and doing anything risky and not just surviving, but thriving, made him appreciate things that much more.

Then, that spring, Ryan was invited to climb Denali and snowboard partway down with some serious mountaineers, including the climber

Conrad Anker and writer Jon Krakauer, author of the book *Into Thin Air*. At the time, Ryan didn't even know who Krakauer was. But the whole way up the mountain, the two connected. Ryan and Krakauer shared stories and became friends. They came from radically different starting points but found so much commonality.

Three hundred feet from the summit, an electrical storm rolled in, and the team had to turn around. They raced down the mountain, dragging anything containing metal, from caribeeners to ice axes, behind them with a rope so they wouldn't get electrocuted. Eventually, Ryan snowboarded sections toward the bottom. The experience taught Ryan that, even though he and the other climbers on the expedition all came from different starting points, he could hold his own.

In 2021, when Ryan was thirty-three, he went back to Alaska to participate in the documentary film *Mountain Revelations,* alongside professional snowboarders Jeremy Jones and Rafael Pease. They helicoptered to a glacier and hiked up steep mountains, carving their way back down. During the adventure, they talked a lot about the proverbial mountains they'd had to climb, ones involving race and privilege. For so many years, Ryan had been, as he puts it, one of the "token black guys on the mountain."

Being one of the only anything isn't easy. Ryan says things have changed in the last decade. There are a lot more people who look like him in the mountains. He won't say so himself, as he's too humble, but Ryan has played a huge part in that evolution. But there is still more work to do.

While companies have sent Ryan gear since he was twenty-one and a few have paid him, the sport hasn't been the easiest path to a full-time career. Ryan has continued to work side jobs, including at a sushi restaurant, to pay the bills.

Snowboarding isn't like baseball, basketball, or football, where you are guaranteed to make money just for making it to the big leagues. But Ryan has done a lot for snowboarding. And he's been advocating to get more people of color introduced to the outdoors. Recently, he coined the hashtag #StreetsToPeaks to use his journey to inspire others. He also helped fundraise about $25,000 to give to Outdoor Outreach by partnering with a brand and auctioning off a snowboard. It's come full circle.

In his thirties now, Ryan notes that snowboarding is his greatest passion and purpose, and he is incredibly grateful for finding it. When I asked him if it changed his life, he corrected me. "I think it's the choice to choose to have a relationship with nature that changes you," he said. "It doesn't change you alone."

> ✴ ProTip: Volunteer with an organization that takes kids or adults outside on adventures. Start with your main skill. If you can teach surfing, kayaking, or rock climbing, awesome. If not, help pack lunches, chaperone an event, or volunteer your skills with things like accounting or fundraising. See where they need help, and use your strengths to get in. That's one of the best ways to get outside and give back.

A RELATIONSHIP WITH NATURE won't change every person's life course so drastically, and there is still a lot of work to do to make the outdoors more accessible to everyone. There are many organizations dedicated to this, some which are included in the appendix on page 267. Volunteering at one, or donating your time or money, is a great way to get out there and give back at the same time.

For five years, I volunteered for a week every September at the National Veterans Summer Sports Clinic in San Diego, where Surf Diva, the original all women's surf school, was teaching surfing to veterans. Founded in 2008, by the US Department of Veterans Affairs, the clinic introduces veterans to the world of adaptive sports through activities like learning to surf, kayak, cycle, sail, and more. The VA San Diego Healthcare System serves as the host every year with support from numerous sponsors and companies.

Many of the veterans have served overseas and experienced PTSD or were wounded in action. Obviously catching a few waves isn't going to erase someone's trauma overnight, but these small doses of adventure build courage, let people experience flow and awe, and are a small way to support and give back to the people who have served.

A few years ago, I was assigned to teach a veteran who was legally blind how to surf. She was athletic by nature, a former volleyball player and coach, but I was nervous. Surfing requires seeing where you're going, where the waves are, where your board is, and where other surfers are. Before helping her catch a wave, we strategically lined up volunteers from the sand to the deepest part of the ocean like a runway. Still, my student sensed my nerves. "Shelby," she told me, "you don't need sight to have vision."

With that, I pushed her on her first wave and she got to her knees, then slowly stood up, doing a dance that could put J.Lo to shame. I cheered. I learned more from her that day than she did from me. And we both had nature to thank.

HOW TO MICRODOSE NATURE, EVEN IF YOU LIVE IN A CITY

A National Geographic Adventurer of the Year, Stacy Bare is an army veteran who tasted the power of adventure firsthand through rock climbing. He says rock climbing helped save him after his own time serving in Sarajevo and Iraq in the 2000s. Over the years, Stacy has used adventure to help other veterans reframe their interactions with war. He started an initiative called Adventure Not War, taking veterans back to the places they'd served, places like Iraq, Angola, and Afghanistan, to climb or ski—and, in the process, use those adventures to rewrite traumatic narratives. Now the executive director of Friends of Grand Rapids Parks, Stacy is on a mission to help people find nature everywhere, even in the busiest cities.

In that work, Stacy follows what's called the 3-30-300 rule, an idea developed by University of British Columbia forestry professor Cecil Konijnendijk. The premise is that everyone should be able to look out their window and see three trees, live in a neighborhood with a 30 percent tree canopy, and be no more than three hundred meters from a park (which is about a ten-minute walk). Through the Friends of Grand Rapids Parks, Stacy is hoping to bring the 3-30-300 rule to his own city by planting ten thousand more trees and creating more green space and parks. In that way, sidewalks can become trails.

Stacy believes that even if you don't live near a green space, you can find nature and adventure right near your home. His young daughter, Wilder, gets incredibly excited at a leaf, a rock, or even dandelions coming through cracks.

Access to nature isn't always easy, especially when you live in a city. That's real. But even microdosing nature can create real shifts in how you feel. Studies prove that keeping plants has been shown to create profound effects on your mood. It can be that simple.

Plantfluencer "Garden Marcus" Bridgewater, whom I also interviewed, has developed a huge following on social media teaching people life lessons through the hundreds of plants in his Houston backyard. The author of *How to Grow: Nurture Your Garden, Nurture Yourself*, Marcus started posting in 2019, and spent the pandemic spreading the joys of finding peace among the plants you care for, helping them grow new roots and flourish.

Here are some of my favorite ways to get your nature dose, courtesy of Garden Marcus, Stacy Bare, author Florence Williams, and others. Remember: even if it's just a microdose, it can help.

1. Find something amazing to smell outside—an orange tree, a flower, pine needles, wild rosemary, or wild sage, my favorite.

2. Look up at the clouds and study the shapes. Find the nearest tree and examine its leaves, branches, and roots. Look far into the distance at the horizon, tree line, or mountains.

3. Listen to birds sing or waves crash.

4. Keep images of nature as screen savers. (It's not the same, but studies have proven just looking at images of nature helps reduce stress, which is why so many office and hotel lobbies have paintings of nature scenes.)

5. Go to a nearby park for a picnic or tea with friends, or just treat the sidewalk as your trail, admiring neighborhood plants and trees.

6. Ground out by putting your feet in the sand, a stream, a lake, a river, or the dirt.

7. Get some houseplants. One thing Garden Marcus advises is to practice caring for them as you would also care for yourself. Plants can be great teachers. You have to water the roots, like you would yourself.

8. Study the birds on your next walkabout. Bird watching is way cooler than you might think, and it can be highly beneficial for improving your distance vision.

9. Want to literally ground yourself in nature? Next time you get to a beach, lie down in the sand, making yourself a sand angel. Or, better yet, dip yourself in the water and then roll around on the sand, making yourself into a human corn dog. It's one of my favorite activities to make myself feel grounded, even though sand gets everywhere, and I mean everywhere. My friend Liz Clark, a badass sailor, Patagonia ambassador, and author of the book *Swell*, calls it "sand therapy." Liz believes sand is just ground-up crystals that charge your body and heal it.

10. When people ask how much time in nature is enough, author Florence Williams gives this

advice: "Go outside, often, sometimes in wild places. Bring friends or not. Breathe."

My version might go something like this: Get outside into nature, make a sand corn dog, light a campfire, look up at the sky, jump into the waves, ditch your cell phone, or just drop in and get dirty. Find it wherever you can. Nature always feels good.

CONNECTING TO NATURE EVEN WHEN EVERYTHING ELSE IS CLOSED

from author and Outdoor Afro founder Rue Mapp

Rue Mapp is the CEO of Outdoor Afro, a not-for-profit organization that celebrates and inspires Black connections and leadership in nature. What started as a kitchen table blog in 2009 is now an organization with over sixty thousand participants. Rue is a sought-after speaker, public lands champion, and author of *Nature Swagger: Stories and Visions of Black Joy in the Outdoors*. With Outdoor Afro, she also came out with an entire clothing line with REI made to fit more bodies, with style that brings her and her community more joy. The tagline is "WE ARE NATURE." Rue is a force of nature in the outdoor world. She's advocated for public lands at the White House, and even taken Oprah hiking. Like many of us, Rue turned to nature in the pandemic, and I love what she had to say about it:

> One thing I learned during the pandemic is that Nature never closes. That became a mantra for me and my work, and to remember the bigger thing that's not just about me. During the pandemic, we were all trying to find and hack connection in ways and times that were hard to come by. I've had many inflection points in my years. Nature has been a teacher and a healer, but I recognized nature in that time, especially as our country felt so divided, as a unifier. I know that when I am out

in nature, the trees don't know I'm Black. The flowers are gonna bloom no matter how much money is in my account. The birds are gonna sing no matter who I vote for. So, I elevated my consciousness around the real way nature is not separate from who we are. Being people comprised of mostly water and governed by the lunar cycle, as tides are, we aren't separate from nature, WE ARE Nature. Even if you can't go to that trail or iconic public land (because it was closed), there is nature at hand all the time. We just have to shift our consciousness to recognize it. That became an important thing to think about for me in my own life and work, and an extension of how we can connect to each other.

CHAPTER 5

MAP YOUR TRAIL

An investment in knowledge always pays the best interest.

—Benjamin Franklin

Having a why will keep you committed to your plan. But you're going to need a map to keep you from getting lost. Some wild ideas are fairly linear in their planning: you simply buy a map, draw a line, and point your body, board, or bike and follow it. Others require the creation of the map itself. Everyone starts from a different place with different skills, resources, and amount of time. The common steps that most adventurers have told me were helpful in charting and staying their course are these:

- Write your wild idea down. Say it out loud and go as far as to tell someone else to create accountability.
- Write down everything you need to learn and accumulate to make it happen.
- Get educated (fast). This includes contacting others and listening to their podcasts or reading their books.
- Plan (with deadlines). Plot your course and gain the skills you need.

- Come up with a Plan B for safety. If your adventure is more risky, you may need a Plan C, and D as well.
- Invest in yourself. That means investing in education and/ or gear.
- Learn to pitch.
- Cultivate vision, motivation, and faith.
- Find your team.
- Face fear.
- Start.

I've outlined these in greater detail in the box at the end of this chapter.

All of this can get overwhelming, but don't make it too complicated. As many adventurers have told me, when it comes to planning, speed can be your friend. Sometimes, when the project seems too daunting, too big, too cumbersome, or too scary, we can get sucked into a vortex, overwhelmed by the task at hand. This is what is called analysis paralysis. Obviously, you don't want to set out totally unprepared. But eventually, you do want to start. And momentum will keep you going. Get educated and chart your course as safely, but also as quickly, as possible.

ALSO, MAKE SURE you define your own adventure. Guidebooks are full of gear lists, but they don't always include what's essential to *you*. A few years back, I gave a talk at the Girl Scouts of America in San Diego. The speaker before me talked about the essentials you need to go ultralight backpacking, which allows you to travel light and fast without carrying a heavy load. A young Scout raised her hand. She was sure the ultralight hiker had missed something in his presentation.

"What about the emergency candy?" she asked him.

He paused with skepticism. Then, after thinking about it for a few seconds, he looked back at her. "Yes, you absolutely need emergency candy in your kit," he replied, suggesting something light like jelly beans or hard candies.

When you gear up for your adventure, don't go so light that you miss things that make your trip fun. It's not supposed to be a sufferfest (unless that's your thing?!). You will need your own version of emergency candy or proverbial joy to keep you going. I always pack my own chocolate and coffee. I also try to leave a cold kombucha and some watermelon in the car in a cooler for afterward (as long as I am not in bear country). Watermelon just tastes so good after a long day of hiking! On long days of back-to-back podcast interviews I try to reward myself with cold brew in between. And those evenings I plan for a surf, a hike, an outing with friends, or an indulgent comedy show because I just love laughing.

Emergency candy can go beyond actual candy, food, and beverages. Have a playlist or certain song that pumps you up. Download photos that make you laugh out loud. Call a friend you share daily accountability messages (or dirty jokes) with to keep you upbeat and on track. You can go as far as to plan and pack for celebrations at key milestones, have a dip at a lake, or a dance at a summit. My little niece throws her arms in the air and yells, "Congratulations! We did it!!" Don't forget to bring whatever you need to pick you up at that lowest moment of your journey.

NOW YOU'RE READY to get started for real. You have your wild idea. You know your why behind it. Maybe you've told some friends.

One thing that nearly every wild idea involves is some investigation of what you're getting into. A great thing about living in the 2020s is the vast amount of information out there. You no longer have to go to business school to start a business. You don't have to do a twelve-week National Outdoor Leadership School class to learn to backpack. You don't even need a guidebook to hike the Pacific Coast Trail; there are phone apps for that (though I would still take backup maps and read actual books). You can join meetup groups, follow people on social media, read blogs, and watch YouTube videos to learn skills.

Once you've covered the basics through the Internet, nothing substitutes for the hard-earned wisdom of real live people, especially those who have done something similar. Read their books or blogs; listen to their podcast interviews; follow them on social media if you can; try contacting them directly or showing up at their speaking events (but no *actual* stalking, please). You can volunteer to work for them, intern for them, or trade a service in exchange for their expertise. If they get paid to coach or teach a course, sign up. Don't be offended if they are busy. Some people get dozens of pitches a day.

Over the course of my life, I have direct-messaged and pitched hundreds of people, some of whom have become invaluable mentors. I am genuine about my interest and always try to offer something in return. If you can offer something valuable to someone you look up to, you can learn along the way.

Over a decade ago, for example, I met Chris McDougall at a book signing in San Diego. I'd read his barefoot running memoir, *Born to Run*, and wanted to profile him for a magazine, and also ask him for advice about writing. Once I had the okay from my editor, I asked Chris to participate in a profile. And in the same breath, I also invited him to an underground event in San Diego—a run around the city's coastline, swimming around the rocky places without a sandy shore. The idea caught his attention.

Chris couldn't make the event, but he agreed to go for a barefoot run. On our run, we happened to pass the beach where I taught surfing in La Jolla for years. The weather was impeccable, and my friends were teaching lessons, and had an extra surfboard on the beach that was tall enough for Chris's six-foot-plus frame.

Chris agreed the conditions were pretty perfect, and although neither of us had on swimsuits, we had on running clothes, which would quickly dry on the run home. About thirty minutes later, I'm proud to say, Chris rode his first wave. We built a friendship from that interaction, and over the years Chris has given me invaluable advice about writing stories and eventually books—and most of all just encouragement.

If you ask someone for advice, be genuine in your interest and respectful of thier time. Sometimes people are busy and sometimes the timing doesn't work out, but often when you are doing something wild and are motivated by the right intentions others will help. When they do, be sure to send a thank-you. Ideally, a handwritten note or a token of appreciation with something they'd like. For me it's dark chocolate, quality coffee, or surf gear. And if they are someone who gets asked for advice a lot, and they offer a consulting service or class, it will be worth signing up for their expertise.

The wilder your idea, or the more dangerous, the more education you may need. And the more important it may be to find the right people to help you on your way. Asking for help is a part of living wildly. It's one of the bravest things you can do.

I GET THAT AT first glance research might sound like a lot of home-work. But learning and growth is, for me, the best part of pursuing a wild idea. When you have a wild idea, you will often have to put yourself out there to make it happen. That can be vulnerable, and scary. One way to ease into a wild idea is to invest in a coach or a guide or join a group with like-minded people doing what you want to do. For example, if you are learning a new sport like rock climbing, you can try it on your own, take a class, join a rock-climbing gym, or ask a friend to teach you. Or you can just hire a guide.

When I was in my twenties, I planned most of my adventures totally on my own. Now that I'm in my forties, I do a mix of solo adventures and ones where I hire guides. Recently, I decided to hire a guide to take Johnny and me rock climbing in Mammoth Lakes, California. One, I had no idea where to rock climb because I was visiting on a whim. Two, I don't own much rock-climbing gear. Three, I didn't have that much time to learn everything I'd need to do it on my own. Finally, I didn't want to get hurt and I definitely didn't want Johnny to get hurt. In three hours, and a sliver of what it would have cost to buy gear, our guide provided everything we needed to climb, showed us the best route, taught us the proper technique, and kept us safe. Our guide also pushed us to try more technical routes and ensured we had a good time too! It felt like an awesome investment in exchange for a totally stress-free, rewarding experience.

Part of why I am such a fan of hiring guides is that it's not just a way to fast-track your way into an adventure. I have also been a guide myself. After I quit my job at Vans, teaching surfing in Costa Rica seemed like a pretty silly idea, at first. But being a surf instructor at Surf Diva was one of the best jobs I ever had. I taught so many incredible people to surf, and helping people get over their own fears helped me get over mine.

Being a guide is also a unique opportunity. You are in charge of other people's safety. You are teaching them something valuable. And you will likely help them overcome huge mental blocks, and be there for a life-changing experience. There's not a lot of jobs that let you do all that, and meet such cool people along the way. I've taught so many people who have become good friends to surf, some whom I even later worked with. I mentioned earlier I even once taught the then vice president of National Public Radio to surf; he's the guy who first mentioned the idea of a radio adventure show, which first sparked my idea to start an adventure podcast. And I am still friends with not only former students but also my fellow instructors, whom I keep in touch with decades later.

In short, being a guide is a great way to also get into the outdoors, get educated, gain skills, and help enable other people to have their own life-changing adventures (altruism and fun). This is exactly how Laurie Watt, a physical therapist and a mom of two, became an ice-climbing and mountaineer guide at fifty-five, an age where she says she has never been more fit in her life.

Laurie had a full career as a physical therapist on the East Coast and was an empty nester before she decided to start embarking on outdoor adventures on a grand level. When she was a little girl, Laurie's uncle took her and some family members hiking in the mountains of New Hampshire. She will never forget how free the wilderness felt, the vastness of the trees, the smell of pine and maple overpowering her senses. She remembers the moment vividly. She was eight years old, and once she reached the very top of the mountain, Laurie was rewarded with M&M's (the emergency candy). Fueled with a burst of sugar, as the rest of the group started to head down, Laurie sprinted the entire way back.

"I felt like I was flying, and it was the most incredible feeling," she told me. "I did not wait for my family, and I did not wait at trail junctions. And so I waited at the car, and when my parents got there, they were pretty angry."

Even though she got a serious talking-to, that moment on the mountain and the freedom she felt never left her. Laurie went on to pursue the life she thought she should. She played soccer in high school, went to college, got married, started a career as a physical therapist, had kids. "I got into the rhythm of what my family and cultural expectations were, and I was going along on that path that was expected. I enjoyed it, and I don't regret it. But during that time, I was neglecting this whole side of myself, which is the side that needed to move and be in the outdoors."

When she was forty-four, Laurie's family relocated to Europe when her husband took a finance job for a biotech company overseas in Switzerland. It was the first time Laurie had been back to the mountains, and she went on her first hike since grade school. As far as mountains go, the Swiss Alps are pretty radical, with their steep faces and idyllic villages. Every vista looks like a postcard. Being there sparked a fire Laurie remembered from childhood.

She also met other moms from her kids' school who were pretty badass hikers. After hiking in Switzerland, one of them suggested they try to climb Mount Kilimanjaro in Tanzania in 2009. At 19,340 feet, Kilimanjaro is often an entry point for hikers who are venturing into the world of mountaineering. It was Laurie's first big mountain adventure. And after that, she was hooked. Laurie loved getting out in the elements, exploring new places, and proving to herself that she could take on some pretty big challenges. The freedom Laurie felt in the mountains made it clear that it was time to prioritize getting outside.

She and her family moved back to the states in 2011, which is when Laurie decided to expand her skills. She signed up for an REI trip, a winter ascent of Mount Washington, which was contracted with a small guide agency in New Hampshire. "Being up on top of Mount Washington in the winter is like being on the moon. It's a completely different landscape. Not only is it the tallest mountain between the Rockies and the Atlantic Ocean; it's also the convergence of three major wind patterns. Although it's only six thousand feet high, the mountain for many years had the highest recorded wind speed of anywhere on the planet." It was dangerous, but Laurie liked the challenge. "There was something about putting yourself up against those elements, learning to manage them, learning to stay comfortable and move through those elements no matter what the mountain provided, that was incredibly appealing to me and challenging."

The guides on that trip left a remarkable impression. They made her feel comfortable, kept her safe, and were so encouraging that she hired them and others she met over the years countless more times. As time went on, she developed relationships with certain guides, which spurred her to try rock climbing, and then ice climbing. Laurie still had her physical therapy practice but scaled it back because, as she says, "I wanted to learn new ways to interact with the mountain environment."

During a navigation course, her twenty-four-year-old instructor, who had seen Laurie on a few trips, looked at her and asked, "Have you ever thought about becoming a guide?"

Laurie admitted right then, she'd been harboring a secret desire to make it her job, to scale back her physical therapy practice so she could be outside in the mountains every day and get paid for it. It just seemed so improbable.

On every trip she'd been on, from Kilimanjaro to Mount Washington, all the guides were young, fit, and male, with years of climbing experience. "I was female, middle-aged, and suburban," she said.

Still, the idea sparked something inside her. She emailed the owner of a guide company she'd booked trips with previously, telling him not to laugh, but that she'd really like to become a guide herself, asking if this might be possible.

She needed to learn a lot of new skills, especially when it came to climbing, but the folks at the guide company were incredibly supportive. Over the next three years, Laurie shuttered her physical therapy practice and dove in, becoming a full-time guide based in New Hampshire at age fifty-five in 2021.

Women started signing up to take lessons with Laurie in droves. It's pretty amazing what happens when we see people who look like us. Laurie told me she loves taking groups of women climbing together. There's an instant support system, not just a lot of fun lady banter. "Everyone wants everyone to succeed," she says. She absolutely loves watching women conquer their fears and realize how capable they are.

Today, not only is Laurie an experienced mountain, rock-climbing, and ice-climbing guide, but brands such as NEMO Equipment have hired her as an ambassador to get other women outside. Sometimes the path to getting educated leads you to become an educator.

 ProTip: **Fast-track your way to learning a new outdoor sport by taking a class, hiring a guide, or joining a group.**

LEARNING FROM A GUIDE is a great way to learn fast, and to meet amazing, like-minded beings. But what if there is no map, no guidebook, or no class you can take, because you are doing something no one has ever done? That's when you're going to have to get creative.

In 2015, when twin brothers Casey and Ryan Higginbotham were seniors in college, as part of a conversation over beers they started talking about adventures to do next. The ideas escalated as they kept drinking (which I do not endorse as a way to make life decisions). One of the ideas was riding horses across Mongolia, but neither knew anything about horses, so they nixed that one. By the end of the night, they landed on their wild idea: paddle twenty-two hundred miles from Alaska to Mexico on prone paddleboards, using their hands to propel them, not actual paddles. Then, not only did they say it out loud (step one); they toasted and shook hands on it too. After that, they were fully committed.

For those who don't know what a prone paddleboard is, imagine a longer, thicker version of a surfboard, shaped to handle distances rather than ride waves. You paddle it while lying down on your belly or sometimes kneeling, using your hands to propel yourself. No actual paddle is involved.

The twins were twenty-two when they had the idea, but despite their young age, they were already above-average adventurers. As beach lifeguards in their hometown of Pismo Beach, California, they knew a lot about ocean safety. They'd also raced in IRONMAN Triathlons and finished a few adventure races. That experience had taught them how to navigate with topographic maps and a compass. So they had plenty of skills.

Still, it's a long way from Ketchikan to the Mexican border. Plus, no one had ever done a multi-month prone paddle trek, at least no one they'd heard of. To understand how ambitious this undertaking was, Jimmy Chin, one of the most well-renowned adventure filmmakers and storytellers of the modern era, said as far as expeditions go, the Higginbothams' trip was one of the most difficult trips of any kind.

There was no playbook to follow and nothing to Google. To get educated, the brothers had to get creative and DIY their education and plan, which you may have to do too. They looked into the most similar adventure to theirs that they could find. The farthest long-distance prone paddling event in the United States is the Molokai2Oahu, where racers paddle thirty-two miles across open ocean between the two Hawaiian Islands. Ryan found an old how-to guide from the race and followed it step-by-step when preparing. But the differences were substantial. People don't do that race with gear on top of their boards. And Hawaii's climate is a heck of a lot warmer than Alaska's.

Still, it was a start. The brothers then had to figure out what gear they'd need, keeping safety at the forefront. They read a book called *Point to Point: Exploring the Inside Passage by Kayak*, by Denis Dwyer, who had paddled from the San Juan Islands of Washington State to Alaska. The only difference: Denis had used a kayak, which usually has storage compartments for gear and is designed to go through waves more easily than a paddleboard. A rogue wave or pounding shore break can easily break a paddleboard in half. Dwyer's book was helpful. It was full of information about the route, his safety gear, the weather, and how to navigate.

The twins messaged Denis about their wild idea through his website, and he returned their message immediately, sharing information on what gear worked best and how to navigate through the most grueling sections. When you are undertaking a grand adventure and you're genuinely excited and committed, people are usually fired up to help out, especially if they've done something similar. And of course the twins sent Denis a thank-you.

Because they would need to have food dropped at different ports, Casey and Ryan also read books and blogs by Pacific Crest Trail hikers, who pre-ship food to outposts miles ahead on their own journeys.

Then they called Joe Bark. In the sport of prone paddleboarding, Joe Bark is one of the best paddleboard builders around. The twins hired him to build two eighteen-foot boards, each with a small rack to hold more than seventy pounds of gear: a camping stove, a satellite phone, two sets of rudders, a medical kit, a tent, sleeping bags, and a 12-gauge shotgun in case of bears. They brought one thick wetsuit each, booties and gloves, an EPIRB (emergency position-indicating radio beacon) to alert search and rescue services, flares, and a weather radio.

This stuff cost money. A lot of money. The food was also expensive—$6,000 for several months of freeze-dried meals. The Higginbothams could have collected sponsors to help offset costs. Some brands did donate gear here and there, but the twins decided they would rather just work extra lifeguard shifts to save up. When you have a wild idea, it is sometimes going to cost some money. Pitching funders, as I'll talk about later, can be more hassle than just paying for it yourself.

Once they got educated, they plotted their course, literally. For every day, they also made sure to have a backup plan and a backup landing point (Plan B) about halfway toward their mileage goal. Each spot had to be protected from big waves, with access to a freshwater source.

They also had a hard deadline to get started. The twins gave themselves one year from March 15, 2015, the day they shook on the idea to leave from Alaska. It would not be enough time to fully prepare, but enough to learn the most important things. On March 18, 2016, when the twins were twenty-three years old, they left.

At the last minute, a friend, Kellen Keene, decided to make a documentary film, *By Hand*, about the expedition, giving the twins GoPros and a camera to record themselves along the way, which was exciting but added some extra gear to deal with.

"We planned really well," Casey told me. "But you don't know what you don't know. We didn't know what it was gonna feel like in Alaska with all that gear."

Though they had practiced paddling some serious distances, the twins hadn't actually practiced two things: first, paddling their boards fully loaded with gear, a mistake that would surface the minute they took off from Alaska. The second was working together as a team every day for such an extended length of time.

The twins did their best, got some great video footage, and had some serious close calls (which you will hear more about in chapter 9). Because they'd been educated and had a Plan B (and a Plan C) with a strong vision, and lots of motivation, and faith, they made it in about seven months.

> *ProTip:* If doing any sort of multiday backcountry excursion, consider taking a Wilderness First Aid class and a backcountry navigation class. You will learn invaluable skills that can help you get you out of serious jams in the wild and might save a life.

THERE ARE THOSE kinds of trips where finding help is scarce, and those where there is zero margin for error whatsoever. As intense and dangerous as the Higginbothams' adventure was, they were usually within sight of land—meaning it was at least possible they could find help when they needed it.

Chris and Marty Fagan, a married couple from Washington State, would have little ability to get help when they decided to ski unsupported to the South Pole. I realize that few of us are going to paddle from Alaska to Mexico or ski to the South Pole. But the way Chris and Marty Fagan had to prepare for every detail of their trip offers a master class in planning, something we can all use as inspiration for any kind of adventure we take.

In 2013, Chris and Marty Fagan skied 570 miles each, taking forty-eight days to reach the South Pole unaided and unsupported, meaning they would have no one carrying their gear, no one to help them navigate, and nowhere to resupply their food, or gear, including camp stove and fuel to melt snow for water, along the way. In doing so they would break a record, becoming the first American married couple to do so. But the expedition would test them as individuals, as a couple and family, and take everything they had to get them there.

It would also require in-depth, meticulous planning, and an outline that could rival most successful start-up businesses. In fact, that's exactly how the couple approached their prep. Chris and Marty Fagan aren't exactly weekend warriors. The couple had built a life around adventure. They met in May 1998 while climbing Denali, when Chris was in her early thirties.

It was a classic adventure love story. Chris had left a big ad agency job in Chicago to start her own firm in Seattle, leading brainstorming sessions for corporations. She met a group of adventurous women while taking an intermediate mountaineering course in Seattle, and two of the women suggested climbing Denali, so Chris took a month off to join them. Chris had already done a few climbing trips and traveled around the Cook Islands, New Zealand, Australia, Malaysia, Thailand, and Japan by herself. In her early thirties in 1998, Chris was in good shape and thought Denali would be an awesome adventure. Plus, she'd just completed a six-month mountaineering course with her new friends from Seattle, so it would be a great place to test her new skills.

Marty was a police officer in the bicycle division of the Honolulu Police Department. Two years older than Chris, he was on Denali with a group of buddies a tent over. Every day, Marty and his friends would ask the ladies how they were doing, and Marty continued to flirt with Chris specifically. He even made pancakes that he delivered to her tent.

The day they came down the mountain after summiting, Marty asked Chris to meet him for a drink. After talking well into the night and re-alizing how much they had in common—mostly a love for all things adventure—they both decided to change their flights back home. Six weeks after that, Marty packed up, left Hawaii, and moved to Seattle. He thought he'd get a job with the Seattle Police Department but ended up getting a great job at a tech company instead.

At that point, Chris said she and Marty had the equivalent of a college degree in adventure. But they thought that together they might be able to combine their double passions and get a PhD, so to speak, learning to-gether and testing themselves in the wild. They married, and over the years together climbed mountains around Washington, fast-packed around Mount Blanc, sailed to Alaska, and finished dozens of ultramarathons.

But in 2010, when they were officially middle aged, Marty came up with a really wild idea. One day in the kitchen, he casually asked Chris, "What do you think about going to the South Pole?" Initially, she was taken aback; it took her a few weeks to even agree to consider it. In fact, the two of them didn't officially decide to commit to the adventure for a full year while they researched it. Sure, they'd done some crazy adventures, but aside from the open ocean, the South Pole is about as untrammeled as it gets. They would have to drag sleds 570 miles, all alone without a store, human, or sign of another human for months.

The two had built a family together and lived thirty minutes outside Seattle, in North Bend. They had a son, Keenan, who would be in middle school when they made the trip. They were worried about leaving Keenan for an extended time. Some people also thought they were crazy to leave their kid behind to do such a wild adventure.

Still, the idea of the South Pole was pretty alluring, and they didn't want to wait for a number of reasons. They realized that climate change was threatening the South Pole quickly. They also knew Marty's knees, which had been bothering him from years of distance running, were not getting better. They were at their peak of fitness and not getting younger.

They gave themselves two years to plan, which seems like a lot of time. But this quest was ambitious and wound up taking three years total, including an extra year to plan more, and to gain and vet their skills. They also needed more time for Keenan to grow and get comfortable with the idea.

"We wanted to get educated fast, but also not dive into the deep end right away," Chris told me. They also had to save money, because when they tried to get sponsorships, they found the process too tedious. Chris and Marty both had good jobs, so they decided to just keep working and save up. "The key thing we did," Chris said, "is we kept moving every day to keep reaching toward this big wild idea."

Small steps add up. The important thing, Chris told me, is to keep going. Every small step matters. Momentum is crucial to turning a wild idea from dream to reality.

Like the Higginbothams, they also approached people for advice, seeking out those who had already gone to the South Pole. When it comes to doing anything proficiently, it's helpful to go straight to the smartest people you can find. (That's not to say they'll always call you back.) Still, there is always someone to call who will help. All you need is someone one step ahead of you. One polar expert even agreed to meet Marty in Norway, where he filled a notebook full of tips and information. It's also where Marty picked up custom fiberglass sleds for their trek.

Because you can only really test yourself for the South Pole in the coldest and windiest of conditions, Marty and Chris took separate turns in separate locations—Minnesota and Norway—at the height of winter, each spending a week with a guide to work on their fitness, fortitude, and endurance. They also wanted to have the guide vet their skills to make sure they'd be okay in the wilds of Antarctica. This was all part of their education and planning.

At home, they ran hills, pulled tires to simulate sleds, and hiked endless miles. They invested in good gear, from the fiberglass sleds to quality skis and poles, weatherproof tents, cold-weather parkas, and other attire.

For food, they ran hundreds of calculations. They'd be burning 8,000 calories a day, but they could only carry 5,400 calories a day. That's about 2.5 pounds of food a day for forty-five days—about 100 pounds total per person (about half the total weight of their cargo). They also gained weight before setting off, knowing they'd lose it skiing.

In diving into their plan, they created spreadsheets and to-do lists for food, gear, medical kit, and repair kit. They filled another binder with spreadsheets for getting themselves and all their gear to and from Antarctica. They organized various family and friends to stay at home with twelve-year-old Keenan during the two months they'd be gone. They left copious notes on his daily schedule and a lot of "what to do if X happens" scenarios.

Part of the reason why planning was so important is there was little margin for error. They would have to bring everything that they needed with them to Antarctica. Even if they did radio for help, it would take many hours, if not days, to reach them. All energy would also be used skiing and surviving. They wouldn't have the calories for any more complicated planning aside from going to the next destination every day.

Also included in their binders of information left at home were pre-written notes to Keenan so he could read a sweet message from his mom and dad every day. Chris and Marty brought a satellite phone, not only for safety but also to check in with Keenan every other day. The last thing Chris included was a sealed letter to Keenan, in case something went terribly wrong. Writing that one letter became a great exercise in sharing their family's values, their why for adventuring, and their love for their son. On a grand adventure that involves risk, you just never know.

Chris and Marty set off in winter of 2013. Once they started, they actually realized they could break a record for being the fastest American married couple to reach the South Pole, but while skiing for forty-eight days they did run into some unexpected challenges you'll read about in chapter 9. Even with contingency plan upon contingency plan, they almost didn't make it out.

BACKYARD MAPS

You don't need to go to an exotic place to have a wild adventure. So many inspiring adventures ignited during the pandemic, but one that excited me most took almost zero planning: REI's Tiniest Mile challenge. The goal: to ignite the spirit of adventure while social distancing, and without requiring participants to invest in almost anything. Some people ran around their block. Others ran around their driveways, having to do multiple laps. One guy even ran around his couch.

I have many friends doing similar feats: running their own marathons, half marathons, or even triathlons by using the terrain outside their door. It takes less planning to do an adventure outside your living room and you can come back in between the swim, bike, and run to refuel from your own fridge and use your own bathroom. I often run as far as I can at low tide on the beach and ask a friend or take a rideshare home. My map is just the coastline, and I can stop in stores to use the restroom or buy food along the way.

In the same vein, there's also the David Goggins's 4x4x48 challenge, which is to run four miles every four hours for forty-eight hours, so the only real preplanning you have to do is map out four miles. I have friends who do this every year as a tradition, having potluck meals in between. You can riff on this how you want, even doing one mile every four hours for forty-eight hours, or even one mile every hour for twelve hours to try something during daylight hours.

Another one: the entrepreneur and ultrarunner Jesse Itzler holds an annual event in his backyard called Hell on a Hill, where participants simply run up and down an incredibly steep (40 percent slope) grassy hill that's about eighty yards in his backyard one hundred times (or as much as they can) for charity. He's also the co-founder of 29029 Everesting, an event where participants go to ski mountains and get to simulate climbing up to the distance of Mount Everest (without the extreme cost or distance to get there) by running or walking up a ski hill and taking the gondola down until they've reached the 29,029 feet of climbing distance.

OKAY, before you say, "Whoa, Shelby, I'm not going to the South Pole, or go paddling from Alaska to Mexico . . . ," well, I'm not either. Not everyone's wild idea involves such high risk and planning. But all wild ideas involve getting out of your comfort zone and exposing yourself to some risk.

If you are going to free solo El Capitan like Alex Honnold did (please don't), you risk death immediately after you start. Low risk might be going for a 5K run outside your house. Once you get out the door, regardless of how hard or not you've trained, you'll still have to slay that inner voice inside you telling you to stop.

Our bodies want us to be comfortable. That's how we survive. But sometimes we have to break that comfort to reach a higher reward: internal growth or a view at the top of a grand mountain. That means pushing through discomfort, crushing that inner voice that tells us we need to quit, and pushing through. We also have to make a plan, so we don't get hurt and we actually enjoy ourselves along the way. And a Plan B and even a Plan C and D if your adventures involve more serious risk. If all wild ideas were easy, everyone would do them.

When I started *Wild Ideas Worth Living* in 2016, I'd completed a few wild ideas, ones that involved getting outside and out of my comfort zone.

In starting a podcast, I was not blazing trails by any means, but it still felt like a pretty wild idea to me at the time. Plus, I had a strong why. I wanted to tell stories of people truly going for it, and I wanted it to be my business full-time. I loved interviewing people, even more than writing, and over the years had built up a decent Rolodex of people whose stories I wanted to tell in a bigger way. A few of my stories had been edited down to sound bites and I had a feeling that podcasting was the perfect medium to tell stories in a fuller form. I also had taken an online strengths finder test, the results of which showed me that I had the skills to launch a show and gave me the confidence to do so. And humming along in the background was this: I knew life was short.

While I had plenty of journalism and marketing experience and had interviewed plenty of people who'd started businesses, I didn't know how to actually start a business myself. I came up with the title *Wild Ideas Worth Living* while hiking in Central California (the best ideas often come outside in nature). As soon as I did, I bought the URL on GoDaddy off my cell phone. (It was my fourth choice—the first three were taken—but I've grown to love it.)

What I needed to do next was invest in myself more, something I was scared to do. Being scared to invest in yourself is common. If you invest in yourself and you fail, you might feel like you just blew your money. But if you invest in your own education or personal development, it's the best investment you will ever make. And betting on yourself is risky. But who else is going to bet on you?

In 2016, podcasts weren't new by any means, but a lot of people still hadn't heard of them. Going to business school to learn how to start one seemed silly. Shortly after I bought the domain name, I was surfing with a friend when she told me about a twelve-week business entrepreneurship accelerator program she'd completed, one that was run by a woman for women. The only problem: the class started that day.

I knew enough about listening to signs by then that I got out of the water and called the director, Sylvia Mah, right there from the beach, while I was still dripping wet. Somehow, she let me in the class, and I showed up with wet hair only two hours late. She even gifted me her salad for lunch. (That's a trail angel right there, something you will learn more about in chapter 10.)

The twelve-week course was exactly what I needed: it was long enough that I could form my idea but not so long that I would bail on the commitment. On day one, I wrote my business plan on a giant posterboard. Having to create one right on the spot and lay it out visually was incredibly helpful. I knew what I wanted to do, so it was straight from the heart. Using the posterboard allowed me to visualize all the tedious things I'd need to do reach my goal so I could focus on the steps along the way rather just on the end result. Funny enough: it was very similar to what I would write if I had to create a new business plan today.

On the last day of the class, three months later, we would have to present our "product" live to a team of investors. That meant I had to have my podcast done and ready in three weeks. Which, in the podcast world, meant I needed three episodes and a trailer. That seemed daunting.

The entrepreneur Ramit Sethi, author of *I Will Teach You to Be Rich*, says, "If you get tired of walking up the hill, just run." Sometimes going faster is easier because you don't get caught up in your own head.

I have a bit of a perfectionist in me, and I know many of you will relate. I am especially a perfectionist about my work. I want it to be so good that sometimes I get paralyzed by the fear of failing. I either sabotage myself, procrastinate, or beat myself up the whole way through, making the process unbearable.

Luckily, three months didn't give me a lot of time to overthink it. I just had to work as fast as possible, and I wasn't about to get bogged down. This is part of what lured me to podcasting. I loved the fact that I would have to record a new show every week. The pace meant that I couldn't stress about making each show perfect—I'd just have to make another one the next week. I thought it would be the ideal cure for my own perfectionism complex. And in many ways, starting a podcast was.

The accelerator program was one of the best investments I made. It forced me to look at my podcast as a business from day one. Having a deadline kept me motivated. Having a place where I showed up, did the work, and was accountable to others kept me in the game. Creating a business plan and having a teacher gave me both a guide and a map to follow.

Because I had so much to learn, I also invested in a podcast producer to help me edit and launch my first three shows. There was no way I was going to learn sound editing and figure out all the tech that quickly. And I needed the money to finance it.

THIS IS WHERE we get into the art of pitching, which could be—and probably is somewhere several times over—a whole book in itself. But I do want to share what I've learned to help you make your pitch for your wild idea.

It's scary to ask people for money. Most people don't want to do it unless they have to. But if the idea is something you believe in and you believe that your idea can also benefit the people you are pitching, it can be a win-win. In my case, I decided to pitch companies that I thought might want to sponsor my podcast. I started with ones I had worked with, and then some that I was just a big fan of. Luckily for me, I wasn't starting from scratch. I did have some experience after decades of pitching stories to magazines.

What helped the most was that I really believed in what I was doing. I offered companies rates that I thought were fair. Even though a few rejected me at first, I had so much passion, had such a genuine pitch, and got noticeably better at podcasting, that sponsors said yes and signed on. I also had a unique angle—at the time, no one I knew of had a podcast about adventure and actions sports that targeted both men and women, and was hosted by a woman.

When people said yes to support my show, I was ecstatic. The podcast was a culmination of everything I wanted to do, using every skill I'd built to that date. Having others buy in also gave me serious faith in myself and my momentum. Because I was paying most of the initial start-up fees out of my savings, and now had companies behind me supporting me, I had even more accountability to make a standout show.

All of these things really helped me get going. I announced my idea. I had a plan. I got educated fast, which gave me momentum, skills, and confidence. I had a few Plan Bs, and Cs in the form of backup sponsors. I invested in myself by paying for my business course, a producer, equipment, a website, a hosting platform, and more. I pitched not only sponsors but also people to be guests on the show whom I didn't even know. One of my first guests was Pete Kostelnick, whom I'd read about in the newspaper and emailed after he finished running across the United States.

Maybe you'll be funding your wild ideas on your own. Maybe you'll need help funding them. Either way, at some point you will likely have to pitch someone about your wild idea. And it might not be a big idea either. You may need to approach your boss for time off, or your partner to help juggle responsibilities at home while you are training for that marathon or speed-walking coast to coast, or just taking a weekend to hike your local mountain. Or maybe you'll need to pitch someone as an accomplice to join in on your idea. These lessons still apply there.

In my case, I had one ideal sponsor, REI Co-op, who I thought would reach my future listeners—women who wanted to get outside. This was in 2016, and a friend told me about REI's new women-centered Force of Nature campaign. Well, *helloooo!!* I am a woman. I am outdoorsy. I'd been covering women and the outdoors since I was nineteen. It seemed almost tailored to me. I used all my skills to find and pitch the right person at REI, and while I had high hopes, all I got was a polite, "No thanks." Or more like, "Shelby, you seem really enthusiastic, but we aren't in the podcast business."

With wild ideas—whether you are trekking up a mountain or starting a movement or even a small podcast—you will likely hear a no, or a lot of nos, from potential sponsors or mentors, or from a boss, a family member, or someone else. This shouldn't deter you. Nos can be helpful. Sometimes people say no because the timing is just off. Or because it's not a good fit. Pitching is a lot like dating—sometimes there's chemistry, and sometimes there's not.

The key is that your pitch has to be valuable not just for you, but for the other party. I particularly wanted to pitch REI because my goal with *Wild Ideas Worth Living* was to encourage more people to get outside and find their own wild ideas and I couldn't think of a better catalyst. That's what the company already did, and they had a lot more reach than I did.

I went on to pitch more companies and get a lot more nos. But after I launched my show, improved it, made a great pitch deck, and started pitching ten companies a day, I started getting some yeses and partnered with a lot of great brands.

So what does this all mean? Well, sometimes you are going to get rejected. You have to keep going. Sometimes a pitch doesn't work right away. Sometimes the timing isn't right or your own pitch isn't quite motivating enough, and you need to refine your ask. Sometimes it's about finding the right person to pitch. Sometimes it's about making your pitch stand out. And it's learning that sometimes "no" just means "not now."

Six months after launching my show, I called REI back. Turns out they were just getting into podcasts. REI ended up becoming a sponsor, and today REI Co-op Studios owns and produces the whole show, while I continue to host it. What started out as a no became a "not now," and then an incredible partnership that continues to grow.

I know I am making it sound easy, and like it all fits together like the pieces of a puzzle. The reality is that in addition to a little luck and good timing, it took months of focused effort and decades of working in the outdoor industry to make my wild idea a reality. Hard work is inevitable when you do something you love. But the important thing I learned is to never take rejection personally. Also, that many things will happen, just not always exactly as you imagined in the exact timing you may want. Stay the course anyway.

WHILE ALL THESE newfound skills are great, they are not the most important things to bring on a wild adventure. For that, you need to look within yourself to find vision, motivation, and, most of all, faith in yourself and your wild idea. These are all things you can't buy and you can't out-source. But you can cultivate them.

First, vision. You have to be excited about your wild idea. If you are not, it's going to be very hard to pull off. And if you are doing something for ulterior motives or because it seems "cool" or you think it's something you "should" do, or something someone else wants you to do, it's going to be very hard to make it happen. Your idea should excite you. Yes, it might scare you, but you must also be stoked about it and have the vision that you will make it happen. So do what you can to make it fun! Listen to music that gets you pumped up. Add some jelly beans to your survival kit. Don't forget your emergency candy! Also consider the steps you will need to take along the way. A lot of people make vision boards with pictures of their ultimate goal: the summit of a mountain, a fully formed business, a house on the beach. In your mind or on an actual board, also visualize what you'll need to do to get there (e.g., training for your goal, getting your gear, or studying your trail map).

Motivation is key as well. Having a deadline, some momentum, and skin in the game will help you stay on track. Having friends who support you (more about that in the next chapter) and people who have your back can help keep you going. But sometimes you will be totally alone, and this is where you need to dig deep and find your own drive to keep going. Go back to your why. Write it down. Stick it on your bathroom mirror or your computer keyboard. Make your wild idea bigger than just you if that helps. Just do what you have to do to stay motivated and keep going.

Lastly, faith. That big staircase leading to nowhere. There's a lot of unknowns in adventures and wild ideas. There are no guarantees. Not every trail map is going to have straight lines. Faith is a surrendering to the unknown. It is a release. That is something you need to have when you want to see a wild idea through.

And when you are fueled by vision, motivation, and faith, that's when serendipity steps in. Often, when you start out on a wild idea, something even better happens along the way. For me, starting a podcast led to another podcast, this book, the most incredible friends, and so much more. When you really care, you are going to put your all into it. You might not make a lot of money or even progress at first. But if you stick with it, just like if you stick with a steep trail up a mountain, you just might get to the top. Even if you don't, you will likely connect with some awesome people or, more important, with a deeper, stronger, more authentic, and more vulnerable version of yourself. No matter what, you'll learn something great along the way.

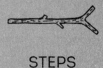

STEPS

Every person's journey will be different. But after launching my own wild ideas and after hearing about so many others, I've found that the same guidelines seemed to apply for almost all adventures. These are general guidelines. Obviously, this is your trail. You can go down as many winding roads as you want. These are just suggestions to get you going and keep you on whatever path is best for you to get the view you want.

Step one: Say your wild idea out loud, and then write it on a piece of paper. It's been proven by dozens of different studies that if you write something down you'll remember it better and follow through.

Step two: Now, write your why behind it, which will help you keep going even when you want to quit. Go even further by telling someone else. This will also keep you accountable because now other people know.

Step three: List all the things you'll likely need to learn to make it happen. This might include how to read a topographic map, drive a stick shift, tie boating knots, or ride a bike with clip-in pedals. It could be a new language, a skill, or something else to boost your mental game. While you're at it, make a list of the things you might need to get going, from a rain jacket and tent to a pair of running shoes.

Step four: Get educated—as fast as you can and as much as you can. This is where you start gaining the skills you will need on your journey, including knowledge. You're not going to be able to learn everything you need to know, but you need to learn as much as possible quickly. I have found that, if it takes too long it's hard to stay motivated. Any amount of new knowledge will not only help lessen fear of the unknown but will also help you stay safe and have a deeper experience.

Don't know where to begin? Start typing out your questions in a search engine. You will be amazed at how much, and how fast, you can learn online. Then research whom you might be able to approach with questions. I find that learning from people who have done something like your wild idea before is very helpful. If they teach a class or course online, consider taking it. Read books—accounts of people's own experience as well as how-to guides. (Books in some ways can be better than the Internet. Books generally take someone a year or more to research, and usually a year or more to write. The Internet—well, it's the Internet.)

Step five: Plan your course and set deadlines. You can do this however you want. Some people like to use Excel spreadsheets (I'm not one of those people). Some just write something down on a piece of paper or in a note on their phone. I use a calendar and enter the dates for when I need to get things accomplished. The calendar holds me accountable. Otherwise, if you're like me, you might drag your feet. With wild ideas, you are never going to be as ready as you want to be. Eventually, you have to actually start (more on that in chapter 7). Having deadlines will keep you on track and give you something to look toward. When you combine your why with an actual deadline, it creates a powerful combo to turn your idea into reality. Sometimes, when you have a wild idea and you think it will take too long to achieve, it can impede you from actually doing it. Sometimes you're going to have to invest more time or some of your own money. Either way,

I believe momentum will also get you there faster. And a plan or map of sorts will keep you on track. Lastly, remember the seven Ps, a saying my partner, Johnny, loves: prior proper planning prevents piss-poor performance.

Step six: Make a Plan B. If you have a Plan B, Plan A generally works out. Plan B can be a looser plan, but having an alternative can often get you out of a jam. If your wild idea is to hike a certain trail and find water at a certain spot, Plan B might look like having extra water in your pack, plus taking a filter. If you're starting a podcast, as I was, Plan B might look like having a backup recording in case your recorder dies or your memory card malfunctions (which definitely has happened more than once). If your adventure involves serious risk, you may also want to have a Plan C, just in case.

Step seven: Invest in yourself. It's the best investment you can make. This might mean paying for a trainer, a course, a plane ticket, or gear that will keep you safe. You don't have to buy the most expensive gear, but don't go cheap when it comes to important things like mountaineering boots or crampons for ice climbing, strong ropes for rappelling, or a rain fly for stormy conditions when sleeping outside. Take it from me: I recently agreed to hike down the Grand Canyon in the spring when it was still snowing and only brought my trail running shoes. It would have been a great investment to spend a few bucks to buy a pair of crampons at the camp store, rather than slip and slide, raising my heart rate the entire way down an icy trail to the bottom.

The good news is that products today are really well-made; with a little searching, it's easy to buy good used gear without breaking the bank. For most of my life I only ran and hiked in cotton tees and hand-me-down soccer shorts. You don't need name-brand gear: you need gear that works. And if you don't have any gear, then start with what you have. Don't let that be a deterrent to getting you outside.

Step eight: Work on your pitch. You're likely going to have to pitch your idea to someone—a boss, a spouse, a kid, a parent, a co-worker, a partner, a potential sponsor, or even your own self-doubt. When you work on your pitch, do it with love. Be genuine. Always let people know why you are doing something, and if you want something from them you have to be able to offer something to them in return, whatever that looks like for you.

Step nine: Cultivate vision, motivation, and faith. This might be the most important step of them all. Education and planning will only take you so far. You can spend years on a plan. But eventually, you need to start. Skill will take you far. But vision, motivation, and faith will allow you to do things you never thought you could do and make the journey that much more fun. When it comes to visualization, don't just visualize reaching the summit of the mountain; visualize all the steps you need to get to the base of the mountain as well.

Step ten: Don't forget to pack your own version of emergency candy, something I learned from a Girl Scout. This may go beyond gummy bears, chocolate, or your favorite coffee. The joy is in the journey, so pack the things that make it more fun and celebrate along the way.

PLAN AND PRACTICE A MINI-ADVENTURE

One thing I recommend is stepping up like you are the Scout leader and planning a mini-adventure with your friends. This is a great way to test your skills. You can divvy up duties, but try a night or a weekend trip on a smaller scale. Here are some things you could also attempt:

- Plan a mini road trip with and stay at a cool glamp-site or rental. You can also check out sites like Hip-camp for alternative camping destinations.
- Plan a short day hike with some friends. Have a cooler of snacks packed for the end and bring some extra treats to keep them motivated.
- Book a guided trip and invite your besties along. That way you all get to learn from a pro and share in the adventure together, but you take the initiative.
- Book your nearest campsite, or the nearest park with a fire pit that allows actual fires, gather ingredients for s'mores, and invite your friends to a potluck dinner on a weeknight when sites are more available.
- Or try one of my favorite adventures, the birthday adventure. You get to do your adventure in the distance of your age. You can use decimal points to break that up or spread out your attempt over the week or even month. For example, if you are turning forty-two? Spend that week trying to catch forty-two waves,

running forty-two miles, or doing forty-two sends at the climbing gym. You can also do this over the week, the month, or the day, or use a decimal point (example 4.2 miles) to scale it for your liking. You can even do something like forty-two wild ideas in forty-two days. It's a great way to celebrate a year around the sun with some adventure.

CHAPTER 6

CULTIVATE COMMUNITY

**Friendship is like wetting your pants.
Everyone can see it, but only you feel the warmth.**

—The Golden Girls

You have stoke; you have motivation; you have faith. You know your why. You've gone outside. You have a plan. Now it's time to find your people. Sometimes you find your people after you start. Sometimes you find them before you even begin and they lead you to your wild idea and help carry you along. Either way, finding your community is a big part of living wildly and carrying out a wild idea successfully.

Now, you don't *have* to have a community to pursue a wild idea. But if you want to sail across the Pacific, it's helpful to be around sailors and to look out for one another, warn one another about pirates or coral heads, and to share that "it's five o'clock somewhere" margarita. If you're hiking the Pacific Crest Trail, knowing there are people like you who want to spend months walking along a trail and camping every night is incredibly refreshing. You can also trade tips, gear, snacks, playlists, meals, and more. If you want to run a 5K, a marathon, or an ultramarathon, having others to commiserate with makes running a whole lot more enjoyable.

Pursuing wild ideas can be superlonely, and at times you may feel like a total weirdo. Finding others who are pushing themselves, who can share ideas with you, and who are equally as weird makes it all go more smoothly. I'm not saying you need to ditch your friends and make new ones, but often it helps to be around others who are also wilding themselves. When you find a community of people that makes you feel so utterly yourself, you automatically can do so much more, and lift others up along the way. Together we can always achieve so much more than we can on our own.

COMMUNITY IS CURRENCY. While on a work trip to Australia, I went on a sunrise run in Manly Beach when I passed a dozen surfers rocking bright neon full-piece swimsuits. We're talking bold outfits here—they wore animal prints, tutus, butterfly wings, and had bright pink-and-green Zinka sunscreen plastered over their faces. My host had told me about this group, OneWave. They got together every week to surf in fluorescent colors and talk about the invisible issue of mental illness. They called their sessions Fluro Fridays, and I wanted to learn all about it. So after they got out of the water, I asked the group's founder, Grant Trebilco, a surfer originally from New Zealand, if I could join them the next week. "We'll bring you a onesie," he said, knowing that I probably had forgotten to bring anything fluorescent with me to Australia.

The following Friday at 6:30 a.m., Grant greeted me with a bear hug and handed me a bright yellow-and-pink Lycra jumpsuit bearing an image of a lion. How he owned that suit, I had no idea, but the Australians clearly have some fun style. I wasn't sure if I'd be able to hang with these Aussie surfers, but I instantly felt happier and more relaxed just slipping the costume over my wetsuit. It looked ridiculous and awesome at the same time.

As the group gathered, I looked around and saw mostly young professionals in their twenties and thirties, people who looked just like me. They laughed, exchanged more hugs, and passed around tubes of bright sunscreen. Then, as is tradition, the group formed a small "anti–bad vibes" circle before paddling out. That's when Grant shared words of encouragement.

"It's okay to not always be okay," Grant told the group. While this is a more socially accepted mantra today, at the time I'd never heard an athlete, especially a male surfer, talk so openly about mental health. "Wellness is a lifelong journey," Grant said. "Everyone has bad days." A few members of the group shared gratitude, but nothing was preachy or heavy. The whole interaction lasted about five minutes, and then we jumped into the ocean.

As I looked around, I saw people from all different backgrounds and ages donning superhero costumes, electric blue leggings, dresses, and more. They worked in different industries and were at various surfing levels from total beginners to semi-pros. While surfing a new spot usually feels intimidating to me, the costumes put everyone on more equal footing. I instantly felt at ease.

The waves were average-sized, and the group was respectful of any serious local surfers. Most of us stayed on the inside, away from where the best waves were breaking. We exchanged "party waves," where we all rode the same waves to shore. There were a lot of *yeeww*'s and *wahoo*'s in the air.

These Fluro sessions were something that the surfers looked forward to the entire workweek, rain or shine. They told me it made them feel less alone, introduced them to new friends, helped them open up—and, of course, get better at surfing. One surfer recounted leaving his house in West Sydney at 3:30 a.m. to take the train and then the bus two hours to come to Fluro Fridays. He'd been struggling with depression, something he never talked about, until many Fridays after joining the group. Now every Friday, he wore his pink business suit and actually loved it when people on the train and bus asked him about it.

After my first Fluro Friday session, I grabbed a coffee with Grant. A few years prior, he told me, during a manic episode that involved paddling into the lineup of a professional surf contest as a spectator and causing quite a scene, he was hospitalized and then diagnosed with bipolar disorder. After Grant was discharged from the hospital, he says surfing saved him. Riding just one wave a day was enough to make Grant feel a little better. Having friends to surf with was also really important. They kept him accountable; they motivated him to get out of bed and show up to the beach.

For a lark one early evening as Grant was recovering, he decided to wear a suit and tie when he paddled out. "This guy started asking me about it," Grant said, "and I just told him my story and then he opened up about how mental illness affected him too."

Grant loved the idea that his outfit had started a conversation about mental health, something he'd never discussed. He began surfing in more wild outfits, mostly fluorescent colors. Soon after, he and a friend started OneWave, so named because all it takes is one wave to feel a little better. Grant quickly realized that wearing bright colors acted as a highlighter for a traditionally invisible topic.

When I met Grant in 2014, a year after he started OneWave, the community had spread to nearby beaches in Bondi, Byron Bay, and throughout Australia, New Zealand, and Bali. Since then, the group has gone global, with meetups at over two hundred beaches worldwide. Through their weekly Fluro Fridays, the group offers free surfing and yoga sessions to share joy and reduce the social stigma around mental health issues. The recipe they post on their website—"saltwater therapy, surfing, and fluro"—has helped many members around the globe. OneWave has also started running "Free the Funk" programs to raise awareness about mental health issues in schools and workplaces, having impacted over 30,000 people.

Looking back, surfing with Fluro Fridays was a milestone for me. I even hosted a few OneWave sessions in California and Costa Rica. In those days, I had just started to talk about my own struggles with mental health. It was wild to hear other surfers opening up. It was welcoming and nonjudgmental, and I felt more connected and vulnerable in a way I'd ever experienced.

ProTip: Finding your community can also mean finding your people. I tell all my friends who move to a new city or want to meet new friends that there's no better place than an outdoor community event or organization where you are doing something good for others outside. You don't have to pay too much attention to what you're wearing, as you would at a typical networking event. You're usually doing something active that boosts your endorphins, and you will likely meet other good-hearted, kind, adventurous souls.

A COMMUNITY WILL KEEP you accountable, keep you going, keep you healthy (even when you don't want to show up), and give you something to look forward to. They will also help you be less afraid to try new things, go further distances, keep pushing, and make you laugh when you need to. When you join an existing community, they'll also just help you to feel less alone and less afraid to do scarier things, push you to be your best self, and defend you when you need.

Surfing, of course, has been a key part of my own will to wild. In 1996, I started teaching surfing at Surf Diva, the original all-women's surf school. I was sixteen. A woman named Izzy Tihanyi, who was my favorite camp counselor at that water sports camp I went to as a kid, had started Surf Diva that same year, with her twin sister, Coco. They now also teach men and kids to surf too.

Back then, though, most of the instructors were women. And besides Izzy, I didn't know many other women who surfed as much as she did. Sure, I'd played on women's soccer teams growing up and I knew the power of being part of a team of other confident women, but surfing is such an individual activity. To meet other women who faced the same issues of having sand in every orifice, dealing with the occasional weird comment some guy made in the lineup, always trying to find wetsuits that actually fit, and sharing the same fears was incredibly refreshing.

The women were also confident, fun, and had a connection to nature and themselves that I admired. When we all surfed together, just like when the OneWave Crew got together, it was a giant party, with hooting, hollering, and lots of laughing. If anyone said anything mean to us, my friends would give them hell. And when the surf was bigger and the other women were charging, I felt so much more at ease to paddle out and catch bigger waves. Plus, since most of them were older than I was, they also gave me grief if I didn't paddle out. That in itself was motivation to get out there. If they could do it (or were going to tease me for not paddling out), you bet I paddled out. I still keep in touch with the original Surf Diva crew to this day. Many of their own kids now surf with us.

While finishing writing this book, I spoke with open-water marathon swimmer Melissa Kegler. The IT specialist told me she went from being an average pool swimmer to someone who had swam around Manhattan Island, across the English Channel, and so much more after finding a supportive swim group who pushed her and supported her efforts. When Melissa moved to Seattle for a job almost a decade ago, she joined the Notorious Alki Swimmers, which meets weekly at Seattle's Alki Beach to swim in the Puget Sound. The group's few dozen members are a mix of all shapes, sizes, colors, and speeds—people training for national and world records alongside people learning to swim for the first time.

"The group is a safe zone," Melissa told me. "We all have different opinions on different subjects and politics, but when we swim, we're all respectful of each other. We know no one is going to judge you for your politics, religion, profession, or sexual orientation. Everyone is bonded by water. We all share that same passion, and we respect each other for it." It's a true community.

Finding your people is joyous. Sometimes all it takes is seeing someone who looks like you, doing what you want to do, to get you motivated to get out there. Sometimes you join a community and it totally changes your life. Unintentionally, sometimes you even end up creating one.

When Mirna Valerio started running, she didn't fit the stereotype of a typical distance runner. She's a larger Black woman, and there weren't a lot of people who looked like her at races and events, especially as she got into ultrarunning and trail racing. Mirna discovered running in high school as a way to get in shape for the field hockey team. But then after high school and college, life took over: she became a conservatory-trained musician, an opera singer, a teacher, a resident adviser at a boarding school, and a private music instructor, in addition to being a mom and a wife. She achieved so much. But she was always busy. And in putting the needs of so many others first, she had put her own health on the back burner.

In her early thirties, she was driving in the car with her son when she thought she was having a heart attack (luckily, she was not), but the event was a catalyst to get Mirna to prioritize self-care and lace up her old running shoes again.

Mirna started with just a mile or two but quickly increased her distance. She loved moving her body the way it was intended, whether she was outside or on a treadmill, and she loved the euphoric feeling you get after miles on end, the famous "runner's high." She also started feeling better and more energetic all around. She set goals, and soon running became not just self-care, but an act of joy.

She began sharing her journey on a blog she created called *Fat Girl Running* in 2011. The goal was to share, as she put it, "being an active larger girl in a thinner world via the individual yet universal sport of running." Mirna wanted to let people know that *anybody* with *any* body could be a runner. Her blog proved as instantly popular as her personality.

When you meet Mirna, you notice right away that she has an infectious and outgoing personality, a magnetic smile, and an amazing voice. She's also funny. She naturally draws people to her, so it makes sense that she soon had running companions. It started with just work colleagues and friends who saw the joy Mirna experienced while running, and wanted in on the fun. She welcomed the company. Soon she started to find more runners who looked like her.

Mirna continued to work multiple jobs as she started increasing her distances, from 5Ks to 10Ks, to half marathons, to full marathons. In 2013, she completed her first ultramarathon. The ultramarathon running community is on a whole other level from the regular running community, with a different set of bonding. It takes a certain kind of person who wants to run more than 26.2 miles, just for fun, on trails, and camp overnight at races. Mirna loved everything about it, especially the camping part. Many times at these races, Mirna got last place, but she didn't care. It aways felt amazing to finish. She came across most finish lines with a giant grin, fists in the air, cheering for herself, the kind of finish that *starts* the party. It's that level of joy Mirna brings to a sport that is pretty grueling that's made so many others want to be around her.

That level of joy and magnetic humor also came through on her popular blog, *Fat Girl Running*. Readers loved her humorous approach and candid demeanor, and as Mirna kept showing up to more races, and sharing about them, the response was overwhelming.

Mirna's following and community grew quickly. Media outlets such as the *Wall Street Journal, People* magazine, and *Runner's World* all wrote stories about her. REI Co-op Studios made a documentary about her.

One thing that drew so many people to Mirna is how authentic and candid she is about her experience. When she writes about race recaps, she posts hilarious pictures of her trying to climb over boulders, admits that she sometimes trips over twigs and rocks, that her hands swell after fifty kilometers, and she makes you feel like if she can do it, you can too. The teacher in her has a natural way of also helping people get excited and learn along the way, so she regularly features content like how to prep for a race, what to eat on race day, what to wear, and more. She also describes the majestic routes and awe-inspiring landscapes of her runs, speaks about the kind volunteers who help cook for and feed runners during an event, and discusses how she deals with altitude and more. She admits when races are hard, when she wants to quit, when she doesn't finish, and also speaks about when she feels in the flow. She made something incredibly intimidating so much more inviting.

Part of it, Mirna told me when I interviewed her for my podcast, is that she's always been comfortable in her skin. Mirna said she had the privilege of being raised in a family and around people who never tried to make her someone who she was not. She knows that body acceptance isn't part of everyone's upbringing, but it was part of hers, and Mirna loves who she is. She wants other people to love themselves as they are too, no matter what.

"We just have to be authentic to ourselves," she said. "So if you want to go out and be a runner or a hiker and that's an identity you have always wanted to have, you can create that for yourself. It does take some confidence and a swift kick in the ass, but once you go out and do it and you enjoy it, it becomes part of your DNA," she told me. That sense of confidence is contagious.

For Mirna, the magic was always in the messages she got from others too. From people who read her blog and told her they made a decision that *today is the day*. "That I am gonna walk outside, or run outside, even though my family or doctors have told me I am big. I am just gonna go outside and move my body and feel good about it."

Those kinds of messages that thanked Mirna for giving them the courage to get outside and do something for themselves felt incredible, and helped inspire Mirna to run farther and to continue to share her messages.

Unfortunately, along the way, Mirna did get the random hater. That can happen with wild ideas. When you go after what you want, some people can be threatened by you, or the idea of you, or they are just incredibly insecure. Often they are not living wildly themselves and so they become jealous, or scared, or resentful. It's generally never about you—it's about them. Still, haters suck.

In 2017, about six years after she started her blog, Mirna was at a 50K race in North Carolina. She was in the zone, nearing the finish line, and she was elated, as the race had been hard, with freezing and relentless rain, which made the trails muddy and slippery.

She pulled out her phone to take a picture, but that's when she saw a nasty email come across her screen. The sender wrote saying she was running slower than the sender could walk, with some added profanity letting Mirna know she'd never be a professional runner.

The fact that someone had taken the time to find her work email to send such a vicious message hurt a lot. Mirna was in shock, but she kept running. And at that exact moment, Mirna was surrounded by beautiful friends, who'd come to pace her on the last lap of the race, and a bunch of other tired, cold, and supermuddy runners who still managed to say something kind along the way.

After she finished the race, though, Mirna decided to share that awful email comment she received on Instagram. She wanted to let people know that sometimes people are going to try to stop you from being your best self. By that point, Mirna had more than one hundred thousand followers. After she posted the message, thousands of people responded with kind, supportive notes back to her. Mirna realized she had an enormous team behind her. The comments were proof that the running world and the greater outdoor space are filled with supportive people. There is a bigger community of people who matter.

Mirna did eventually respond to the troll. Her response was direct, letting the troll know Mirna gets to decide what beauty and success look like, and that running was something that person could never take away. Mirna learned that she didn't have to accept that cruelness.

"My mantra is *Don't be an asshole*," Mirna told me. She believes in spreading joy. That's how she approaches and grows her own community, and I agree, it's the best way. Some people may try to grow communities otherwise, but living wildly is only about spreading goodness.

If you get haters, don't give them any of your precious time. Keep doing you and keep surrounding yourself with your community—not the people who throw you shade. And if they do throw shade, you can lean on your community to lift you up.

Mirna is still being true to herself. She's still running. She's still sharing her story, and she's lifting others up along the way. She's recruited hundreds, if not thousands, of new runners to the sport. She has over 140,000 followers on Instagram—a pretty big community—and she still gets notes from people who thank her for single-handedly getting them into running. A few years ago, Mirna wondered if she could quit all her jobs and just be a full-time speaker, writer, educator, and runner. It was another wild idea on top of becoming an ultrarunner, and it took a leap of faith, but she did it.

While Mirna's story has continued to reach mainstream media, as of 2021 she has left her teaching job and side hustles, and is living out her most wild of wild ideas: She gets paid to run, to write books such as *A Beautiful Work in Progress*, to be a diversity coach, and to speak all over the world. I just saw her on a billboard at Lululemon, where she is one of the brand's main running ambassadors. Someone inside the store told me Mirna influenced them to start running too. By showing up and being authentically herself, Mirna continues to build a community of runners based on authenticity, kindness, inclusion, and a lot of fun.

A COMMUNITY WILL keep you going and defend you when you most need it. But your community may also move you to stand up for something you believe in, whether it's fighting for preservation of the trails you spend time on, for cleaner ocean water, or to make room for more people like you in the outdoors. Sometimes, like Mirna, you end up building a community, and sometimes you also end up advocating for other communities that need support as well.

Photographer and activist Wyn Wiley knows this firsthand. On October 3, 2018, Wyn had a wild idea. The former Eagle Scout, who is six feet three, ginger faced, Nebraska born and raised, put on a pair of black patent-leather boots with six-inch platform heels and went outside in the dirt while on a backpacking trip with friends on the Continental Divide Trail.

Wyn felt electric in the platform boots. The whole experience was trailblazing, if you'll forgive the pun. Wyn had been venturing outdoors since he was a Scout, but he hadn't seen a lot of queer people outdoors, let

alone a drag queen. When he thought about what nature meant to him—
but also what it had meant to him to not see anyone like him in that space
for so many years—ideas flooded in.

Wyn made a video in the outfit shortly after wearing the boots with
heels as if they were the best new hiking boots around, and declared himself the first outdoor drag queen, naming her Pattie Gonia (The North
Fierce was his second choice). In the video, Pattie, who in addition to platform heel boots was also wearing a green technical shirt, carrying a hiking
backpack and hiking poles, was dancing to Fergie's "London Bridge" while
munching on Cheetos.

Wyn, who refers to himself with male pronouns and to Pattie as
"she"/"her," showed the video to his mom, who thought it was fun, and
posted it that night. The response was overwhelming. People loved it. It
had just enough humor and just enough pizazz that people ate it up. I remember watching it for the first time and I continued to hit "replay." It was
such a contrast to outdoor hiking videos with dudes climbing mountains.
This was so different, so fun. The video went viral.

Pattie Gonia created her own Instagram account. Within a week she
had twelve thousand followers and quickly became bigger than Wyn ever
imagined. Originally the idea was something Wyn made just for himself.
But soon after, he realized he could have more fun with it. He got a wig, recruited friends to help with makeup, and even made videos wearing dresses
made from recycled materials to bring attention to climate change and
other issues. All were set in wilderness scenes with music from artists such
as Beyoncé and Ariana Grande, who also started following Pattie.

In one post, Pattie's strutting down the Brooklyn Bridge during fashion week in New York wearing a tent as a dress and riding a scooter. In
another, she has an image of the earth, reminding us that we only have
one home . . . and that it also has Beyoncé on it. In another post, Pattie's
a park ranger who picks up trash, dances to hip-hop, and admits she's not
totally plastic-free. Pattie is an imperfect environmentalist and advocate
encouraging us that we can do our part to help too, even if we're not perfect
about it.

Being Pattie Gonia provided joy, and a chance to explore multiple
things Wyn loved at once—performance, photography, his own identity,
and shaking shit up! Wyn remembered being a little kid on the playground

and performing, and this was really no different. He just had a different stage: social media. As momentum grew, and more people started following Pattie Gonia, Wyn realized Pattie could be used for something greater than his own creative pursuits. Pattie represented a way to bring more awareness about inclusivity in the outdoors. Pattie used her influence to bring attention to other people advocating for equity and protecting the climate.

I interviewed Wyn and Pattie in 2019, right after Pattie Gonia started going viral. We went surfing, which was a blast. Pattie surfed in platform boots. She was a natural. (The heels made only one small, easily repairable dent in the surfboard.) Being around their energy made me want to be a better person. Here was someone not afraid to be themselves and stand up for others. To me, that's wild and admirable. We made a short video and I was incredibly impressed with the level of professionalism and desire to help others Wyn and Pattie had when it came to the work they were doing.

In 2021, I spoke to Wyn again for this book. Wyn told me that back in 2019, when all this greatness was happening, he'd left something out in our podcast interview: Wyn and Pattie had haters. He was also getting hate mail and losing friends. Some were strangers. But unlike Mirna's, some were people Wyn actually knew.

"When Pattie was going viral and the community was growing, it was so beautiful," he told me, "but at the same time I was losing almost everyone from my past life—people that I thought were my friends and who'd one day be in my wedding party—because they couldn't accept me for being my true queer self. I was also losing clients. Like literal clients were canceling photo work with me, and my house was getting egged."

Wyn didn't share this with me at the time because he was still in the middle of it. It's incredibly unfortunate, but Wyn learned a lot from having haters. Sure, he lost people he thought were part of his community—that part stung. But he used his platform to make space for others. In many ways, his community self-sorted—and became much bigger.

As Wyn explained to me, behind a lot of people's wild ideas they have a more authentic self they want to chase. That can scare people. He also realized that sometimes when you do something wild, you can make room for so many other people to follow after you. That's been one of the biggest gifts he's received through Pattie Gonia and the community that's come from it. It's also propelled Wyn to what he does today.

Wyn developed a barometer for the haters. If they are in the arena doing the same work he is, he'll listen. He'll think about whether he's wrong, and respond appropriately. He also knows that sometimes people project their own insecurities. "Pursuing your wild idea when someone else isn't can make someone feel uncomfortable," he said. "It's like RuPaul says: 'Unless they're paying your bills, pay the haters no mind.'"

I can't say it any better than Wyn and Pattie through RuPaul. You may have haters. When you have a wild idea, it may scare those who love you most because they don't want to see you hurt. It may scare some friends and acquaintances because they want to be living more authentically themselves.

Pattie Gonia has continued to grow over the last few years, helping a lot of other people and communities with their wild ideas. In fact, Pattie's community on social media has helped fund dozens of National Outdoor Leadership School scholarships for queer kids and worked with dozens of nonprofits to push for more inclusivity in the outdoors.

Pattie has also been to the Met Gala, launched brand campaigns, spoken at schools across the country, and led group hikes, for which at least two of my friends drove three hours to hike with her. She even convinced Alex Honnold to rock platform heels (pun intended), and recruited another friend to dress as Pattie's twin and rappel in platform boots in Yosemite.

The impact has been phenomenal, but Pattie always emphasizes that it's Pattie Gonia's community, not her, doing the work. In November 2021, over the five days surrounding Giving Tuesday, Pattie Gonia's community raised over $500,000 for five BIPOC, queer, and environmental nonprofits—donating 100 percent of the funds directly to each group. I know this because I'm on the board of Outdoor Outreach, an organization that received over $100,000 in donations after Pattie Gonia ran a campaign on Instagram, with the participation of 15,277 individual donors.

"When you chase your wild idea," Wyn says, "it's probably going to be incredibly uncomfortable. It's going to be a new butterfly blossoming. But when you go out and do something wild, you shed the skin of a lot of your past lives." You might lose pieces of your old life, but what you gain is worth so much more.

One of the wildest things about the Pattie Gonia community is that it just keeps growing and making room for others. That's where the power in your community lies. Even as I'm going through edits on this book, Wyn has rallied leaders in the outdoor industry to create the Outdoorist Oath, a public commitment that anyone can take to create a more inclusive, better place for one another and the planet, with actionable steps to make that happen. Part of it is a two-hour seminar people attend that teaches how to be a better ally for the planet, inclusion, and adventure. It's a wild idea that has spread like wildfire and just keeps giving.

A COMMUNITY CAN lift you up, and it can help so many others along the way. And by showing up and being authentic, you might even create a community or inspire one in pursuing a wild idea.

That's why it's so important to feed your wild idea like you feed yourself. We're often really careful about what we put into our body. But what we put into our brain—from what we watch and listen to, to what we say to ourselves and whom we choose to spend time with—adds up in the same way.

And even if you want to or have to (hello, pandemic lockdowns) be alone, you can still surround yourself with good content. Read books, watch great movies, or even listen to podcasts until the hosts feel like your friends. (I'll be your friend!)

If someone in your life is holding you back from going after your wild idea, let them go, for now—you can always pick up a friendship after you do the thing you want to do. But if someone is in the way of you chasing your dreams, you might have to give them a time-out.

Remember: community is currency. Choose good thoughts. Choose good teammates and friends. Choose and be part of a great community.

STARTING AN OUTDOOR GROUP
FROM A WILD IDEA

A community can start small, but with the right intentions, it can seriously grow, and even turn into your life's work. One November morning in Boston in 2011, Brogan Graham met an old crew buddy, his fellow Northeastern University alumni Bojan Mandaric, for a 6:29 a.m. workout at Harvard Stadium. The pair made a pact to meet at 6:29 a.m. every day of November, tracking their workouts on a Google spreadsheet called *November Project*.

The workouts became a habit, and Brogan, who is a true extrovert, started to invite others. People showed up. Brogan and Bojan had been college athletes, and both coached Division I rowing after graduating, Bojan at Syracuse and Brogan at Northeastern. They had no idea so many people would enjoy the free workouts—which came with a few booming "Fuck yeahs" thrown in, which can take a little getting used to so early in the morning in some parts of the world.

What started as a team of two and some friends is now a legit movement providing free workouts at predawn hours in nearly sixty cities and ten countries. Plus, it's gotten megasponsorships over the years from brands such as The North Face and Brooks Running. The workouts motivate all types of people, from those just starting their fitness foray to Olympic medalists. They also use humor and fun as well as monthly sessions where they spray-paint the November Project logo on tee shirts people bring to workouts. Many people have said the community of the November Project has changed their fitness and their entire life.

I'm constantly learning about badass groups that are making the outdoors more fun and welcoming. In my own town of San Diego there are women's skateboarding meet-ups—like the one started by Kateboards founder Katie Adams, who takes women of all ages and levels out on free sunset skate sessions—and Textured Waves that shares waves with "people of all shades" through surfing. And recently, my friend, *New York Times* best-selling author Caroline Paul, told me about a seniors boogieboard group, the Boogieboard Wave Chasers, with older women ages fifty-six to ninety-six who meet three times a week to boogieboard. Many of them are grandmas, but they trade and share waves like a bunch of rowdy twelve-year-olds, and their joy is contagious.

A recent podcast guest, Faith Dickey, told me how she created the Women's Highline Meeting, a festival to introduce more women to the sport. The first year, in 2009, only six women showed up. In 2022, more than forty women from all over the globe filled a cabin in Europe, some even with their kids. They slacklined, highlined, made music, skinny-dipped in the lake, and had a wildly wonderful time. As Faith told me, "There's nothing like gathering a group of people who all share the same passion together in one spot."

The pandemic allowed a lot of outdoor groups to flourish, and also helped ignite new ones.

While finishing writing this book, I went running with the Santa Mujeres, a group started by two young Mexican American women named Priscilla Rojas and Virginia Camacho. Both women are badasses in their own right. Priscilla works as a molecular biologist, while Virginia runs several retail shops in San Diego. The pandemic finally gave them some free time to create their dream: a safe space for women of color to grow and get active together.

Virginia started running as a way to improve her physical and mental health, having experienced depression after the sudden loss of her mother. Priscilla found running when a stranger told her about a Triple Crown half-marathon series that she entered in 2018. Training for and finishing that first series was so empowering, Priscilla then recruited Virginia to run it with her the following year. They loved it, but afterward they stuck to themselves. "There weren't a lot of people who looked like us," Virginia said.

That's part of why they wanted to start their own running club.

"We're young women in our thirties," Virginia said. "We specifically wanted a place where any woman could come and feel comfortable, get some steps in, even if it's just walking a mile, or running a 5K. And we wanted to have a crew to hang out with at finish lines—to do things like dance and drink mimosas and listen to good music." They also wanted to avoid membership fees, like many run clubs in the area had.

When the pandemic hit in 2020, Priscilla and Virginia found a window of time to pursue their wild idea. They formed the Santa Mujeres, which translates from Spanish to "holy women."

"We wanted a name that shows that all women are sacred and magical, and the name keeps us close to our roots, which is why we wanted it in Spanish," Priscilla said.

They meet after working hours in an easy-to-find location in downtown San Diego. All the runs are led by women, and they aim to give anyone in any type of body a space regardless of pace. Priscilla and Virginia are meticulous about answering any question from anyone who asks—whether it's about how to train, what to wear, proper nutrition for running and racing, or just directions to get to a location, with expediency and kindness. Their goal is to make everyone feel welcome, safe, and to have fun. Priscilla and Virginia firmly believe that your love for what you want to do has to outweigh everything else, even being scared to show up if you are the only one who looks like you, and then you can make space for others too.

At my first Santa Mujeres run, we all ran a 5K through Balboa Park in San Diego. At the end, the people who'd finished first set up an arm-linked tunnel for the rest of us in the back or who ran longer distances to run through. I felt like a total rock star.

The group multiplies their community by joining with other running groups in the area such as Black Men Run, Black Girls Run, Unity Runners, the Badass Lady Gang San Diego, and more. They recently put together their very own USA Track & Field team.

As a club, they even went back to the event where Priscilla and Virginia ran their first half marathon. They were no longer the only two at the finish line wanting to dance and party their own way. The Santa Mujeres had their own tent with music, yummy food, and mimosas for all.

UP YOUR GAME AND SURROUND YOURSELF WITH PEOPLE WHO PUSH YOU

Every time I talk to someone who is pushing their limits, I want to push my own limits too.

This happened to me in early 2016, when I flew to Hawaii to cover Bethany Hamilton as she prepared to surf Jaws, one of the biggest, most terrifying waves in the Pacific. For those who don't know Bethany, she is one of the best surfers in the world, despite having lost her right arm to a fourteen-foot tiger shark when she was thirteen. There's a book and movie, *Soul Surfer*, about her life.

Jaws, also known as Pea'hi, is on the island of Maui. Winter swells there can reach up to seventy feet, pushing speeds of 30 miles an hour. When a wave breaks, it sounds like a thunderous roar. Jaws is an unpredictable wave that shifts at a moment's notice, but it's also beautiful and magnificent to watch, especially from the cliffs above or in a boat in the channel.

Also there for this event was filmmaker Aaron Lieber, who was making a new documentary, *Unstoppable*, about Bethany's life since the shark attack. Basically, it was about her being a bad-ass. In observing Bethany for a few days, what struck me most was the level of professionalism with which Bethany approached everything—from surfing to parenting to being a wife and handling a film crew around her. She was able to lift everyone up but also perform on the highest level at all times. Aaron was the same. He'd hired one of the best helicopter pilots and cameramen on the island to capture footage from above. He'd stationed extra camera-men on the beach and cliff with walkie-talkies to coordinate different shots. He helped make sure Bethany was comfortable too.

These were people who knew exactly what it took to pursue a wild idea, and had all the ingredients to pull it off, despite the whims of Mother Nature. But who also enjoyed performing at the highest level.

At the time, I also wanted to start playing at a higher level. I'd left office life and was working alone. I missed having a team around me.

When I met Bethany, not only was she about to surf Jaws; she was also a new mom. She'd just given birth to her first son—she's had two more children in the interim—and her abs were still healing from childbirth. Spending time with Bethany, I watched her nurse her son and give him a kiss goodbye before heading out on the boat. When we got to the break, the waves were roaring. I'd never heard anything like it. Bethany put on an inflatable vest over her wetsuit, kissed her husband, and hugged her dad. Then she quickly turned to me, the only other woman on the boat, to help put her hair into a ponytail before she paddled out.

That one simple request drove home for me that not only was Bethany going to surf a giant wave, but she also was going to do it with one arm. It was clear that didn't stop her from anything.

Bethany paddled out, got on the back of a Jet Ski, and laid on her surfboard when a monster set of waves rolled in. I couldn't see her get towed in, but I watched her drop into the wave, stand up, and slide down its steep face. With a huge grin on her face, she turned and faded back into the biggest and scariest part of the wave, with style like no one else I'd seen. I've never seen anyone catch a bigger wave up so close in my life.

Even her dad got teary-eyed as we watched Bethany catch a few more waves, each bigger than the last. When she got back, the energy on the boat was amazing. Once we got back on shore,

Bethany instantly grabbed her son and went right back to nursing. He was six months old and hungry. I felt fueled with a whole new sense of hope and a brand-new bar for what was possible.

A few days later, Bethany went back to Jaws. This time she paddled herself into a few big waves, while another surfer waited on a Jet Ski in case anything happened.

Which it did. Bethany got caught inside and had to take a monster set on the head. She was held underwater, but when she eventually came up for air she was laughing. She said she wanted to experience what a beating at Jaws was like—and she had.

"I don't need easy," Bethany said. "I just need possible."

I got home from that trip and started making bigger pitches to companies about partnering with me on my podcast. I didn't want to keep funding it myself and get small sponsors here and there. This is the time I finally got in touch with and partnered with REI. Having a community and people around me raising their bar made me raise my bar too.

CHAPTER 7

START

There are two types of sailors.
Those who untie the dock lines. And those who don't.

—Ryan Levinson

There's a cartoon I once saw that's stuck with me. It had four squares, each with a stick figure jumping off a high-dive platform into a pool. In image one, the pool is full of sharks. In the next image, the pool has no water. In the third image, there are angry people blocking the pool. In the final image, the figure jumps. There is a small splash, and the figure is smiling.

Jumping is scary—you can never be quite sure what the landing will be like. But thinking about it is always much scarier than actually making the leap.

You can always be more ready. You can always have a bigger cushion in your savings account. You can always have more knowledge. If you break it into numbers and then plot it on a calendar, and actually pay a deposit down on a trip, a plane ticket, or a cabin or campsite in the woods, you are way more likely to show up, the same way you will be more likely to show up at the gym and workout if you hire a personal trainer.

"Starting lines are the hardest," says Steph Jagger, the woman who broke the record for skiing the most vertical feet years ago. Looking back

on her adventure, she realized that starting had been by far the most difficult part. Just getting there can take an immense amount of courage, will,
and sacrifice. You can delay it forever, but once you start, you get to grow,
and that's where the magic happens.

"Sure, the ego loves the finish," Steph says. The finish line always provides for great conversations at the bar and a checked box on a résumé. But
getting to the starting line, deciding *when* to go, usually requires you to
do something scary: to face it. That's when the real journey begins. That's
when you learn more about yourself.

You are never going be as ready as you want to be, so sometimes you
just have to leap.

USUALLY, SOMETHING INSIDE US creates the itch to start. Maybe
it happens slowly and over time the urge to make a change grows larger
than the fear we feel about leaving the familiar behind. Maybe, as I did,
you just feel so stuck that you have to do something, anything, to break up
that inertia and create some momentum. Maybe you see and feel the signs
and you finally listen to them, even if you buried them for years.

That's where Noami Grevemberg was in 2016. Noami had immigrated
to the United States from Trinidad as an adult. When she was growing
up on an island in the Caribbean, so much of her childhood had revolved
around the natural world. But that all changed in college. She'd gone on
to follow the path she thought she was supposed to, the one that everyone
said would lead to happiness. She graduated from college. She met a guy,
Dustin, at a tailgate party. She landed a great job as an environmental scientist. She and Dustin got married. Dustin, meanwhile, had grown up in
the South and also followed the expected path, getting a job as a project
manager at a construction company in New Orleans, where they lived.

The couple initially bonded over wanting to travel the world in a van
after graduation, and visit all the national parks, "someday." They did travel
when they had time off work and even got engaged on the Appalachian
Trail. But over time, they both found themselves growing unsettled and
bored with their lives.

Noami found herself developing depression and anxiety. One day,
Dustin found her curled up in a ball on the couch, having a panic at-

tack, something she'd never experienced before. It was on that day that she started to reevaluate her life and wonder if there was more. Yes, the path she was on was fine. There was nothing wrong with it, but what if it was no longer the path she wanted to keep pursuing? She decided maybe it was time to revisit that old dream.

A few nights later, after dinner, she told Dustin she needed to talk to him about something. Dustin responded that he also needed to share something with her. They both shared the exact same vision: "What if we could quit our jobs, live in a van, and start traveling like we talked about when we first met?"

They could not believe they were thinking the exact same thing. They decided right then: "We have to do it now, or we'll talk ourselves out of it." That's how it is sometimes with wild ideas. And why deadlines come in handy. When it's wild, it's easy to talk yourself out of it. If you want to actually start, you have to give yourself the motivation to do it. The faster your deadline, the less time you have to second-guess yourself.

Noami and Dustin gave themselves three months to quit their jobs, sell their stuff, buy a van, and get on the road. If they'd been living in California or somewhere else on the West Coast, this might have been easier. But they didn't know anyone who was living in a van where they were living, in New Orleans. They'd never even heard the term "van life."

Every van they found was superold and in terrible shape. They even went to check out an old Volkswagen all the way in Colorado, but it wasn't the right fit. They were starting to get nervous. Luckily, two weeks before they had planned to leave, they found a 1985 Volkswagen Vanagon right in their neighborhood. It was the epitome of freedom, of revolution, and of radical living, Noami told me. It already had beds and a tiny kitchen, but it was thirty years old. Even so, the previous owner had it in his family for a while and had taken really good care of it. He was sad to let it go, and because Dustin and Noami realized the owner had such a strong personal connection and so much love for his van, they realized they'd made the right decision.

The last step was the biggest leap: actually quitting their jobs. When the time came, Noami and Dustin worked up their courage together, planning to quit on the same day. But when Dustin got home that afternoon, he had some unexpected news. Dustin tried to quit, but his boss decided he could work remotely. That ended up being a blessing—they would have guaranteed income on the road, while Noami could start from scratch.

Financial concerns can be the strongest deterrent to starting anything. You can always save more money and have more funds. But you can also just live with less, as Noami and Dustin decided to do, even before his boss agreed to let him work remotely.

They also had to leave their life as they knew it. You can't carry around a lot of "stuff" when you are living in a van, so they were forced to become minimalists almost overnight. And because their deadline was so tight, they were able to let go of things more easily.

For Noami and Dustin, the whole experience of van life felt more sustainable than the life they led in a stationary home. As she was an environmental scientist, that's part of why Noami had been so depressed. She felt like she wasn't making a big enough difference on the planet. Now she could do her part in a bigger way by just practicing the change she hoped to see in the world.

Noami and Dustin planned to live in the van for a year. But one year turned into two, and two turned into three. As of this writing, they are still at it, in the same van, and have become evangelists for the lifestyle. They have also figured out a way to make a living as digital nomads, practicing a zero-waste lifestyle as much as possible and traveling slowly, experiencing communities for longer periods of time before chasing wherever it's 70 degrees and sunny, or wherever their hearts lead them next.

Because Noami had met only one other person of color living the van-life lifestyle when she started out, she was also inspired to create a platform called Diversify Vanlife, a movement that encourages and supports BIPOC and LGBTQ van lifers on the road, and shares info for those who want to try it out themselves. That community has grown to thousands of van lifers in many different intersections. Noami and Dustin are a perfect example that when we start one thing it often leads to something so much bigger.

ProTip: Give yourself an unreasonable deadline and you will be amazed at what you can accomplish. Speed is your friend—don't waste time.

STARTING AS FAST as possible for Noami and Dustin was helpful in getting them to leave, but when you choose a wild idea with more risk, like crossing an ocean, where there will be no help if something goes wrong, there is always more to do in order to be ready. So choosing *when* to start can be a lot harder.

Ryan and Nicole Levinson developed the wild idea of sailing across the Pacific in their forties. The two met in college at a geography class at San Diego State University, and both taught at that summer water sports camp I attended as a kid in San Diego. I was actually a Counselor in Training (CIT) and helped Nicole, who's about ten years older than I am, teach a basic sailing class when I was a teen. Ryan, who became her husband, is the guy I later called in traffic when I was thinking about quitting my job—the one who was surfing in the middle of the day.

Ryan has a pretty inspiring story, one I didn't learn until I was assigned to cover Ryan's brand-new kiteboarding school for the local newspaper, when I was nineteen. While I thought we were going to just talk about kiteboarding, which was a newer sport in 1999, I learned something else about Ryan then. He had a rare genetic disorder, facioscapulohumeral muscular dystrophy (FSHD), that causes his muscle cells and tissue to weaken and atrophy.

Throughout his teens, Ryan had been a fit, athletic surfer, and a promising cyclist. But in his twenties, he noticed that despite his constant activity, clean eating, and hours of surfing, his muscles weren't as defined as when he was younger, and one of his calves was shrinking. It took six years of doctor's appointments and taking various tests before Ryan was officially given the diagnosis of FSHD in 1996.

Doctors told him to stop doing strenuous activity altogether—the prevailing medical theory at the time being that the more he used his muscles, the faster they'd atrophy. Ryan could have quit everything and found a desk job. Instead, he set out to prove those theories wrong.

At the time, Ryan already knew the benefits of the outdoors. He even majored in outdoor recreation in college, and he was willing to test the theory himself. Along the way, he discovered firsthand that muscles don't actually atrophy faster if you use them more. His experience helped transform the way many doctors talk to FSHD patients about continuing with their lives. In some ways, Ryan says, having FSHD gave him a more defined deadline than someone who is fully able-bodied might have. Even so, sailing across an ocean is a wild idea with hefty risk, even more as Ryan's ability to get in and out of a boat with ease was lessening.

By the time he hit forty, Ryan's disease had progressed to the point that he could barely lift his arms over his head, paddle a surfboard, or perform adequate chest compressions as an EMT, which he became after selling his kiteboarding school. But Ryan knew he wanted to keep pursuing adventure. He also knew he felt most alive in the sea.

Ryan told me that he and Nicole had several conversations about wanting to sail and had a pretty big why. For one thing, early in their relationship Ryan asked Nicole what she wanted most out of their life together. "Adventure," she'd replied.

Over the years, the couple SCUBA-dived, kiteboarded, raced paddleboards, competed in triathlons, and, in Ryan's case, competed in adaptive surfing events, some of which he helped start. Nicole had been teaching at an elementary school and worked as a San Diego City Ocean Lifeguard.

Aside from adventure, Nicole and Ryan were both looking to escape the hustle-bustle of life as they knew it in San Diego. They'd met a few sailors who'd crossed the Pacific to French Polynesia, where they described the crystal-clear water, abundant sea life, world-class waves, lush green hills, and kind locals.

Ryan was also looking to keep testing his limits outside despite losing his muscles. The allure of the raw wildness of a voyage like sailing across the Pacific toward Tahiti lured him in. "There isn't really anywhere more untouched by man than the middle of the ocean, where you are so remote, nobody can help you even if you were able to contact someone," he said.

In many ways, Nicole and Ryan's why was similar to why the Fagans wanted to travel to Antarctica and the Higgenbothams from Alaska to Baja.

But if anything went wrong, Ryan said it would be a "true rescue-free wilderness," like those he'd studied in college. They'd have to prepare the boat for their abilities and also prepare themselves as best as possible. Plus, because Ryan was still losing his ability to push his body up or lift Nicole out of the water should either of them fall overboard, the risks would be even greater. They'd have to learn even more medical knowledge and have the proper medical equipment should anything go wrong.

There was so much to do: buy a boat, get it and themselves ready to cross an ocean, make it more adaptable for Ryan, get their house ready to rent, and deal with putting their life in San Diego on pause. Nicole was most afraid that, in leaving her teaching job, she'd be leaving behind her entire career. But when she learned she could take a three-year sabbatical, she was in.

Now their biggest obstacle became *when*. It was all so overwhelming: saving to buy a boat, learning how to use all the parts, then getting it ready to cross an ocean.

Deciding *when* is challenging.

> ★ *ProTip:* Put down a deposit to reserve whatever you want to do. A campsite. A plane ticket. A class you want to take. If you have some financial skin in the game, you are more likely to show up and actually start the thing you want to do.

LOGISTICALLY, it took two and a half years to save enough money to buy the boat that would take Ryan and Nicole to French Polynesia. While they kept their day jobs, they started with a smaller boat, a twenty-five-foot monohull where, using manuals and YouTube videos, they taught themselves and practiced the basics such as plumbing, sail repair, navigation, and fiberglass repair. Why all these skills? Well, first off, fiberglass is pretty important: one hole and the boat (which is made from fiberglass) sinks, so you need to know how to work with fiberglass and repair it. You are also pretty bummed if your sail rips far offshore. Sailboats only carry a limited amount of fuel, so you have to either jury-rig a repair, or drift aimlessly until you're (hopefully) rescued.

In 2012, Ryan and Nicole traded up to a thirty-eight-foot monohull they named *Naoma*, after Ryan's grandmother. Built in 1988, *Naoma* needed a lot more work. She also had a dinghy with a gasoline engine they'd need to learn to repair in addition to the diesel engine for the main boat. They installed a high-frequency radio and reequipped *Naoma* with solar panels and a wind generator. They added extra safety lines and installed multiple autopilots, radar, a weather fax receiver, a chart plotter, and cabin fans to help offset the oppressive tropical heat they'd face crossing the equator.

It was brutally tedious work. There was always more to learn, especially when it came to electrical engineering. Their to-do list was always full of unchecked items. They kept extending their start date, a few days slowly creeping into a few months.

The harbormaster at the dock where they kept *Naoma* had spent fifteen years at sea, in the days before GPS. She used to walk by and ask them, "When are you gonna go?" Ryan and Nicole always had something that was deferring them—usually something about improving the safety or performance of the boat. Every project felt important.

"There's always stuff to do," the harbormaster told them. She'd seen hundreds of sailors spend all their time tinkering with their boat without ever leaving the dock. She gave them a tip: they could always finish the rest of the projects at anchor.

That harbormaster was right. Timing is key to anyone setting out on a wild idea, and a great question to ask yourself. What would happen if you *don't* go? Ryan and Nicole started to realize they could be either the sailors who never left—or the ones who set sail knowing they would never be fully prepared.

"I learned you can be unready forever if you let yourself," Ryan told me later. One reason, he realized, was fear. They weren't just leaving the dock. They were leaving their life as they knew it. Comfort is addicting. Leaving that behind can be scary.

"To actually leave, to do any adventure like this with such high stakes, is hugely risky," Ryan said. "Not just existentially, but there's also professional risk—will I get a job when I come back? Then there's relationship risk—will we survive living in this small vessel together? Will I still have my friends? You're leaving that all behind, not just to face physical dangers, but to face yourself and the people you are with."

This is where the importance of a good deadline comes in. A friend of theirs was getting married in Mexico, and Ryan was due to officiate. They decided that the wedding would be the perfect nudge to untie the dock lines and start. It was December, a good time to begin their crossing with the prevailing winds. Even so, they were incredibly nervous. They worked countless hours making final adaptations to the boat.

"When you set out on a wild idea, you are going to definitely change," said Ryan. "You have no idea how, but you will, and that's also terrifying."

Eventually, Ryan and Nicole got to a place where they were more afraid of what it would mean if they did *not* go than of the actual voyage itself. Going means jumping off into uncertainty. But staying home means losing all that momentum, and wondering *what if?* We often regret the things we didn't do more than the things we actually did do.

On December 13, 2014, Ryan and Nicole went to the grocery store and stocked every last compartment of the boat with nonperishable food. They'd already had a bon voyage party and said goodbye to friends a few times now. Any more farewells would just delay them further. They knew if they left in daylight there'd be more stalling. It was time. So at midnight on December 14 they let out the air of the dinghy, and they untied the dock lines at 3:00 a.m. They were off.

It was exhilarating to start in the dark. They took their time sailing down the coast of Mexico, ultimately reaching the wedding after two weeks of exploring the Baja peninsula. Then they set off for French Polynesia.

Most of the time, they reveled in their new adventure, the endless horizon of deep blue. Of course, no adventure is an adventure until something goes wrong. Ten days or so after they began the Pacific crossing, a rogue wave knocked *Naoma* on her side. It was a terrifying moment. Sinking a boat in the middle of the ocean is every sailor's biggest fear. A window had been left open, and water flooded in. Somehow, the boat righted herself and the wind vane steering got them back on track. But many of their electronics shorted and numerous other items were soaked. It was definitely a close call, but one that made them thankful for the time they'd spent studying electrical engineering.

Luckily, the rest of the trip was mostly smooth sailing. There was a lot of fishing, laughing, some naked time (because why not in the middle of the ocean?), and of course a lot of learning. About twenty-three days later, Ryan and Nicole made it to the Marquesas, a group of volcanic islands in French Polynesia. After experiencing true awe at the beauty of the islands and finding a community with the French Polynesian people, the couple decided to stay in French Polynesia for much longer than they'd imagined. Grocery runs can take all day or more—that is, if there is food at the grocery store and a nearby ship has stocked the shelves—and many other things are harder on a boat in the islands, but they love the life they've created.

Nearly a decade later, they are still sailing around this area, diving with large sharks, surfing remote tropical waves, learning to wing surf and foil board, and facing challenges together.

As of this writing, Ryan's muscles are still shrinking. He no longer surfs a regular surfboard, and he has a hard time getting out of the boat. They may eventually move to land. But he and Nicole have learned an immense amount about each other, and about what they are capable of. And most important, they've learned about having a greater purpose.

I asked them if it got easier, the starting part. As they continue setting out for new remote atolls, starting is always hard, they told me. "At sea, you are so vulnerable," Ryan said. "We are one tiny mistake from not existing anymore." But that can apply to any part of life. "Why just have a life when you can have an adventure?" they both always say.

Many of us have our own dock lines we tether ourselves to. You will never be as ready as you want to be. Eventually, you have to untie the lines and sail.

 ProTip: Ask yourself, *What's my life going to be like if I don't go?*

SOMETIMES WE GET TO create our own starting lines, but sometimes life imposes its own starting lines on us. You might not feel strong or ready at all. But sometimes in those cases, just following a wild idea and actually getting to the starting line can have a lot more meaning.

Tate MacDowell had a clear sign. In the hallway of the clinic where he was receiving radiation therapy for rectal cancer, there was a three-by-three-foot photograph of a line of mountain peaks sticking out of the sky. It was the Teton Range, capped by the Grand Teton, which rises 7,000 feet from the meadow up to its 13,776-foot summit.

When Tate saw the sign, he knew instantly it was meant for him.

There were so many reasons. First, the image was stunning. Second, Tate shares the same warped sense of humor I do. The Grand Teton—the name given to the highest of the peaks by French-Canadian trappers in the early 1800s—literally translates to "Big Tit" in French. It's just funny.

Most important, Tate had history with the mountain. In his twenties, he'd lived in Jackson, Wyoming, on the eastern side of the Tetons, working as a skier and filmmaker for companies like Teton Gravity Research. He even named his son Wilson after the nearby town where he met his wife, Lora, at disco night at the Stagecoach Bar.

For all these reasons, Tate knew instantly that the image was meant for him, and that he'd found his trail sign. He later learned that the image had been taken by Bernard Lewinsky, a radiation oncologist (and the father of Monica), who believed that viewing images of nature during intense cancer treatments might prove healing for his patients, and so donated his photographs of nature to cancer centers all over the country.

When I spoke with Tate for the podcast in 2019, he remembered thinking, *Wow, Dr. Lewinsky, you basically put that there for me.* Staring at the image, Tate formed his wild idea right then. The sign was clear. He was going to climb the Grand Teton.

I'd known Tate for a while by the time he was diagnosed. His wife, Lora, helps brands like Red Bull and Protect Our Winters with their media strategy and outreach, and I randomly ran into them in Costa Rica on the day they got engaged in 2010. They went on to buy a house and start a family in Cardiff, California, my hometown.

Like many of us, Tate never imagined cancer would be part of his story. After leaving Jackson, he'd gone on to start his own film company and make his own films, including *Junk in Public,* a documentary that features H2O Trash Patrol, a squad of surfers who stand-up paddle around San Diego's waterways picking up floating trash. It's an awesome movie.

Then, in 2016, when he was thirty-five, he was diagnosed with Stage 2 rectal cancer. Like many who face cancer, he tried everything once he got the diagnosis: finding the best doctors, eating even healthier than he already did, undergoing radiation and chemo to shrink the tumor, having surgery to cut it out, starting immunotherapy. Tate thought cancer would just be *part* of his story, a chapter in his early years.

When Tate decided to climb the Grand, he figured that by the end of a year of treatments and surgeries he'd be done with cancer. Throughout, he continued to make movies and started to train for the climb, running the beach stairs up the cliff from his favorite break, Barney's. He also started working out at VITAL Climbing Gym mentioned in chapter 4, the one founded by Dave Sacher. Tate and Lora also bought a 1973 Dodge Balboa van and parked it at the beach on weekends and after school. Now they could spend as much time as they wanted surfing and playing in the sand with Wilson, and have a sweet space to hang out, play chess, and eat snacks afterward.

Getting to the top of the Grand takes many people two to three days. It's about two miles from the high camp to the summit, with half a mile of vertical gain and a sketchy section at the top. It's a tricky route, usually requiring a guide, who can help with navigation, gear, and meals. You need a harness, ropes, and safety gear to climb to the top. Even so, Tate told me, "It seemed like a low bar to go and climb the Grand. I wasn't saying I was gonna climb Everest." Tate planned his climb for the summer after his diagnosis. He created a film concept, and his old filmmaking friends at Teton Gravity Research jumped in to help make the movie about the trek. They'd call it *Mountain in the Hallway*, after the photo that inspired his wild idea. The film would also raise awareness about a disease that takes a lot of young men by surprise.

Through friends in Jackson, Tate met another young father who'd been diagnosed with rectal cancer the month before Tate: Brian McDonnell, a Jackson local in his forties with two kids. Brian and Tate became confidants, cheering each other on, trading funny butt jokes to keep their spirits light. They made plans for Brian, who had climbed the Grand before, to join Tate on the climb.

"It started out as sort of a high-five film," said TGR co-founder Todd Jones. "The boys were wrapping up their Stage 2 treatment; they'd climb the Grand, high-five at the top, and then go back to their life, with cancer in the rearview mirror."

But cancer had other plans.

During surgery to remove the tumor, Tate had been given an ileostomy bag to reroute stool outside the body while his rectum healed. But three months before the climb, in his surgery to reverse the ileostomy, he contracted *C. difficile*, an antibiotic-resistant bacteria that causes severe diarrhea and colitis. Worse, doctors found two tiny new spots—this time in his lungs. Not only had the cancer spread; it was now Stage 4.

Tate flew to Wyoming that July anyway. He wanted to at least get to the starting line of the Grand. Starting lines he knew were important. It meant he was actually pursuing his wild idea and not giving up on it.

When he arrived in Wyoming, Tate's friends threw him what was supposed to be a "Tate Beat Cancer" party, back at the infamous Stagecoach Bar. They thought it would be a celebration that his cancer was in the rearview mirror. Unfortunately, the disease had taken hold of the wheel. Tate couldn't even eat at the party.

He went with Brian to the Grand Teton trailhead, a mile down a dirt road at Lupine Meadows. He was happy to be in Wyoming, a place that brought him so much joy. He was happy for his friend. He was happy to get to the starting line. But he was too weak to climb. He turned around one mile in at the big rock, which he would later call Gravy Rock. Brian climbed without him, and the two men shared a giant bear hug when Brian got back down. At that point, Tate still thought that maybe he'd have another chance. "The Grand isn't going anywhere, and neither am I," he said.

THE NEXT MAY, Tate stopped chemotherapy to try a promising immunotherapy program. But that August, an MRI showed more new tumor spots, this time in his brain, causing double vision. To adjust, Tate threw a pirate patch over one eye: if you only have one eye, he figured, you can't have double vision. He talked in a pirate voice and made his son, Wilson, smile. I thought it looked pretty badass when I saw him wearing it when we recorded a podcast together.

The news kept getting worse. The cancer had spread to his lungs and bones. At the advice of doctors, Tate decided to go back to chemotherapy. He was absolutely devastated. Still, he saw a crack of light even in the midst of this dark news. Snow was about to fall any day in the Tetons, closing the climbing window. But in going off immunotherapy and back on chemo, he figured he'd have a seventy-two-hour window when he might feel okay enough to make a climb happen. It would take a lot of work to pull off. The time to start was now.

Tate looked at his wife, asked her to fly her mom out to watch their son, and said, "Let's do this."

"Absolutely," Lora said.

Climbing the Grand for a fully healthy person isn't easy. It's possible to do it in a day, but most recreational climbers take a few days and sleep in one of the guide companies' huts. You need a harness and ropes to climb to the very top—and you have to pack out your waste in a WAG bag.

Going to the bathroom in the wild is challenging. Going with unpredictable digestion from surgeries and chemo while ascending jagged walls of rocks would provide an even greater challenge. Add in an eye patch, tumors in your lungs at altitude, a tumor in your knee and clavicle, and a full dose of chemo inside your body and Tate had the odds stacked against him.

"My main goal," Tate told me, "was to simply go as far as I could, and not become disappointed if we didn't summit. I set the first goal pretty low: just get past the rock where I'd turned around last year. I'd claimed then that everything after that point was gravy, which is why the rock eventually became known as Gravy Rock. I kept reminding myself that none of this is about the summit; it was just about trying and if I didn't summit, that was perfectly fine. Just go as far as I can, enjoy the experience, and try to live in the moment." All Tate really wanted was to start and actually move forward.

"Starting lines are so much more important than finish lines," he told me. "If I'm going to be successful at something I really have to worry more about the starting line, in being prepared to begin something."

ON THE MORNING of Friday, August 17, Tate was detached from his chemo pump. Hours later, he and Lora boarded a flight to Jackson. Teton climbing legend Greg Miles would help lead the way, along with two friends from Tate's Teton Gravity Research days, who were first timers, like Tate. By Sunday, Tate's crew had gathered all the gear. Tate would carry his own ropes, food, and tent in what Greg called a "big-ass backpack." They hiked four hours to Petzoldt's Caves, a series of boulders at about nine thousand feet with a great view of the canyon. They settled in one of the caverns underneath the boulders, ate a small meal, and slept for a few hours. At 2:00 a.m. Monday, they woke and started to climb.

By sunrise, they had made it to the lower saddle at fourteen thousand feet. There Greg told Tate that he'd made it pretty damn far and that this would be a great time to turn around. After this point, he said, there was no going back. It wouldn't be safe. Tate would need to scramble over boulders, climb over ledges, tie into ropes, and rappel. He needed to decide.

"I guess I was waiting for an excuse to appear. A good one," Tate wrote in his blog. "One that I'd be able to walk back down the mountain with and live with for the rest of my life. But it didn't present itself. So I answered, 'Yeah, let's do this!'"

As with many adventures, this one didn't go exactly as planned. They lost the trail at points. The path was terrifying, especially on the Belly Roll pitch, which has thousands of feet of exposure. Luckily for Tate, who was afraid of heights, his eye patch was on the cliff side, so he didn't look down too much.

Over ten hours later, Tate made it to the summit. This is where people usually stop, take a picture, and celebrate, but Tate had one last thing to do. He'd carried with him a vial of ashes with a photo of one of his best friends: skier and wingsuit pilot Erik Roner, who died in a skydiving accident in 2015. Erik's wife, Annika, had given Tate some of her husband's ashes to spread somewhere meaningful. There was no better place than the top of the Grand.

The day had started with bluebird skies. But as Tate approached the summit, a storm rolled in, filling the view with clouds and mid-August snow. Tate tilted the vial with Erik's ashes, and in an instant they were taken by the wind, as if Erik were still flying by.

After the fact, many people asked Tate if he was bummed he didn't get the epic view at the top. Tate said no. "Eric came, and was like, *Hey, man, it's all gonna be all right.*"

On the way down, the clouds, which had come in swiftly, creating sideways snow, cleared as fast as they'd come in. "Tate was amazing," Greg told me. If climbing up a mountain is challenging, getting back down involved rappelling one hundred and thirty feet and then making it all the way back to camp, through switchbacks and over a steep ridge. The sun set when they still had a few hours to go, so they walked on into the night using headlamps.

They were totally spent and starving, but Tate felt an incredible sense of calm and accomplishment. When they finally arrived back at the trailhead, Tate's, Dave's, and Greg's wives were there to greet them all with pizza, tequila, and beer. Tate didn't have much of an appetite, but he was full of gratitude. He thought back to a year prior when this climb had been impossible. Heck, it would have been impossible a week earlier.

So many people view cancer as a battle, Tate told me. He hated that term, as if there were a clear winner and loser. No one wins or loses with cancer. He thought of cancer more as a climb. He wrote this in his blog:

> We all begin at a trailhead, and we embark on our journey with a full understanding of the challenges that lie ahead and the potential consequences. We'll get blistered, beaten, hungry, snowed on, tired, happy, sad, and we might not necessarily make it to the summit. Sometimes we find ourselves at the end of our rope and don't think that we can possibly go on, and in that moment you feel the tug of a hip belay and know that someone who cares an awful lot about you is pulling on the other end. But the bottom line is that you go as far as you possibly can, and try to enjoy the climb for all of the happiness and hardships that come with it.

Tate not only got to the starting line. He started. Then made it to the top and back down. The important part, he kept telling me, was that he finally started on his dream, and it was a bonus that he made it happen.

Tate passed away on October 4, 2019. He was thirty-nine. At his memorial in Cardiff, hundreds of surfers paddled out to Barney's, below the stairs where he'd run those steps to train for the Grand. Lots of parents with small kids showed up, along with Lora and their son. I was toward the back. Later, I looked at some drone shots and saw that our flotilla formed a perfect heart.

When fact-checking this book, I messaged Bernard Lewinsky, and he mailed me the very photograph of the Grand Teton that inspired Tate's climb to give to Lora and Wilson, to remember Tate's wild idea. Tate's starting line wasn't perfect. But he knew that even if he had to turn around halfway, climbing the Grand and his climb with cancer allowed him to achieve a lot of what he wanted in life. Yes, I imagine he wished it could have been longer, but we don't all get to pick our finish lines.

When I interviewed him for the podcast, Tate left me with this powerful message: "Life is short. Don't waste any time."

BREAK DOWN THE NUMBERS

If you have a wild idea, but you are stuck on starting, break it down into numbers. How many years will you have to do what you want to do? How many months? How many days?

Jesse Itzler, an entrepreneur, speaker, ultrarunner, and author, says that numbers help him get more done in every calendar year. Say, for example, you have aging parents. Let's say that they are about seventy-five. And that they'll live to eighty-five, which is longer than the average life-span. Let's say, for example, you see them only twice a year. Well then, using Jesse's math, you'd have only twenty visits left. When he first shared this with me, I booked a trip to Hawaii with my mom, the first trip I'd ever planned for just the two of us. My mom drove me slightly crazy at first, but we made sand angels, saw an Elvis impersonator, went on an outrigger canoe ride, and threw flowers into the sea to honor my grandma. We ended up having an amazing time, and still talk about it today.

START WHERE YOU ARE, EVEN IF YOU ARE IN YOUR EIGHTIES

Janice Gray is a real estate agent and former ski patroller at Mammoth Mountain who started surfing in her eighties. Janice had surfed before—from the 1950s right on through the mid-seventies—but that was before her knees were wrecked from skiing.

Janice was spurred to try again as she had two grandkids who were taking surf lessons at Surf Diva in San Diego. When her grandkids asked if she'd surf again, she figured, why the heck not? Janice was certainly sporty: a former beach lifeguard who lived in southern California and who later became a ski instructor in Mammoth, Janice had been windsurfing every summer for years. But as she reached her eighties, the windsurf sail was getting too heavy to pull up. Skiing was too hard on her knees. Surfing could become her new sport.

To get started, Janice simply hired an instructor and showed up at the beach. She wasn't sure how she'd do. Just putting on a wetsuit was a challenge. But out at sea, she felt invigorated. She didn't have the strength to paddle herself into a wave, but the instructor pushed her into a nice one that had already broken, and Janice stood up. She smiled from ear to ear. She fell off her surfboard immediately afterward, but she got a taste.

"I didn't surf, but I got up," she said. "That was exciting for me. And of course, the grandkids said they were so proud of Grandma."

After the lesson, it took Janice an hour to recruit enough energy to get up from the sand and walk back to her car. But she booked more lessons that summer. As she and I were talking, she crunched some numbers Jesse Itzler–style. She told me her mother had lived on her own until she was one hundred years old.

"I've got at least seventeen more years," Janice told me, smiling. I am guessing she may have even more than that. One piece of advice Janice said was to get an instructor and get outside. As I mentioned before, hiring a guide, putting down that deposit, and having someone to keep you accountable is a sure way to encourage you to show up and start.

CHAPTER 8

FACE FEAR

Courage is fear that has said its prayers.

—Karle Wilson Baker

It's day four of the surf trip to the Mentawai Islands in Indonesia on the boat that I've talked myself onto after quitting my job at Vans. I've already pulled the *I'm just a journalist, not a surfer* card too many times to count. It's time to get out of the boat and actually ride some waves.

The problem is that I've never been in waves this big in my life, much less ones that break over a sharp coral reef full of fish that could rival those of any aquarium. I've spent the last five years working from a cubicle. It's like going from skiing gentle bunny slopes to a steep black diamond.

In Indonesia, the waves are so different from home. They grow fast and often break abruptly, creating a tube or barrel that experts surf inside of. The waves I am used to come up gently and slowly, with easy slopes to the side that allow you to paddle with ease and stand up in a leisurely fashion, riding the face of the wave instead of inside the fast-breaking barrel.

We are at a wave called Mutts, which I later learn translates to "vagina" in Aussie slang. Despite its sexist name, Mutts is no pussy wave. It's named because it forms an almond shaped barrel to ride inside of. Doing so is no easy feat.

At the previous spot our boat pulled up to, I tried to surf, but every time I fell I got held underwater, a terrifying feeling. Every second underwater feels like ten. A five-second hold-down feels like fifty. The guys I am with are surfing on huge standup paddleboards, and I can only imagine a hold-down for them is even more intense.

Luckily, Brian Keaulana, a regal-looking Hawaiian former pro surfer and lifeguard, is on the trip. It makes sense that Brian looks like a king: he's actually descended from Hawaiian royalty. He's a big-time lifeguard, and helped invent the rescue sled, which is essentially an oversized boogie board with handles to transport and rescue surfers and swimmers towed behind a Jet Ski. Brian is also the lead stunt coordinator for almost every movie and TV show filmed in the islands. He even coached the actress Kate Bosworth for the movie *Blue Crush*, one of my favorites. There is no better person to be stuck with in the middle of the ocean.

"Shelby, fear is just lack of knowledge," Brian tells me. I don't have much experience in open ocean waves, like these pros. The only way to solve that problem, he says, is to get some experience and go for it. Sometimes the fastest way to get educated on the trail is to actually get in the dirt (or, in this case, the ocean).

Brian coaches me through it. After I come up from one wave gasping for air, my eyes bugging out of my head, he says, "When you get held underwater, sing a song."

Don McLean's "American Pie" has just been playing on the boat. The only phrase that sticks, however, is *This will be the day that I die. Oh, this will be the day that I diiiieee.* Not the best song to sing when you're pinned underwater.

Brian laughs when I tell him my choice. "Pick a different song," he says. I look up at the sky and decide "You Are My Sunshine" is my new hold-down song. *You are my sunshine, my only sunshine. You make me happy when skies are gray. . . .*

Brian has an aura around him that is calm and somehow makes me feel bigger than I am. I imagine hanging out with Dwayne "The Rock" Johnson would feel similar. I just love being around his energy.

By day four, I'm feeling more confident, and I really want to get barreled. I've also finally borrowed a bigger board: a 6x10", much better for these waves than the 5x10" potato chip–thin surfboard I'd brought with me. I catch a few smaller waves, but they are so fast that as soon as I get to my feet I fall straight over the front of my board, back underwater singing "You Are My Sunshine" until the wave lets me back up for air.

"As soon as you stand up," Brian suggests, "start saying, 'Make it, make it, make it.'" He and I have the ocean to ourselves; the rest of the guys have paddled back to the boat to eat lunch.

The waves are picking up, and I know that paddling back in when I could have waves to myself would be crazy. But I am just so afraid.

MY DEFAULT MODE when I'm scared is to be neurotic and ask a million questions to distract myself. The waves are growing bigger. I begin giving Brian the Barbara Walters treatment—I ask him how he got Kate Bosworth, a rookie surfer, to ride big waves for the movie *Blue Crush*. If she could do it, I think to myself, so can I.

"Oh, that's a good story," he says. "I took her to Waimea Bay the first day." If you know anything about surfing, you know that the waves at Waimea Bay are ginormous. "That way," he tells me, "Waimea would be her normal. But if I started her off at Waikiki, where it's generally smaller and easier, well then, that would be her normal."

I don't get to hear the rest of the story—that he actually only took her out on a Jet Ski, away from the breaking waves, and that all they did was merely look at the big waves, not ride them. Just as I am busy imagining this dainty beginner careening down a fifty-foot wave, a triangle of water juts up from the horizon in the Indian Ocean. It is huge and headed right toward us.

Brian looks at me with serious eyes. He looks back at the approaching wave. He looks back at me again.

"You gonna go?" Meaning: *You better go or you're gonna be sorry.*

I do not want to go. I do not want to flail in front of this Hawaiian god, miss the wave of the day—or, worse, get absolutely worked. I also do not want to wreck the boatman's thousand-dollar surfboard he let me borrow. The nearest surf shop, not to mention the nearest hospital, is hundreds, if not thousands, of miles away.

I am terrified, but I lie on my surfboard, and I paddle my little heart out. I look back once—big mistake. The wave is huge. I look ahead. Another mistake. All I see is jagged coral.

I start singing. *"You are my sunshine, my only sunshine."* I paddle a few more times, looking ahead, not behind or below, as the wave picks my board up, and I start zooming at what feels like lightning speed. I quickly pop to my feet, going so fast it feels like I'm on a small skateboard going down a steep hill. It's starting to wobble.

Make it, make it, make it. The board's fins make a hissing sound as they speed down the line of the fast wave. *Make it, make it, make it.* I'm now finding my balance and getting in the groove, somehow riding in the perfect spot of the wave. Suddenly, the wave speeds up even more. It gets incredibly steep, so steep I think I might fall face first over the nose of my board. *Make it, make it, make it.* I keep going faster. I try to stay high on the wave, but it feels like a roller coaster.

My gut reaction is to close my eyes to prevent getting dizzy, but I keep them wide open, and I am grateful I do. All of a sudden, the triangle tip of the wave lifts up so high in the air, it throws itself over my head. By sheer luck, I am enveloped in crystal-clear blue water.

I am inside the barrel! It is like nothing I've ever seen. The feeling is magical. It lasts for maybe a nanosecond, but I feel changed. My cells are electrified.

"Hoooo, nice one!" I can hear Brian shouting in the distance. He is behind me, but I wonder if he saw me through the clear water. At least he knows I am still standing. My head, and not my feet for a change, is at the surface. I am elated, beaming, reveling in the glory of the experience, and wanting this feeling to last forever. *Damn, if only there had been a photographer to capture this moment,* I think.

When the wave ends and I catch my breath, I look up. I see sunshine, more blue sky—and then a hand sticking up out of the ocean. Attached to it is a camera with a water housing.

"I got it!" yells Dana Edmunds, one of Hawaii's most legendary photographers, who happens to be in the perfect place. I watch the still frames on his camera, and the wave looks even bigger than I imagined. I have the worst stance in the world, my butt is sticking out in what the captain calls "poo stance," but I am wearing a huge Cheshire-cat grin.

I would later interview an old professional surf legend, Mickey Munoz, for a surf magazine. Mickey was in his late seventies at the time, and he told me he once caught a wave so good in Indonesia, he came out the other side ten years younger. I knew exactly what he was talking about. At this moment, I also understood why surfers go to such great lengths to chase perfect waves. There is no better feeling than surfing one.

That wave would carry me the next few years. I learned that fear is one of those things that, if we never face it, can hold us back and make us angry and bitter. But if we do, it can change us forever.

Ryan Berman, a motivational speaker and author who talks about fear and courage, says that to get over fear, you have to have three things to cultivate courage to do so: knowledge, faith, and action.

In the Mentawais, I had some knowledge about surfing because it's a sport I'd done on and off since age eleven, just not in such big waves. Faith was paddling in, even though I had no idea if I would fall. The mantra *Make it, make it, make it* and the song "You Are My Sunshine" gave me something to hold on to when I didn't have anything else. Brian was there to feed me more morsels of knowledge and the faith that he'd be there to help.

The last step is action. I had to get off the boat, where the only sure thing I'd get was seasick. Then I had to drop in and take the wave. Yes, there was a chance I would fall. I could have hit my head on the surfboard, hit my head on the reef, who knows. But there was also the chance I'd catch the ride of my life. I haven't caught a wave like it since.

For the rest of the trip, I have newfound confidence. The waves grow even bigger, and Brian coaches me to dive under one that is three times higher than my head, and to catch a double overhead wave twice the size of my body. It is the biggest surf I've experienced in my entire life.

The next few nights I radiate. Adventure does that to you. So does doing the thing you think you can't. And getting outside your bubble. I feel like I am firing on all cylinders. I am telling funny jokes. I quit being totally neurotic and asking millions of questions, and I feel completely comfortable in my own skin.

It's like the monkey on my back—my depression and anxiety about the job, about what's next, about the money I need to make by a certain date, about my past and my future, all the fear and bullshit occupying my brain—is lifted. I am in the present moment. I feel alive.

ONCE YOU START on your wild idea, you will likely face fear more than once. As I learned in the Mentawais from Brian Keaulana, most of that fear is just the unknown. The more we can prepare for the unknown, the more adept we will be to handle it.

There are a lot of additional tools you can use to cope with fear: things like breathing, humor, singing songs, and visualization. But the foundation that holds together all those tools is developing the knowledge and skills, and eventually the mastery and courage, to deal with fear. Sure, you are going to be scared rock climbing if you have never attempted it before. But if you actually go, use a harness, attach yourself to ropes, and learn to do it, every time afterward will be a little less scary.

Perhaps one of the most extreme recent examples of *facing fear* is rock climber Alex Honnold. As anyone who has seen the Oscar-winning documentary *Free Solo* knows, Alex famously climbed Yosemite's El Capitan, a granite wall over three thousand feet, with zero ropes and harnesses, defying what anyone thought was possible. Alex is an anomaly of a human being, but he presents a good case study on fear, primarily because he does actually have it, just like the rest of us. But he approaches fear by getting knowledge and then facing it. To get knowledge about a rock face he could die climbing without ropes, Alex climbed it almost one hundred times. He climbed Free Rider, the route that he ultimately free soloed, fifteen times with ropes. He also spent many days rehearsing the most difficult sections over and over again.

Alex first had the idea to free solo El Capitan around 2009, eight years prior to doing it, and he made it his mission to get as comfortable as possible with ropes, so that when the time came he could do it without them.

On our podcast he told me, "It always looked scary, because it wasn't that certain. There was always a good chance that I might fall off and die, and I obviously wasn't willing to take that chance."

He probably could have free soloed El Cap sooner, he said. He had already done Half Dome, the famous granite dome located in the eastern part of Yosemite Valley, in 2008. "Had I tried to free solo El Capitan in 2009, there was a seventy-five percent chance I would have done it. But I wasn't comfortable with that other twenty-five percent." He laughed.

Half Dome provided good training though. It's one thousand feet shorter than El Capitan and less sheer, with more ledges and holds, making it easier to climb. He still could have died, but Alex basically lived in a van in Yosemite and trained as much as someone could.

Preparation, more preparation, and years of training helped Alex face fear. Before the actual climb of El Capitan, he deleted his social media accounts (a big part of his personal brand) for a month. He wanted to be fully focused. He also made sure to keep the same schedule every day, so that when conditions were right he'd have eaten the same thing for breakfast that morning and been able to go to the bathroom before starting. Because his friends Jimmy Chin and Elizabeth Chai Vasarhelyi would be filming him for the documentary, they also filmed him during practice, so nothing would change.

"I think, for anybody, the key is to differentiate between well-founded fear and irrational fear," Alex says. "Fear is your body giving you some information. It's up to you whether you keep that information. Sometimes it's incredibly useful; sometimes it's not. The challenge is to know when to use fear and when not to."

One thing Alex told me is that you can always prepare if you are resourceful. For example, want to hike to the South Pole, but you live in a tropical climate or a desert, where it's hot? You can figure out ways to simulate training for cold weather, like sleeping in a sleeping bag in a meat locker. Okay maybe that's a little extreme, but there is always a way to prepare at least a little bit.

Yes, eventually you will need to start. But starting doesn't always mean diving in headfirst. Try making small steps. If you want to hike the Pacific Crest Trail, get over your fear by hiking shorter sections. Try a few overnight camping expeditions. Set up your tent and sleeping bag in your living room, then your backyard or a neighbor's yard. Want to ride a bike one hundred miles? Start by riding a few extra miles a week and build up to it. Want to surf bigger waves? Practice holding your breath underwater so if you do wipe out you feel more comfortable holding your breath underwater for longer periods of time. When it comes to adventure, even a little bit of preparation can boost your confidence. This is why most people run 5Ks before entering marathons.

You can watch YouTube videos or take a class, but when it comes to adventure, the more hands-on experience the better. Sure, if you want to learn to climb, for instance, there are high-tech learning tools such as virtual reality. But what will be most impactful is actually going rock climbing with a guide or teacher and learning to do it yourself in the wild.

ANOTHER TRICK Alex Honnold uses is humor. It's something I've seen a lot with top climbers and surfers, who often make fun of one another during perilous moments to ease the tension.

"Climbing can be so hard," Alex says, "especially a multiday climb, when you are sleeping on ledges, surrounded by hazards. At times it can be really foreboding and intimidating. Humor can be a great way to manage that stress and stay focused and keep things in perspective." When Alex and his longtime climbing friend Cedar Wright go climbing together, there's a constant soundtrack of smack talking. It deflates the fear, releases pressure and makes the intense climbing a lot more fun.

"You know that things are approaching full near death when I stop reminding Alex that he has gotten soft since the Oscars," Cedar told me, laughing. When I asked Cedar, who is also known for many of climbing's most daring first ascents, about the power of humor, he agrees it can be incredibly helpful.

"Being able to laugh at yourself and your climbing partner, especially when the going gets sketchy, should be considered a superpower," Cedar said. "When you electively choose to put yourself through the risk and suffering of type-two entertainment, you better have a resilient sense of humor. I really believe that being able to laugh in the face of adversity is a priceless life skill. I definitely don't trust people who can't laugh at themselves."

Even if you are not climbing giant rocks without ropes or surfing giant waves, humor is helpful. Humor has gotten me out of a variety of sticky situations and helped me when I'm most scared. It has been a salve that's helped me break through my own barriers, including the ones in my head.

About six months after that fateful trip to Indonesia, I found myself in Costa Rica teaching surf lessons to a group of women at Surf Diva.

I've always loved teaching surf lessons, as it's the one job where you can completely change someone's day or even life, by just pushing them into a wave. But in 2009, it seems irresponsible to go off and teach surf lessons, especially when I am supposed to be proving myself as an adventure journalist.

When I am speaking to her about my hang-ups, Izzy, who was also my babysitter after she was my camp counselor and who has become one of my dearest friends to this day, reminds me, "Shelby, this is *why* you quit your job. So, you could go to Costa Rica and do this." It was true, there'd been plenty of opportunities to go before, but my day job prevented it. Plus, I am able to use Skype and write from the jungle, from the pool bar, or in a hammock. This is years before working from home is normal, and I think I am truly winning.

The clients at Surf Diva come from all walks of life. For all of them, learning to surf is their *wild idea*, and they all have to get over some sort of fear to make it to Costa Rica and ride waves. One woman stands out. Chandra is an agent at the federal Drug Enforcement Administration and a natural athlete. She isn't scared of surfing, but she seems like she is battling some demons in her life at the moment.

For whatever reason, she is struggling to stand up on the surfboard. At this point in my life, I've taught surfing to enough people, especially women, that I know what works and what doesn't to help someone get to their feet. I also see patterns. For example, triathletes and other uber athletes frequently think learning to surf will be so easy. They are usually okay once they finally stand up, but many tend to get in their heads when they don't excel immediately.

I can tell Chandra also thinks surfing will be easy. When it isn't and she struggles to stand up, I watch her get extremely frustrated with herself. On the second afternoon, all of the other students are standing up and riding waves to shore except for Chandra. Many of the women are not athletic but have low expectations of themselves. They just let go, move with the flow, stand up, and enjoy the easy, warm Costa Rican waves.

While the other women are cheering one another on and starting to paddle themselves into their own waves, I see Chandra get pissed and yell at herself. I imagine she is saying something to herself along the lines of, *I can't even surf; I'll never be able to do X*—something I've said so many times myself. But a protip here: beating yourself up never works.

So I tell her a story about a former student. My best surf student ever could not stand up the first four days of a five-day camp. I was nineteen years old, teaching at Surf Diva's Tofino, Canada, surf camp the summer after my freshman year of college. This student was a professional cyclist and snowboard instructor, but she was in her head. On day five, she finally stood up and rode a wave to shore. She celebrated with everything she had that evening. A few months later, she quit her job, moved to San Diego, became a surf instructor at Surf Diva, and now surfs better than I ever will.

Telling Chandra this story does little. As the rest of the ladies continue catching waves in the heat of the afternoon session, I see her eyes well up with more than salt water. This is a woman who can shoot a handgun with utmost precision and isn't afraid to break down doors to bust drug deals. Something is up.

Just then, a set of waves starts approaching us.

"Can you think of something that makes you laugh?" I ask while moving her surfboard into position. I want to disrupt the pattern of negative self-talk.

"No," she says in a whimper.

"Anything? Like any good jokes? What about stuff your kid says?"

Crickets.

The wave starts approaching. It is a perfectly straight line of whitewash, ideal for beginners.

I look to the shore and see a guy I know—a really good-looking guy—run by.

"Think of a big . . .

"Think of a . . . a big, big, giant, luscious . . ."

The wave is approaching faster and faster.

I am not totally sure why this escapes my mouth, but it tells you where my mind is focused in those days. When the wave arrives, I position myself behind her board to give her a proper push, and scream into her ear.

"Big *PENIS!*" I yell. "Now stand up!"

As I pushed her into a wave, the whitewash explodes in front of me, and I cannot see ahead. I wipe salt water away from my eyes, and see a body rise. Behind the body is a noise.

It's a squeaky sound. I can't make it out at first. There are some strange animal noises in this jungle.

"Enis . . . Enis."

It gets louder and louder.

"EEEEEENis. Eeeeeeeeeeenis." Eventually, I figure it out.

"BIG PEEEEEEEEEEENIIIIIIIISSSS!!! Big Penis!"

Chandra screams as she rides the wave standing, pumping her fists into the air and shaking her bootay all the way to the sand.

At that moment, I realize something as clear as the water looks that day. Striving for perfection rips away the fun. Beating yourself up does jack shit. And there is nothing a big-penis joke—or something else that makes you laugh—can't cure.

There's a saying we use at Surf Diva: "The best surfer in the water is the one having the most fun."

Making light of the situation and yourself can be a game changer. It will take you out of your head and help you become your more authentic self. Authenticity is a big part of dealing with fear. So is having a light heart.

> *ProTip:* Try a sport you are bound to fail at like rock climbing or surfing. With rock climbing, start at a bouldering gym or indoor top rope gym so you can get in a lot of reps and where a lot of the variables are more controlled indoors, reducing risk, allowing for easier learning. When I started rock climbing, I learned something important about wild ideas. First off, I suck at climbing, and sucking at something is part of living wildly. You have to try and fail, and try and fail, and try and fail until failure becomes less scary and trying becomes second nature. Pulling your way up a wall over and over, especially one you think you might never scale, changes your level of self-confidence, often immediately. Also, trying something where you have no experience or certainty of the outcome is living wildly in itself.

WHEN IT COMES TO FEAR, having a light heart and using humor will take you a long way. But it's not always easy to tap into those things when you are scared. Being authentic, remembering your why, having perspective, and cultivating a supportive community are also key elements in facing fear. So is just eventually facing and getting over the biggest fear of all—the fear of failure—which you will likely have when you pursue a wild idea.

Take the story of long-distance swimmer Kimberley Chambers, who almost lost her leg in a fall before becoming the sixth person on earth to swim the Oceans Seven channel crossings, marathon swimming's equivalent of the Seven Summits. She even swam thirty miles through the notoriously sharky waters between the Farallon Islands and San Francisco, becoming the first woman to do so.

None of those crossings were easy. Just swimming those distances is scary. How can your body handle all that time in cold water with no wetsuit? What if you get hypothermia? What if you cramp? What if you chafe so bad your skin tears open? Despite all that, Kim's biggest fear was something we all dread: failure.

When I spoke to Kim for *Wild Ideas Worth Living*, she told me she used to be a perfectionist. She trained as a ballerina growing up in New Zealand. She loved pushing herself to her limits, and when she came to the United States for college at UC Berkeley, she joined the rowing team.

When you're a ballerina, you're judged on how perfect your form and performance is. As a rower, if you don't perfectly sync with your crew, you'll lose. In other words, you have to come as close to perfection as possible.

This mindset can be hard to shake. Kim had to do a lot of mental reprogramming after she started swimming in her thirties. Not only did she have to get over the fear of failure and perfectionism, though; first she had to learn to walk again. In 2007, at age thirty, she was living in the Bay Area with a successful career in tech. But she'd become a slave to her perfectionist ideals, she told me. "I was a workaholic, a gym rat, and very social. I was obsessed with training, mostly so I could fit into a pair of the latest expensive designer jeans. I'd become quite shallow."

Then one morning, on her way to work while wearing high heels, Kim slipped down a staircase outside her apartment. The blunt force trauma resulted in acute compartment syndrome, where blood flow is blocked to an area of the body—in Kim's case, her right leg. When she woke up, she told me, doctors were thirty minutes from having to amputate the leg. It took two brutal years and multiple surgeries for Kim to learn to walk again.

Kim had to face the fact that she would never be the same. She had to push through self-doubt, and the doubts of her doctors. She relied on faith and the belief that she would walk one day, an important tool for coping with fear. And when she did eventually walk again, she began to wonder what else she was capable of.

That's when she discovered something that totally changed her life. While doing physical therapy at a local pool, some "cute guys" invited her to swim at the Dolphin Club, a community of open-water swimmers in San Francisco Bay that is home to legends and undercover superheroes—everyday teachers, entrepreneurs, and engineers who swim great distances across waterways like the English Channel. The Dolphin Club is where they've trained since 1877.

That first day jumping into the bay without a wetsuit was scary. With a skin graft on her thigh, Kim was already embarrassed by how she looked in a bathing suit, but she was desperate to find happiness through movement again. It was a brisk 53 degrees in the bay, but Kim couldn't stop smiling for the two hundred yards she swam.

At first, her coach later told her, she couldn't swim her way out of a paper bag. But, he said, she had the "eye of the tiger." The community was so intoxicating that Kim couldn't help but keep showing up. Because of that, she improved quickly.

In 2010, Kim completed her first long-distance swim, the two-mile crossing from Alcatraz to San Francisco. She was scared, but she'd been through so much already that she was getting good at approaching fear head-on.

The next year, she attempted the English Channel—20.5 miles, about ten times the distance she swam from Alcatraz. She wasn't even halfway across when it was clear she had to abort. There was no way she was going to finish. Self-admittedly, Kim was ill prepared. People spend years training for a goal like this.

Failing wasn't fun, but Kim started to soften up to the idea that failure would be part of her journey. After nearly losing her leg, not finishing a swim became less of a big deal. When someone is going after truly wild ideas in nature, failure will be part of it. Sometimes Mother Nature isn't going to let you succeed. With swimming, sometimes it's too windy or too choppy, or there are too many jellyfish. Or there are sharks circling and you have to get out of the water. You might also cramp or simply become too exhausted or malnourished. Perspective can be a useful tool in dealing with fear.

Being out in nature also comes with a spiritual component. Out in the open ocean, there were plenty of chances to experience awe. The more connected Kim became with her surroundings, the more she surrendered to the greater forces of the ocean, and the easier it was to push through each long-distance swim.

This was a lesson she learned in 2012, when she attempted the Cook Strait, the seventeen-mile channel between New Zealand's North and South Islands. The swim would take eight hours and twenty-six minutes.

In the most remote part of her swim, just as she was starting to tire and feeling especially vulnerable to sharks, a pod of dolphins arrived. They squeaked underwater, jumping and swimming all around her.

Whether it's true or not, many surfers and swimmers equate the presence of dolphins with the absence of sharks. Not only did Kim feel safe and protected; she also began to feel so much more connected to everything around her. Awe does that. And because of all that awe and her connection to the greater ocean and animals swimming alongside her, she had faith that she would make it to the other side and be okay.

Naturally, Kim squeaked back at the dolphins for what felt like hours. In many ways, her squeaking was her way of saying thank you. We know gratitude can cause a huge shift in emotions. With all that awe, faith that she would be okay, and the power of gratitude fueling her cells, Kim felt recharged for the rest of the swim.

The experience also helped her tap into her capacity for humor. How else do you spend all that time in the harshest of conditions, just you and the open ocean, trying to move forward with rough currents? You have to keep yourself entertained, or you'll go insane. For someone who puts a lot of pressure on themself to complete such challenging feats, humor can serve as a great release.

Kim said she exchanged a lot of jokes with the dolphins on her crossing. Mostly, she imagined them laughing at her. "I'm sure they were making fun of me and they're like, *George, she can't even swim; did you see that woman? What's she doing? Shall we help her?*"

FOR THE NEXT THREE YEARS, Kim went on a roll. She decided to look beyond one or two marathon swims and go for the Oceans Seven. She leaned on her community, which was invaluable in training for her crossings and manning her support boat. She kept to her strong why, proving to any doubters that she could not only walk again, she could also swim incredibly far. And she gave back, her swims raising over $1.7 million for various charities, including those helping wounded veterans.

In 2014, she completed the Oceans Seven with a thirteen-hour swim across the North Channel between Ireland and Scotland. It was a grueling crossing, in which Kim was stung by hundreds of lion's mane jellyfish, so many that she experienced pulmonary edema, an abnormal buildup of fluid in the lungs that causes shortness of breath. Somehow, she made it to the other side and went straight to the hospital.

Kim told me she kept the faith she'd make it through. She'd faced pain and fear before. She'd learned how to deal with chafing, sunburn, nausea, and more. She knew what to do when she felt like giving up or was in pain. She was prepared. And she was accepting of failure if she had to pull out. But she kept the goal of finishing at the forefront of her mind. She had faith she'd make it and she did.

You'd think that Kim may have stopped after completing the Ocean's Seven. But as wild ideas can lead to other wild ideas, she decided to do something even scarier a year later. In 2015, she decided to swim thirty miles across the Farallon Islands to the Golden Gate Bridge.

No woman had ever completed the swim before. The area around the Farallon Islands is also a national marine sanctuary, home to countless seals and sea lions, and notoriously sharky (probably because seals and sea lions make such great meals for sharks). Just two weeks earlier, her training partner had to abort his own attempt when a great white shark started circling him.

Kim decided to start around 11:00 on a Friday night, so she could finish in daylight the next day. We all know swimming at night would be even scarier, but Kim said jokingly, "Sharks only work during working hours."

To get across the Farallon Islands, Kim used every tool she had to face her fears. Humor to keep her mind away from sharks, who she convinced herself were too busy working to bother her. Faith in nature and awe at the wildness of the Farallons. And gratitude for the team all around her. She used a mantra: *Please, just give me permission to keep going. Please, just grant me permission to keep going. I'm not here for any harm; just grant me permission to move through your waters with grace. Give me the grace to pass through your stretch of water.*

When she finally saw the Golden Gate, seventeen hours into the swim, Kim's goggles filled with tears. She could not believe she was going to make it. Here was a woman who was told she might never walk again, who was told by many this swim would be impossible.

Kim's mom was with her on the boat when she came across the Golden Gate. Kim realized her swim was not just for herself but for her whole community—her family in New Zealand, the charities she supported, all the people at the Dolphin Club, North Bay Aquatics Masters, where she started swimming, and the South End Rowing Club, where she also trained, all the people who had ever doubted her, and all the people who would go on to do wild things because they were inspired by her.

Kim and I talked a lot about fear together, and about that biggest fear for all of us: that deeply ingrained fear of failing. "You hear about people achieving these great feats of swimming the English Channel or climbing Everest, but how many times have you heard about their failures?" she told me rhetorically. "You don't. We live in a society where success is the primary source of adulation. But from my experience, it's through failures that you actually grow and learn the most. I'm the first to say, 'I'm afraid of that,' just like everybody else. I'm afraid of embarrassing myself. I'm afraid of saying, 'I'm going to do that,' and then I fail. 'Failure' is actually a very loaded term, and I would say that, as I look back on it, that it's actually a gift."

Kim told me every failure helped her get to where she is today. If she hadn't fallen down those stairs, she said, she may have never found swimming in the first place.

"We are all a little afraid of failure. We all have fears, and we are all judgmental of ourselves," Kim says. The only way to get through is to switch your mindset. And to actually do the thing you are afraid of failing at anyway. The biggest thing is to realize that you are worthy of going for a goal, even one you don't end up reaching. "It's a beautiful, beautiful gift," she says, "and no gold medal, no standing on a podium, would ever do it justice." The gold is in the going and trying. It's in the jumping in where we reap the most rewards.

"If you are not fearful," she said, "you are not pushing the limits of who you are. And if you are not pushing the limits of who you are, you are not living the limits of you who you are."

ProTip: Don't forget to breathe. Breathing will help calm your nervous system in stressful situations. Try a technique called the "Physiological Sigh." Inhale in regularly. Then, at the end of your inhale, before breathing out, do another short inhale. Then, exhale slowly for an extended period. See how relaxed you feel and repeat as needed.

ONE COMMON DENOMINATOR with wild ideas is that they all have scary components. But we have to pursue them anyway. Failure is often our biggest fear. For many of us, it's rare that our wild ideas will take us to the side of a cliff, or swimming across water known for having an abundance of great white sharks. We are usually more afraid of going broke, leaving the familiar behind, embarrassing ourselves, not being accepted, or even failing at the thing we told everyone, including ourselves, we wanted to do.

There have been so many times I have failed, most of them when I was being inauthentic or too stubborn to take the time to gain more knowledge, or too impatient to take the necessary steps to prepare. I've failed to understand directions and gone the wrong way, even in running races where I was in the lead and ended up behind after making a wrong turn. I've failed and been rejected dozens of times when the company I was pitching wasn't really one I wanted to work with anyway. I've failed in pitching people I did want to work with because the timing wasn't right or it wasn't a good fit. I've failed every time I've made a decision from fear, which never works out.

Once, I was so scared of not having enough money, in 2010 I took a job selling vitamins for a multilevel marketing company as a side hustle. I didn't have the heart or desire to recruit my friends or people I didn't know to buy vitamins from me or sell underneath me. I lasted a month and was left with a box of vitamins that made me pee bright yellow, and the rest I ended up having to give away.

Fear and failure are closely intertwined. In many ways your failures can highlight your biggest fears, pulling them out for you to see more clearly.

About a year after I quit my job at Vans, I was scared of a lot of things: not just of making enough money to keep doing the thing I quit my steady job to do, but also a little afraid of not being adventurous enough.

I went on a tear of chasing adventures outside my comfort zone, and surfing waves that were beyond my means, and it didn't even bring me joy. In some ways, I surfed those waves because I wanted to say I'd surfed them, rather than because I actually did. I also went on a tear dating—mostly lifeguards, stuntmen, and boat captains. Sure, they were all exciting and many were very kind, not just on the eyes, but good people too. The problem: I was partially dating them for their résumés rather than their hearts. I get that this was very uncool, but I learned this the hard way.

One morning, after a night of intense dancing and some drinking, I'd agreed to meet one of my girlfriends, who is a much better surfer than I am, at a break that is notoriously challenging, with a fast wave over a shallow reef. Since I was on a mission to prove myself, I paddled out. My friend was late, and didn't arrive until about an hour and a half later, just as I was paddling back in. I was exhausted, slightly hungover, and I'd actually caught a few fun waves. I was ready to drink water, put food in my body, and get back to being a normal person again.

"Shelby, come on, we just got here, and I brought my friend," she said. The friend happened to be the ex of one of the guys I was dating. Now I am the first to be nice to another woman. I grew up in a family of women, taught surfing to women, and played on countless all-women soccer and cross-country running teams. But I wanted to show off a bit, so I paddled back out even though I was past my exhaustion zone. This is where my ego took hold. Once we got back outside and a wave came, I took it. Knowing that they were watching, I performed a move where I tried to smack the lip of the wave to throw some water spray and fell backward.

What came next happened in both slow motion and fast-forward. My board came out from underneath my feet, and I was now below it with my feet in the air above me. The steep section of the wave then took the board, now above my head, and threw it right down on top of me, smacking the rail of the board into my face, hitting the thin section above my upper lip. I didn't have any time to cover my head or my face.

"Ouch!" I screamed, though I probably just said, "Oh fuuuck!" I looked up and around to see if anyone had seen it, but I was now in the channel, and much closer to shore. My head throbbed. I took my finger to my lip, and it was covered with blood. I guessed it was just a fat lip or a bloody nose. I waved my arms hoping to attract my friend to come look or maybe even a lifeguard, but no one saw me, so I paddled into shore. That's when a woman on the beach greeted me.

"Oh, honey, your face!" she screamed.

"My face?" I wasn't sure what she meant, but I ran back to my car, looked in the driver's side mirror, and saw that the impact of the rail to my face had split my upper lip open. I drove myself to the hospital, where I got seventeen stitches. The experience gave me a permanent scar and crooked smile I still have.

That failure didn't just hurt; it literally changed me. I wasn't respecting my limits, my empathy for my fellow humans, for myself, or nature that day. My ego also got in the way of my abilities.

Nature will often teach you a lesson when you disrespect her. And if you disrespect your fear, you may also get smacked in the face.

Sometimes there is a second chance; sometimes there is not. It's a fine line to push yourself past your comfort zone, but to also not be naïve, reckless, or douchey, because most adventures have consequences.

I know now to always take every adventure, big or small, seriously. And to always be as healthy and alert as possible when doing anything. Alcohol and adventure never mix. Also, to always be kind and authentic.

Fear is healthy. It keeps us from dying. But failure is our biggest teacher.

THERE'S A LINE from a special with comedian Trevor Noah that has stuck with me for a long time. He said, "When we laugh, we are our most authentic selves." Then he made a ridiculous face. "That's why we are ugly when we laugh."

Part of living wildly is being a lot more ugly and authentic. When I am being my most authentic self, I am often not that pretty. In fact, most of us aren't all dolled up in the wild. Often after surfing my best wave, I come up with my bikini twisted, the bottom of my boob exposed like a frog's belly, and a total wedgie, my hair all over the place. When I am camping, I have dirt in every finger- and toenail and I often don't shower for days. These are not my most glamorous moments. But they are often some of my best.

In fact, in all of adventure, if you are doing it right, you might look ugly at times too. There's really not a big place for vanity or trying to be cool when climbing up a rock face or swimming for miles. Often when you try to look cool, or your ego gets too involved, that's when you get hurt. When I smacked my lip open with my surfboard, I realized my smile was something I had to accept, even while now crooked. I could no longer resist or hide my depression, something that was pretty easy for me to hide behind, because I am a fairly outgoing person and around other people, I am generally in a good mood and smiley.

I wrote a blog post after getting my lip smacked open and shared about my struggle with depression. I admitted that I didn't have any easy answers, but that as an athlete I didn't know a lot of people like me at the time who dealt with it, and I was embarrassed to admit it was something I struggled with. I wrote about sometimes not feeling comfortable in my own skin, and that sometimes I struggled to understand my own psychology. I cried the minute I finished writing it, but I could not hide behind a smile that was now a little crooked and had a big scar above. I also could not lie to people and tell them I was always happy when I wasn't. I remember being terrified to hit "post." But the minute I finally did, people started texting me almost immediately. I was shocked. Many thanked me for my honesty and vulnerability. People whom I would least expect told me they struggled. It felt good to know I was not alone.

What I realized is that being vulnerable was probably in many ways scarier than any wave I've surfed. But in being vulnerable, I've been able to connect to others, including guests on my podcasts, in such a more meaningful way.

I also learned that the things that are the scariest are usually the stories you tell yourself. On any adventure, you will have to learn to leave those behind, and embrace your most authentic self, even if it's not pretty. You will also have to learn to accept failure. If you can learn to laugh at yourself, that will help. And if you are afraid to do something you know that will improve your life, you must do that thing anyway, even if you fail along the way. The success is in the actual trying.

As Kim Chambers said, "When you conquer your fear, you not only discover the essence of who you are, but you discover your own personal legacy that no one can take away."

FACE FEAR

- Get educated as much as you can to address fear head-on.
- Have faith.
- Breathe.
- Have a why that will help you get through the how, even if it's scary.
- Develop and lean on your community around you.
- Have perspective when facing fear. Try not to sweat the small stuff.
- Use a mantra or a song. You can use, *Make it, make it, make it.* Or sing "You Are My Sunshine."
- Embrace and accept failure as part of your journey. In fact, failure is often the road to success, so try to get comfortable with failing.
- Use gratitude to remember you are doing exactly what you wanted to do, even though it's scary.
- Use humor to break the tension in perilous situations.
- Respect your fear, but do the thing you are scared of anyway if it will improve your life positively.

HOW TO FACE FEAR

from Ryan Berman, the author of Return on Courage
and host of The Courageous Podcast

Ryan Berman helps people and companies embrace the idea of
courage as a way to excel. Through his research for *Return on Courage*, Ryan developed his own definition of courage that helps you
face your fear. His courage definition is made up of the following
three levers:

- Knowledge
- Faith
- Action

As Ryan explains,

*Knowledge, faith, and action are the matchstick, tinder, and
wood that work together to form the fire that is courage. The sum
of these parts—and it must include all of them—makes up courage. Courage always starts with knowledge. Obtaining knowledge is the true differentiator between doing something careless
and embarking on something boldly calculated. It surely will be
easier for you to take a risk if you are educated on the topic you
need to be courageous about.*

*Since you're never going to be able to gather all the available
knowledge on a given topic, at some point you have to rely on*

that belief system of yours we'll call faith. And once you build that faith, mixed in with just enough acquired knowledge, then it's time to do something about it. This is when you should take action. You need all three—knowledge, faith, and action—to courageously take on fear. The more you grow your knowledge and the more you grow your faith, then it's time to turn all that into action. When you do, that's courage.

CHAPTER 9

WHEN IT ALL GOES HAYWIRE

It's not an adventure until something goes wrong.

–Yvon Chouinard

"*Oh fuuuuuck!*" While I am not a huge fan of profanity, I know that that is the universal sound of things going awry, which they likely will during almost any good adventure. (For the purposes of this chapter, I'll use the most common expletive I hear in the wild, "oh f——," but feel free to insert your own.)

Wild, Cheryl Strayed's memoir about hiking the Pacific Crest Trail, contains one of the most classic "oh f——" moments in modern adventuring. Early on in her trek, her boots were giving her blisters. But when she took one off, it fell over a cliff. *Oh f——.* If there's one mandatory piece of gear for thru-hiking, it's a pair of boots. Not one boot. A pair of boots. Also, this was 1995. It's not like there were cell phones to call for help. Cheryl had no contact with the outside world except the places the trail intersected a town. She eventually got in touch with a customer service agent at an REI store, who shipped fresh boots to her next stop. But until she got there, she had to fashion her own makeshift pair using duct tape and sandals. Cheryl's "oh f——" moment not only made her stronger; it also taught her that she could solve problems on her own. She could make this walk alone.

Those moments when everything goes haywire make for great stories and awesome conversations at dinner parties and even job interviews. But we do not do wild adventures for the Instagram posts. These are the moments that test us and change us for the better. Many of our biggest "oh f——" moments happen when what we expect goes awry. When our funding falls apart. When the plane gets canceled. When all our well-laid plans seem ready to unravel.

Most "oh f——" moments will be small. When we have packed our partner's wetsuit—which is two sizes too big or small for us—instead of our own for a full day of cold-water surfing. When the rest stop that looked so cute and so close by is neither. When we have to go to the bathroom and there is nowhere to go. When our trusted directions lead us to a dead end—or a raging river, which just happened to me and caused me three extra hours of drive time.

Others, however, will be much bigger. Often the emotion behind that "oh f——" moment correlates with the gnarliness of the adventure at hand. A boat capsizing in the middle of the ocean is a lot bigger deal than going the wrong way. While I was writing this, Ryan and Nicole Levinson messaged me from French Polynesia that, a mile out to sea, one of them accidentally poured diesel into the gas tank and gas in the diesel tanks. Two hours later, both tested positive for COVID. That's a true "oh f——" moment.

You have all had an "oh f——" moment, likely outside of an adventure in real life. I have had my share. For one, there was the bathroom incident. In 2018, on a day I was supposed to interview both Cheryl Strayed and a famous skateboarder, I went for an early-morning run in La Jolla. On the way, I used a beach bathroom. Now, the beach doesn't always have the cleanest bathrooms and at 6:15 on a Tuesday morning they haven't been cleaned, but I really have to go. Six of the seven stalls are a total mess, but the seventh has a clean toilet, though the door handle does look a little funny.

I enter and close the door behind me. Just then, it makes a funny click. I do my business anyway, and go to open the door.

It does not open.

I turn it left. I turn it right. Nothing.

Oh f——! It's totally locked and broken from the outside. And my phone is in my car.

There are openings at the top and bottom of the stall door, but each is about three inches high. I attempt to crawl out; my butt is not fitting through. Only my arm reaches out. The floor is sandy and wet, and an incredibly foul smell of raw sewage mixed with salt and seal poop permeates the air.

A full forty-five minutes later, a woman hears my yells, and sees my arm sticking out of the bottom of the stall, trying to get her attention. She alerts the maintenance guy, who arrives eventually and unlocks the door. He feels terrible, but there was no harm other than the fact that I am stuck with my own shit for a while. I run home and eventually laugh it off. But in the moment, it was a real "oh f——" situation.

WHEN YOUR "OH F——" MOMENT happens on a true adventure, it can be very scary. You are often not near your home, a gear store, a doctor's office, a pharmacy, or around other people. You are often out in the elements, alone. You are often going to have to ask for help, even if you don't want to.

Chris Fagan's "oh f——" moment happened three days before Christmas, the twenty-first day of her estimated forty-day journey to ski to the South Pole in 2013.

She and her husband, Marty, had been skiing for eight to ten hours a day, in temperatures ranging from −10 to −50 degrees, pulling 220-pound sleds. That's a lot for someone who, like Chris, is five feet four. Their sleds got a little lighter as they ate through their food and burned cooking fuel, but the South Pole sits at nine thousand feet, so the whole time they labored up a gradual incline.

Antarctica is stunning. It's a big white, vast landscape, but it's also monotonous. With so much whiteness all around, every day was starting to feel like Groundhog Day. Where the snow was sticky and sand-like, it felt like pulling a tire through mud. In patches of sastrugi—hard, wavelike formations formed by wind over freezing snow—it felt like crossing a series of ocean waves. On day twenty-one, the couple agreed to take a recovery day, their first of the trip, and Chris spent the evening painstakingly sewing a pair of custom thigh warmers into her thermal underwear, a defense against growing headwinds that are known to freeze thighs.

The next morning was beautiful, with bluebird skies and light winds, a welcome departure from the usual 15-plus mph headwinds. It usually took the Fagans two hours to get going in the morning, but they made it out in a record ninety minutes.

An hour into skiing, Chris was having issues with her body temperature. She was hot. Then cold. Hot. Cold. Cold. Hot. She was going through perimenopause at the time, and her internal thermometer was whacked.

Then she felt a weird bunching in her thighs. Her carefully sewn thigh warmers had torn away and were now bunched inside her long johns. This wasn't quite an "oh f——" moment yet. Still, it was annoying, and she was tired and emotional. During their first break, she removed the bunched-up material from her pants. But when she squatted to pee, she was greeted by an unexpected visitor: her period. Great.

A woman's period isn't the kind of thing most adventure tales are made of, but every female adventurer has had to deal with it. At least Chris now had an explanation for why she'd been feeling so tired and hormonal.

Chris was on the verge of menopause, so her period was no longer predictable. Packing for Antarctica, she had to prepare for every eventuality, but she didn't want to pull boxes of tampons or pads she might not need, much less pack them out. She discovered the DivaCup, a small silicone flexible cup that, instead of absorbing menstrual flow, collects it. It's washable, reusable, and safe for up to twelve hours without leaks.

Before the trip, she tested the DivaCup on a two-hour run and then on a ten-hour tire pull. No problems. Now, while Marty waited in the freezing conditions, Chris rummaged around for the DivaCup. She inserted the device and went back to skiing.

Nine and a half hours later, the Fagans had skied 15.3 miles, about 3 miles farther than on previous days. Chris was beaming. While Marty made dinner, she went outside to empty the cup in a hole in the ice (standard Leave No Trace practices in Antarctica).

She took off her liner glove—something she rarely did in the 30-below temps—and reached up to pull out the DivaCup, just as she'd done multiple times.

Hmmm, something was up.

She couldn't reach it.

She tried again.

No luck.

She was just able to touch the tip. But that was all.

She tried one more time.

No luck.

Her hand was beginning to freeze.

Panic was rising. Was it stuck?

She tried one last time.

Nada.

She remembered the packaging, which suggested that, in the rare case you are still unable to remove the DivaCup after more than twelve hours, to "seek medical advice." That wasn't a possibility here. Chris had just skied fifteen miles with something stuck inside her. She had many more days to go in the middle of nowhere, and the temperature was far below freezing. There was only one thing to say.

"Fuuuuuuck." Chris sounded the universal alarm. Now her hand was freezing, so she had to stop trying. She pulled up her pants and went back into the tent. This was crucial because, at 40 below, exposed skin can develop frostbite in five to ten minutes.

In the tent, she told Marty what was happening. His face turned a little white. What was *he* supposed to do?

As Chris's hands started to warm up, she went out into the tent's vestibule and tried again. Somehow, she found the tip. But when she went to pull it out, the cup slid out sideways and tipped over in the snow. The whole area looked like a crime scene, but that didn't matter. Immensely relieved, Chris laughed a little to herself as she cleaned up.

While the mishap felt like a pretty big "oh f——" moment at the time, it turned out to be a funny story in hindsight. The best moments when things go haywire often are. The memory would come in handy as a reminder that every problem can be solved with a pause and some patience. And Chris and Marty soon had bigger problems.

Two weeks later, on day thirty-six of their trek, the couple realized that, even as their sleds grew lighter, their pace was still too slow. The terrain was growing tougher, and they were going about two miles slower per day than expected—averaging 13 instead of 15 miles a day. Even though they'd packed for five extra days, they were at real risk of running short three to four days of food. They'd already lost so much weight.

Oh f——.

The Fagans had prepped and trained, but you can't know what it's like to ski in Antarctica for days and days until you actually get there and do it. On top of that were the anxieties of navigating themselves in low light and whiteout conditions—and worries about their son, Keenan, back home.

They rationed food, cutting their calories from 5,400 to 4,000 calories a day. Then 3,600 calories. They were burning over 8,000 calories a day and losing weight faster. The weather was also terrible. The skiing was harder than anything they'd imagined. The whiteouts became mind-numbing. Skiing so far with so much gear for so many hours and so few calories, their bodies were breaking down.

Day thirty-nine was predicted to be the last night of their forty-day journey. But they still had 109 miles to go. Many adventures take longer than expected. There are so many things you can't plan for until you arrive.

Chris wanted to take a day off. Marty told her that if they stopped now they'd never make it. Chris disagreed. She couldn't move any faster. They had a standoff in the tent, both of them getting a little irrational and raising their voices. This was rare: they never fought at home, and in tough times they usually leaned on each other. This time, they were spent.

Then Chris remembered that, when things go awry, the best thing to do is to pause. She had paused with Diva. Now she and Marty paused again and, in doing so, realized they weren't getting anywhere together. They decided to call a mutual running friend, Leni Karr, via their satellite phone. Leni had been there with the couple through ultramarathons when the Fagans both struggled to go on. Leni knew how to help her friends dig deep and get going again. She diffused their angst with a compromise. Marty would need to have more patience with Chris's pace. But they would keep going forward without another rest day.

"What I learned," Chris told me, "is that sometimes if you keep going, even if it's just plodding, it will get better unexpectedly. Maybe not right then, but often the next morning or day. You tap into mental and physical resources you didn't know were there."

In the end, the expedition took forty-eight days. It added another layer of strength, resiliency, and even love to the couple's bank, something that can't be learned in school or bought in a store. And their "oh f——"

moment made for one of the best chapters in Chris's 2019 book, *The Expedition: Two Parents Risk Life and Family in an Extraordinary Quest to the South Pole.*

It's in those moments, the ones when you think you might have to quit, where the growth is. That's what the best adventures are made of.

ProTip: If you're doing an adventure with serious risk, have a Plan B, and consider having a Plan C and D. You should also have bailout points and strategies defined. Plan a few worst-case scenarios with solutions, and then practice them just in case. If you're adventuring with a partner, talk to them ahead of time about how you hope to communicate if you get into a jam. This might make for an awkward conversation to start. But it will help you iron out kinks in your communication styles so you can work together as a team *when*, not *if*, things do go wrong.

AS YOU MIGHT EXPECT, Ryan and Casey Higginbotham, the twins who paddled from Alaska to Mexico, also had their fair share of legitimate "oh f——" moments. Like the Fagans', their expedition had little margin for error. They were carrying their own gear, far from stores and hospitals, and at the mercy of the elements.

Even though the brothers had practiced, gotten educated, and mapped their trail, you can only do so much from California when your expedition starts in Alaska.

Their first "oh f——" moment came before they even set off, at the dock in Ketchikan. When Casey loaded his gear on his paddleboard, it tipped over, nearly drenching his tent and gear, which thankfully were in a waterproof backpack. It was at this moment they realized how tippy their paddleboards would be with all that gear (about seventy pounds), and how difficult that would make the whole expedition.

Day four provided a more serious "oh f——" moment. The brothers were paddling along the Inside Passage in their 5mm wetsuits, neoprene hoods, booties, and thick 6.5mm gloves when Ryan stopped to take a picture. To do so, he took off one of his gloves. Just then a tidal push hit him. He saved his board, his gear, and the camera, but the glove was gone.

The water off the Alaskan coast is freezing cold. And Ryan hadn't thought to bring a second pair of gloves. It was lost in the churning, dark waters.

Without a wetsuit glove, Ryan had a serious problem. And that meant Casey did too, because they were doing this whole thing together. Ryan was in shock. Casey was pissed. "You sandbagger!" he yelled at Ryan.

You can't paddle for long without gloves in Alaska. It's not a matter of *if* you will get frostbite; it's *when*. So Ryan took off his bootie and put it on his hand. He then put a wool sock on his foot. He was really worried he'd lose a toe or a finger. It's not like you can stop and do a lot of adjusting on a small paddleboard at sea with so much gear on top. There aren't shops or even access roads along the Inside Passage either. The stretch of coast that runs from the southeastern part of Alaska, through western British Columbia, to northwestern Washington State is full of thousands of islands, coves, and inlets with huge tidal swings.

Now the Higginbotham twins are tough. They come from a family of military veterans, and grew up pushing themselves to the extreme by cave diving, cliff jumping, and competing in IRONMAN Triathlons and off-road adventure races—but this was a whole different realm of extreme psychologically.

Ryan just pushed through. His fingers were cold, but his foot felt really frozen in the wet wool sock. The whole time, he visualized sending warmth into his foot. Those moments of suffering added a big deposit to both twins' resiliency banks. After sixteen long and freezing-cold miles of paddling, with Ryan's hand in a wetsuit bootie, the twins pulled up to a cove, which had a lodge. This in itself was incredibly lucky. There are not that many lodges between Ketchikan and Prince Rupert. The lodge was closed, but a caretaker just happened to be there.

After they warmed up, Casey and Ryan called the nearest dive shop, in Prince Rupert, which was about forty-five miles away farther down the coast. The dive shop just happened to sell the exact same O'Neill 6.5mm gloves Ryan lost. Also, incredibly lucky since this was remote Canada, not California.

But now the twins needed to find a way to actually pick up the gloves, which were forty-five miles away by sea, about four more days of paddling. The Inside Passage is not a direct coastline either, like the stretch between Los Angeles and San Diego, but a raw, wild waterway with countless fjords and serious tidal swings.

Risking freezing hands by paddling without gloves for four more days was not an option. Neither was waiting at the lodge and having the gloves shipped, which would require hiring a plane with money that they didn't have.

But again, as luck would have it, a seaplane was actually flying supplies up to the lodge from Prince Rupert that afternoon. The owner of the dive shop was so inspired by the twins' story, he agreed to drive the gloves to the local airport and hand them to the seaplane pilot, who delivered them to the lodge that very afternoon. The next morning, Casey and Ryan were back in business. Four days later, when they did eventually get to Prince Rupert, they stopped at the dive shop to pay the owner and bought him a beer.

Losing your wetsuit gloves in the middle of a cold ocean is a pretty big challenge. But there would be many more challenges after that. The twins saw plenty of sharks. They broke two paddleboards in crashing waves and had to wait to get new ones. When the rack carrying their gear broke, they fixed it using beach trash—a bottle cap as a washer, pieces of an old crab trap as spacers.

Sometimes they had a hard time keeping down food after paddling 20 miles a day at sea. At other times, they would gorge on food without ever seeming to get full. Casey's back seized up from all that prone paddling. Their wetsuits smelled like urinals. It wasn't always a fun time.

The hardest moment would come around day sixty-nine of their trip. If having his brother lose his gloves was the biggest "oh f——" moment yet, Casey said he nearly lost his mind at the Columbia River Bar, where the Columbia River dumps into the Pacific Ocean, on the border of Washington and Oregon. Known as the Graveyard of the Pacific, the rushing river forms a series of sandbars and shoals with treacherous currents. Since the 1970s, about two thousand ships have gone down there. If a ship the size of a football field could have a hard time crossing, Casey and Ryan were sure to meet challenges on paddleboards.

They had a good idea what they were getting into, but they'd never experienced anything like the Columbia River Bar. At one point, both brothers were getting swept so far so fast, they thought they might die. Caught up in their own fear, they started to bicker. But they quickly realized fighting takes up way too much energy. They decided to use their energy to stay alive instead.

While they usually tried to stay within a mile of land, this day they got swept nearly fifteen miles out to sea, with the outgoing tide and force of the river pushing sideways into the ocean. It was a beast to paddle in, but it pushed them outside the worst part of the current. In a way it was similar to getting caught in a rip current and letting it take you out to sea until it dissipates so you can swim sideways outside of it. Nine grueling hours later, they made it to a safe shoreline. "After the Columbia River Bar, I knew we'd make it the rest of the way," Casey told me.

The wildness and solitude, along with the knowledge that neither would quit on the other, kept them going. Casey told me, the same way so many people undertaking an extended expedition have told me, that he remembered every single thing about the trip. "For all of 2016, I can remember over one hundred specific days of my life because they were all hard. I can think of every day. No section was a blur. Every place had its own challenges."

Once they reached Point Conception, in Santa Barbara County, though, the currents eased and the water warmed. By then, the brothers had learned a lot about teamwork, about each other and themselves. When they pulled up on the beach, they looked at each other, shook hands, then hugged and laughed. On a journey where teamwork can be life or death, they learned the least efficient thing you can do is "bitch at someone." They never really fought again after that.

> ✦ If you are in danger in any way, pull the plug, turn around and go home. No adventure is ever worth risking your safety, your life, or others' lives ever.

IN INTERVIEWING SOME of the most epic adventurers around, I have heard countless stories about how the best times and the best lessons come when it all goes wrong. And that some of the strongest relationships are forged after it does. Sometimes in the midst of the hardest moments, you also realize something about yourself that changes the course of your life. This happened to me in 2011. After a paddleboarding trip on the Amazon, I decided to chill out a bit, for example, and dial back on my attempts to be so hard-core—or at least to look like I was. I was getting a little carried away with pursuing adventures to an extreme, at least extreme for me.

In 2011, I was invited to be part of the first crew to stand-up paddle-board a remote section of the Amazon River as it passes through Peru. I was a last-minute addition to the team, and the others—Mariko Strick-land Lum, a semi-professional paddleboarder from Hawaii, and photographer Chase Olivieri—were both younger and fitter than I was.

None of us *really* knew what we were getting into. We'd all heard tales of the flesh-eating parasites, giant piranhas, disease-carrying mosquitoes, and alligator relatives called caimans that lurk in the Amazon River. I had already gotten dengue fever once from a trip to the southernmost tip of Costa Rica. I wasn't interested in getting it again.

Before I left, I caught the end of an episode of *No Reservations* in which Anthony Bourdain filmed a culinary expedition to the region. He called it "an amazing place, but much better *in retrospect*."

For two weeks prior to the trip, I trained like a madwoman—swimming a mile in the ocean every day and then paddling up and down La Jolla's cove and coast. I also obsessed over gear, calling paddle companies, borrowing stuff from the only stand-up paddlers I knew, and trying to control what I could.

When our group met up at LAX airport, we had enough gear to rival an REI warehouse sale, including three inflatable stand-up paddleboards and paddles.

Four flights, two car rides, two nights, and two long canoe rides up-river later, our guides (yeah, we had guides; we were not idiots) helped us pull the canoes to the side of a river. This was where we'd camp. It was the middle of nowhere, with nothing else around. There were giant trees towering everywhere, noises I'd never heard, and mammals, bugs, and birds I'd never seen. We were far from civilization.

The goal was to paddle back forty miles downriver, ride some standing river waves, camp a few nights, check out birds, get some great photos, and—personally for me—not die or get sick until we got back to a lodge with other people.

Supposedly, it wasn't the rainy season. But just as we set up our tents in the middle of nowhere, it rained on cue—a torrential Amazonian downpour. That was the first little "oh f——" moment.

The next morning, after sleeping for maybe a few minutes, we woke to something that sounded like *Soundscapes of the Jungle* on Volume 100. I noticed that my backpack, which I'd left open in a separate covered tent, was full of leaves. I thought Mariko had played a joke on me. But there were also droppings nearby and paw prints. Apparently, an animal had already set up house.

Even though Mariko and I were both slathered in DEET, we started itching immediately. I looked down at her ankles. They were red and swollen. "I got cankles!" she screamed. Mine were the same. We had both brought paddle pants that did not fully cover our legs. Well, vanity and the outdoors don't always mix, and I had wanted to look cute. The joke was on me. Every exposed patch of skin had been mauled when we were pushing the canoe upriver.

Cursing at the fact that, despite all of our gear, none of us brought anti-itch cream or longer pants (I honestly thought I might even be able to paddle in a bikini, and had brought three with me), my stomach started grumbling. The night before, I had devoured a jar of peanut butter–filled pretzels of Mariko's, and now, I quickly learned, they did not agree with me.

Since we were in the Amazon, I could pretty much go to the bathroom anywhere away from the river, so I walked around a corner and began to squat. That's when I noticed some sort of vulture, one that looked like he might come up to about chest height, walking toward me.

Hmmm. At first, it didn't seem like a big deal. But Big Bird started walking closer. Then he started sticking his neck at me and puffing out his chest like a New Jersey frat boy yelling, *You want some of this?!* (I have no idea if this bird was indeed a vulture or anything about its sex, but stay with me here.)

I did not want any of this giant vulture. I just wanted to empty myself of the peanut butter–filled pretzels, never, ever eat them again, and get back on the stand-up board and paddle back down the river to a real bathroom and not die on the way.

Oh f——.

Big Bird kept watching as I finished my business as fast as possible, finding leaves to use as toilet paper and keeping my eyes on the creature. When I was done pulling up my pants partway, I ran back to the tent fast. I lost my breath. I looked back at Big Bird. He looked at me, then waddled the other way.

It felt like a close call and I was ready to get going and get out of there. After I got back to the tent, we packed up. Then we loaded our gear in the canoes, covered ourselves in the bug spray that the Amazon River bugs didn't care about, and paddled downstream on our inflatable boards. The first section was full of gentle rapids, so we had to be alert. It was a little scary, as at every turn, every lull in the river, and every swampy-looking section our hearts raced in fear of critters and of the unknown lurking below.

Plus, it was hot, very hot. Around 9:00 a.m., our photographer, Chase, spotted a scenic section a few hundred yards ahead and told us to wait so he could set up his camera on dry land.

A few moments later, I saw Chase ahead sprinting across a riverbank. We assumed he was trying to set up a scenic shot fast, but later that afternoon he told us he'd had a much bigger "oh f——" moment. A small caiman had bumped his board, sending him paddling to the bank and running for his life.

We paddled a few more hours, every one of them itchy, hot, and very sweaty. Our guides wanted us to camp another night or two, but it looked like it was going to rain again. We were all pretty miserable, so we asked how far to paddle all the way to the lodge. We could paddle more from there, where they had beds, bathrooms, and mosquito nets. It was about twenty miles away, but since we were going downstream, we hoped we could make it by nightfall. After getting mauled by bugs, having a standoff with Big Bird, getting worked in rapids, and, in Chase's case, being chased by a tiny gator, the idea of a shower and possibly a bed or even a roof sounded a lot better than a tent.

We paddled hard, greeted by more bugs the entire way back. But along the way, I felt something start to happen. In my discomfort and alertness to the area, I felt a shift. I let go. I finally found my flow. It was meditation via paddling, with incredible scenery everywhere I looked, and a soundtrack no concert could come close to replicating.

We had teased one another the whole way down about our cankles, about my fears, about the caiman, but now we remained silent and captivated by the wonders of the Amazon.

This is why people are called to adventure, even when things go wrong, even when they are miserable. It is in that discomfort—the times we are hot, sweaty, scared, and itchy from hundreds of bugbites—that we also find a greater beauty inside us and a knowing of what we can really do in this world. In the less than pleasant moments, we are reminded how alive we truly are.

The guides motored ahead and told us to veer left when we saw a cove. Chase was in the lead with his camera. As we entered the cove, we'd arrived at a *collpa*—a giant clay lick, which is a mineral-rich structure of clay where erosion of the riverbank has exposed clay seams in the soil. Apparently, it's like a candy wall for birds. There were thousands of wild macaws all feeding on it.

As we got closer, the sounds of our paddles sent the birds flying every which way. I looked up and around. All around me swooped macaws— scarlet red headed, teal blue bellied, golden winged, and mixed in so many shades of each. They were chirping and squabbling. The sky was painted in the most magnificent colors. The air was filled with the wildest sounds.

Our mouths dropped open in awe. It was indescribable, like being inside a National Geographic movie. Chase captured the moment perfectly with his camera. In pictures you can see a rainbow sky of birds above. All wild. All free. Surrounded by mineral cliffs above. No aviary would ever come close.

The rest of the way home, I was silent. We forgot about the heat and the bugs and finally relaxed. We paddled through a section of our world rarely touched by humans: thick, green trees towering overhead, the jungle buzzing with life all around us.

We arrived back at the lodge just as it was getting dark. I took the best lukewarm shower of my life and slathered my bites with aloe that Mariko brought from Hawaii.

It wasn't an *easy* adventure. Although I felt safe enough, the trek wasn't comfortable. I spent most of the time not knowing what animals or especially insects I'd encounter, in addition to so many other unknowns along the way. But in pushing myself outside my personal comfort zone, I learned a lot.

I also realized that, in some ways, I'd been trying to become an Amazonian version of myself. I was working like a madwoman, dating a lot, and pushing myself in ways that weren't exactly helpful. I couldn't keep trying to act like a guy to write for mostly male-dominated adventure magazines, and I couldn't keep trying to use nature as something to conquer or a place to prove my worth. That was an old paradigm that I'd have to learn to let go of on my own.

Nature proved to me that it was to be enjoyed in a different way—to experience, to appreciate, to learn from. To let go and surrender to. Not to use as something to conquer or check off a list.

Afterward, I slowed down and started listening more deeply to the lessons that nature was teaching, especially when I went back to Costa Rica later that summer. Like not fighting the current and letting it pull me out in the ocean, so I could paddle to the side and catch better waves. Or laughing and relaxing whenever I got held down by a wave underwater and just surrendering to what came next, knowing I would eventually come up for air. I also stopped surfing on days when the waves were totally over my limits. Instead, I practiced yoga or went for a walk. I paid more attention to birds singing, the monkeys overhead, the way the bright orange and purply blue Halloween crabs opened and closed their claws. The way the rain sounded when it hit the giant elephant ear leaves. I rested more. I slept in later.

I also started talking openly about having experienced depression and anxiety with others, and how I found ways to cope. And I stopped dating like a madwoman. I stopped taking on stories just for the "cool" byline and only said yes to those that felt meaningful to me. I stopped trying so hard altogether. I just started to become more authentically me.

Adventure does that to you.

And in many ways, that's what you have to do when it all goes haywire. You have to slow down. Stop trying so hard and surrender to the moment. It's then you will find a solution and make your way out.

WHAT TO DO WHEN THINGS GO HAYWIRE

- No fighting. Use your energy to solve the problem, not to cast blame.
- Stop and take a breath.
- Reassess the situation. Look at a map. Ask for directions if you can.
- Ask yourself if it's an emergency or an inconvenience.
- If it's a real emergency, for example where you can't extract yourself and you are really stuck, call for help. After that, feel free to scream, "*Oh fuuuuck!*"
- If it's an inconvenience, no matter how big, can you find some humor inside?
- If so, share the levity. *Laugh!*
- Imagine a worst-case scenario and be grateful yours is not as bad.
- Imagine the story, as if you would tell it later over drinks with friends.
- Share the story. Learn the lesson. Congratulate yourself for being on an adventure.

HOW TO TELL IF YOU ARE IN A REAL CRISIS

with Diana Helmuth

We've talked about following the trail. What do you do when there is no trail?

For Diana Helmuth, author of *How to Suffer Outside*, a crisis is when you can't extract yourself from wherever you are. In 2016, Diana was backpacking with two friends on Puyehue Mountain, a volcano in Chile. It was supposed to be a three-day trek, up the mountain and down the other side. On day two, everything was going well. The landscape was beautiful, with sulphur pits and Martian-looking rocks juxtaposed with areas of flowers, butterflies, and awe-evoking beauty.

But when the group reached the cone of the volcano, there were no trees and no dirt. And because there were no trees and no dirt, there was no distinct trail. Atop the mountain, a series of poles had been erected to help guide people, so they could hike from pole to pole.

Soon a giant cloud rolled in, followed by another. Diana and her friends were in fog unlike anything they'd ever seen. So they did what you do when you are a kid and you've lost your parents at the store or Disneyland (at least what I did). They just sat down, hoping the fog would pass. But thirty minutes later, the fog had only grown thicker.

The friends made a chain. One person would walk forward and the person behind would say "stop" when they could no longer see ahead. It did not work.

Diana proposed they go back the way they came. But the group decided to descend below the fog, until they had absolutely no idea where they were. There was no trail, and no poles to be found.

A crisis in the backcountry, Diana explained, is the inability to self-extract. "Knowing that difference can be orienting, grounding, and really calming," Diana told me. And it served as a compass to also help her calm down. They did see a river though, so they bushwhacked down off-trail to the river and followed it down-stream. They camped another night and the next day found a road. Four wrong turns and twenty miles later, they ended up at a farm.

They were ecstatic. They figured someone would take them in, maybe give them a meal and take them home. The farmer who found them was not pleased. He pointed up the volcano and told the group they needed to walk back up the mountain. At that point there was no way they were going up the mountain again.

Eventually, the farmer took them to the road and they hitch-hiked to a hostel. The story made for a great tale, but more im-portant, it taught Diana that knowing if you are indeed in a real emergency is really important in the wild. A real emergency is one where you can't get out. That's when you need help.

CHAPTER 10

TRAIL ANGELS

There is a phenomenon called Trail Magic, known and spoken of with reverence by everyone who hikes the trail, which holds that often when things look darkest some little piece of serendipity comes along to put you back on a heavenly plane.

—Bill Bryson, *A Walk in the Woods: Rediscovering America on the Appalachian Trail*

Jerry Holl couldn't slow down. The retired sales executive was pedaling his bike as fast as he could down the Alaska Highway, especially after seeing a mamma grizzly with two cubs about fifty feet away. He stared straight ahead and kept on riding. It didn't help that the minute he'd arrived in Alaska a woman at the outdoor store mentioned someone had just been mauled by a bear.

Luckily for Jerry, Mamma Bear wanted nothing to do with him. He would end up seeing a total of twenty bears on what would be a 51-day ride, 3,634 miles from Alaska to Mexico.

The whole trip had come together quickly. Jerry wanted to have a grand adventure. He'd been a sales executive for years, working at corporate jobs as he devoured books about the outdoors and people chasing extreme feats. He'd always wanted to do something grand himself. He even admitted to getting a little jealous when he heard of others going out to do something wild.

Over the last several years of corporate life, Jerry found himself looking out his office window when he should've been working. "I dreamed of being in the natural world," he told me, "and of big, hairy, audacious adventures in faraway places.

"I had an overwhelming feeling to jump out of corporate America when I did," Jerry added about his adventure. "I just plain got bored. It was good meaningful work as a cog in a healthy economy. And it took strong developed skills to perform, but it all started feeling the same."

Jerry knew he was incredibly fortunate—blessed with great health, a great wife, great kids, and a series of great jobs—but he was also a problem solver. He felt most alive when he was pushing himself and when he was a little on edge. Over the years, he'd tackled a variety of adventures as a weekend warrior, from backcountry canoeing to skydiving and competing in fifteen American Birkebeiners, the grueling cross-country ski race in Wisconsin. But once he retired and his kids were grown, he (and his wife) knew he was itching to do something. "I simply wanted new 'explosive growth'—something adventurous and something I hadn't done before," he said. "You only live once and I wanted to know what I was made of. Additionally, two big questions kept creeping into my mind. One, what's the story of the rest of your life? Two, will it be a story worth telling?"

Originally, Jerry was going to ride a bike from Seattle to San Diego. But then a friend said, "Jerry, if you go, go big!" On the spot, he changed his itinerary to ride from Alaska down to Mexico.

That decision alone clues you into the amount of time Jerry put into planning his wild idea. So yeah, while I talked about the importance of mapping your trail in chapter 5, some people's maps are a little more of an outline. Jerry knew how to ride a bike. He knew how to camp. He knew how to get in shape and was fit and healthy. He knew how to close big deals and negotiate his way out of a bind. What could go wrong? He was fifty-seven and had two friends who'd nearly died from heart attacks. He knew he wasn't getting any younger.

"It was a culmination of all those small stretches I'd done—that weekend warrior type stuff," he recalled. "You just pile them on top of each other and you make a big stretch out of it. Small stretches shape your future.

Then the big stretch makes your future. I had no idea how I would change or grow, or what would occur after this," he told me when I interviewed him on *Wild Ideas Worth Living.*

Jerry's approach was: "I'm just going to figure it out along the way." It's a refreshing approach. In some ways, he's a good model when it comes to not overthinking your adventure so much that you don't ever start.

But he did hit a few snags. A few afternoons after seeing the bears, Jerry was eighty-five miles into the day's ride. He was tired, straining up a steep hill. His thighs felt heavy on the pedals, and he realized he was in the wrong gear. He reached to downshift, and just then the chain came across the sprocket. He could hear the grind of the chain unraveling, and then a plop and a chink as it hit the ground. He quickly realized he was pedaling air.

Oh fuuuck!

Jerry stopped and got off his bike, then set it down and picked up the chain, which lay like a dead snake in his hand. It was late in the day, and the sun would be setting shortly. Jerry knew how to do a lot of things, but one of them was not fixing anything mechanical on his bike. In this case, some education would have helped, but he figured he could just camp on the side of the road, make do for the night, and deal with it tomorrow. He was stuck. Tomorrow he'd still be stuck.

That's when he glanced in the distance and saw a moving yellow dot. So far, Jerry hadn't come across many people. He mostly rode alone, seeing no one aside from a few big trucks hauling cargo. But the dot kept getting closer.

"Oh my god, it's another cyclist," he realized. Up rode a woman. Turned out, she grew up in the exact same town in Minnesota as Jerry. I personally have never met a mean person from Minnesota, and Sarah, the woman in yellow who was riding her bike that day in Alaska, was as kind as they came. She asked Jerry if he had a manual. He did not. But she looked at his bike and then back at hers. They had the same bike! It was as serendipitous as it comes, especially since Sarah *did* have the manual and realized she could help put Jerry's chain together with a snap-link tool. Of course, Jerry had no idea what a snap link was, but when he'd bought the bike at REI he'd asked the salesperson to get him everything he needed.

Jerry said of the REI associate, "He played the parts rack in the store like a piano and just put everything I'd need in a bag." Jerry never actually looked *in* the bag, but he did jam everything into his backpack before leaving. That is one way to get the gear you need for your adventure. In this case, it worked.

Now Sarah helped him put his chain back together using the snap link. He was able to keep riding with no more terrible mishaps.

Jerry came away with valuable lessons. First, that he has a wonderful self-deprecating sense of humor and was able to laugh at himself. He also learned that "change and growth don't occur in safe harbors and calm waters," he said. They occur instead in the places when everything goes haywire.

Jerry told me his philosophy is to put yourself in a position to hit what he calls "the flameout zones." Then, he says, "rely on your instincts, skills, and some luck, and you'll find out you're so much more capable than you ever thought. That's when your perspectives expand and your capabilities grow, and new opportunities arise."

The episode made for a great story in Jerry's 2017 book, *Downhills Don't Come Free*. But more important, he learned something essential about life on the trail: the power of trail angels, magical people like Sarah who appear along the way—usually just after a serious "oh f——" moment.

"People went out of their way to help me whenever they saw my exposure and vulnerability," he says. "A car would pull in and do a health check on you. They'd top off your water bottles. A guy said, 'Hey, I saw you climbing that mountain. I want you to have this candy bar.'" Those people are called trail angels.

IN THRU-HIKING, a trail angel is someone who arrives just when you need them most to offer a helping hand. They can offer freshwater, fresh fruit, beverages, and sometimes a warm shower, a ride to town, or they can help you get out of a jam. That welcome help is called trail magic. It's what happens when you are in a crappy situation and a trail angel has made it so that your path is clear once again, or has seriously brightened your day. It can also just be something serendipitous, like meeting someone on a remote trail who has the exact water filter you broke and gives you their spare. Or it can even be someone whom you meet on a trail when you're feeling especially exhausted or lonely, and welcome the company.

Like signs, trail angels and the magic they carry tend to show up exactly when you need them. For the Higginbotham twins, for example, their trail angels included the dive shop owner who happened to stock the right wetsuit glove, and the pilot who flew it to them. For Ryan and Nicole Levinson, it was the harbormaster whose advice led them to finally set sail.

Almost every time I've been injured in the wild, mostly from surfing, a trail angel has been nearby. In 2012, I hit my head with my surfboard at 5:30 p.m. on a Friday. In the small Costa Rican town where I was living, there was no hospital and exactly one doctor's office, and it was closed until Monday.

I got out of the water, holding my head and asking anyone who might have the phone number for the town doctor. Immediately, someone pointed, saying, "He's right there."

It was him, Alejandro Gutierrez—or Dr. Ale, as the locals call him—walking with his surfboard down to the water. That's trail magic.

Dr. Ale looked at my head, and decided that yes, I needed stitches—but also that yes, he was going to catch a few waves first. We met at his office an hour later. He was soaking wet in board shorts, with his wife and kid in the car. He put on his medical shirt and stitched me up. To this day, you can't see the scar. I try to bring him Vans shoes (his favorite) whenever I visit.

Almost everyone I know who has completed a grand adventure or even a small hike up a new mountain, or just gone camping, has some kind of story like mine, about a trail angel and trail magic. It can be a person who prevented them from getting lost, or a fellow hiker who told them, just as they were planning to quit and turn around, that they only had a short while to keep going because the view was totally worth it. It could be someone who alerted you to a rattlesnake or another who hooked you up with a hamburger when you were camping and sick of trail mix.

The lesson is not just to always be better prepared, bring manuals, or bring a variety of food. It's that in the wild we are often out in the elements, sometimes exposed to hazards, weather, and all sorts of things that are out of our control. We are usually doing our adventure for the very first time. That's what makes it a wild idea. But we don't have much experience doing it yet.

We're also just more vulnerable. Not just physically, but mentally we are out of our comfort zones. We are sometimes even in the flameout zones. Because of this, we may need more help. We may run into trouble. And we may have to help someone else in trouble as well.

When we are out in the wild, something releases inside us. Without cell phones and technology we are more tuned into our surroundings, but without the creature comforts and easy ways to get help we also rely so much more on one another. So much of our life is geared toward pushing people away—deleting emails, throwing out text messages, blocking spam calls and unsolicited text messages. But humans are the most cooperative and adaptable animals, and in so many ways we become our best primal selves in the wild. We might just be naturally kind.

In the wild, we begin to soften inside even as our muscles grow stronger. We become more vulnerable. We scrape away the outer layer of bravado we sometimes wear—the posturing, the chest puffing—and we begin to open up to all types of things we might not normally be open to, including serendipity and massive kindness. Serendipity and kindness are, in fact, the very essence of what makes up trail magic.

> *ProTip:* I've never regretted packing extrahealthy snacks—on planes, boats, road trips, and any adventures. Food is a gift that transcends languages and cultures (and will help you not get hangry yourself). Add in a smile, a gift that works across every single culture and costs nothing.

JUST AS KINDNESS tends to pay itself forward, trail magic can snowball into a virtuous cycle. When San Diego couple Barney and Sandy Mann decided to hike the entire Pacific Crest Trail, the trail magic they experienced turned them into dedicated trail angels.

Decades earlier, the Manns had vowed to hike the PCT together—someday. They met while working at a summer camp in the San Gabriel Mountains, outside Los Angeles, drawn together by their love of the outdoors. Sandy had found hiking through her family and church group. Barney completed his first fifty-mile hike with the Boy Scouts when he was thirteen. He was the smallest kid, at eighty pounds, but carrying a thirty-five-pound pack made him the other boys' equal. It rained the entire trek, but he fell in love with backpacking.

In 2007, at ages fifty-five and forty-seven, the Manns decided the time had come for their epic hike. They had been married for over two decades and raised three kids. Barney worked as an attorney, and Sandy was a high-school teacher with a PhD in molecular biology. Because Barney and Sandy (or Scout and Frodo, as they are known on the trail) live less than an hour from the southern trailhead of the PCT, they had hosted a few hikers, feeding them meals, giving them rides, and handing out water and fresh fruit. It was never a full-time gig, but something they really enjoyed.

The couple prepared well for the journey. They'd completed several long-distance backpacking trips, including sections on the PCT. They'd educated themselves, built up experience, and made a solid plan. And most of the trek did go smoothly.

Then, just north of the California-Oregon border, Sandy took a bad fall. She had stopped to do her business, and as she stood up to catch up with Barney she tripped on a tiny rock and "fell like a tree," she recalled, breaking her fall with her mouth. The impact knocked out one front tooth entirely and broke the other into pieces.

At this point, the Manns were about twenty trail miles outside Ashland, the next big town. And it was Sunday. What dentist works on *Sunday*?

The other problem: they didn't have a cell phone.

In came the trail magic. A hiker nicknamed Red Baron offered his cell phone to take with them to town. Other hikers offered to take Sandy's pack, an offer she declined; it was her mouth that hurt, she said, not her body.

In Ashland, the Manns walked straight to the emergency room. The doctor told them that, while they had a dentist on call, it was unlikely he'd come out. But the dentist on call that night, David Layer, agreed to meet Scout and Frodo at his office, just across from the motel where PCT hikers usually stayed. Dr. Layer happened to be a Boy Scout himself and was fond of hikers who came through town.

On the surface, it sounded like a simple act of kindness, but Barney's eyes welled up when he and Sandy told me how Dr. Layer spent two hours with Sandy rebuilding the broken tooth and building a bridge to save the other one. The doc shared his love of the hiking trails as he worked. Fifteen years later, Sandy's teeth are still strong.

That episode of trailside dentistry was certainly memorable, but the Manns told me they could share profound stories from every single day on the trail, even when things didn't go so catastrophically wrong. Just as Casey Higginbotham had said about his paddleboarding journey, their memories of the PCT were so much more vivid than those from everyday life. "You look back fourteen years on a day that you're not on the trail, and could you tell a story about that day?" Barney said. "No. You don't remember it. But you remember what happens on the PCT.

"We are all so different out there," he continued. "And unlike most of our life, which has familiar patterns, any moment around a bend the most amazing thing can happen. And they often do out there—whether it's somebody, whether it's an animal, whether it's the most god-awful weather you've been in, or whether it's setting up a tent with the most beautiful view."

That's why the concept of trail magic might be so much easier to find on the trail than in real life.

THE YEAR AFTER THAT TRIP, the Manns began hosting thru-hikers in a major way. They had experienced so much kindness, it made them want to pay it forward themselves.

They started small, with about thirty-five people passing through their San Diego home over the hiking season. Over the next fourteen years, they built up to hosting twelve hundred people, about forty people a day every spring.

The Manns don't live in a mansion. They don't own fancy art or fancy cars. They have a nice but simple four-bedroom on a cul-de-sac in University City, with fake grass and a beautiful tree house Barney built himself. Hosting forty hikers a day in your house for months seems like a giant undertaking to me. But the Manns have just enough room for friendly hikers and they love it. Men and women from all over the world have found a way to stay with Scout and Frodo.

The couple keeps Google spreadsheets of flight information and dietary restrictions. They feed guests two meals a day, including fresh pumpkin muffins and frittatas for those leaving early to start the trail. Their garage is stacked with boxes of gear that hikers have shipped ahead of their arrival. They pick up hikers from the airport and bring them to the AT&T store to get their phone plans sorted out. They have a team of volunteers running shuttles to the trailhead.

They treat each hiker like their own kids going off to college, nurturing them, providing tips, and showing them some fun. At night, they sing campfire songs, beginning with the John Denver classic "Country Roads." ("Even the Europeans seem to know that one," the couple says.)

Barney and Sandy also pass on the trail's Leave No Trace ethos: travel and camp on durable surfaces, dispose of waste properly, leave what you find, minimize campfire impacts, respect wildlife, and be considerate of others. It's like the Golden Rule in nature.

Part of kindness is taking care of the places where we play. We taste the fun of nature's playgrounds firsthand—and also see its destruction more closely. We know how kind nature is to us and how much nature does for our soul. The least we can do is protect natural spaces. Barney and Sandy teach this as much as possible.

When the Manns told me they do all this for free—without fundraising or donations, with their own money—I was even more surprised. They even publish their phone number and address for hikers online.

With forty people a day invading their house for sixty days a year, you'd think there may have been a mishap or item missing. Nope.

"People are basically good when you give them the opportunity," Sandy told me. "When you see someone on the trail—and sometimes you're out in places where the only people are PCT thru-hikers—you know they'd give you the shirt off their back. And you'd do the same for them."

That's not just because being kind is the right thing to do—although that is a big part of it. The Manns also do it because it brings them immense amounts of joy. They love being around people at the cusp of a life-changing experience.

That might be why I loved teaching surf lessons. People would usually come to camp a little pale and beat from their everyday lives. Often they were both scared and ready to do something wild. After a week of surf lessons, many would go home and make a series of small changes that started to add up.

Helping someone do that feels really good. It's joyful. There's no better feeling than watching someone experience the thrill of adventure, riding a wave for the first time or hiking their first life-changing trail. The old saying I mentioned previously is true: you get more from giving than you ever get from getting.

The biggest thing the Manns ask from their guests in return is for people to pay it forward. And people do.

> *ProTip:* Send a thank-you to someone who has done an act of kindness for you. It will go a long way, even if it's a simple text or phone call. Also, do a random act of kindness even on your everyday trail. Try buying the person in line behind you a coffee or juice and see how much that might make their day, or give a compliment that is free.

WHEN I INTERVIEWED Cheryl Strayed, she told me, "I've always taught my kids that kindness is the most important value that I hold. That's the thing I want them to be when they grow up. I don't care if they're a doctor or a lawyer or whatever. I want them to be kind, and they know it." Perhaps part of that is a lesson she learned from hiking the PCT herself.

Kindness is and always will be a game changer. Johnny, my partner, always quotes that old saying that you catch more flies with honey than with vinegar, and it's true. Kindness is *just* one of those things that spreads like wildfire. Once you taste adventure's profound effects, you can't *not* want to help share it with others. And when you share your love of adventure with others, that can be an even more rewarding adventure.

That's how things worked for tech executive Silvia Vasquez-Lavado, the first Peruvian woman to summit Mount Everest and the first openly gay woman to climb the Seven Summits. Those accomplishments are enough to inspire anyone. But it is Silvia's rise up from childhood trauma—and her willingness to guide other young women through that same kind of trauma—that has affected so many other lives.

I spoke with Silvia after the publication of her memoir, *In the Shadow of the Mountain*, which is being adapted for the screen and will be produced by Selena Gomez, who will play Silvia in the movie. Silvia told me about the first time she saw Mount Everest, in 2005, in the aftermath of a breakdown that had been years in the making. The mountain was so awe-inspiring and so mesmerizing, that she knew she would come back. She had no idea, however, how completely Everest would change her life.

Silvia grew up in Peru, a young Catholic schoolgirl in the suburbs of Lima. But starting when she was six years old, she suffered sexual abuse from the family's housekeeper, someone thought to be a trusted friend of the family. For many years, Silvia kept it a secret, until she was a teen. She remembers feeling so confused, so angry, and in so much pain. When she finally told her mother and all that trauma poured out, Silvia went to a psychologist. All of this coincided with the rise of the Shining Path terrorist group in Peru, and things were becoming dangerous in Lima. Several of Silvia's siblings had already migrated to the United States, and with the psychologist's urging Silvia applied to US colleges and won a scholarship at a tiny Pennsylvania college.

Naturally driven and smart, Silvia excelled. She moved to San Francisco and became an executive at SKYY Vodka and then at eBay. For years in her twenties, she pushed away her pent-up trauma. She used workaholism and alcoholism as a way to cope, which was convenient since she worked at an alcohol company. She also binge-dated, using that as another way to cope.

When she was thirty-one, Sylvia's trauma caught up with her. She bottomed out and returned home to Peru for help. Her cousin, a doctor, had worked with the powerful indigenous medicine ayahuasca, and he arranged for her and her parents to attend an ayahuasca session together. There she envisioned herself reconnecting with her inner child, walking together in the high mountains. The experience was so impactful, she decided to see the world's tallest mountains firsthand.

Silvia joined a trek to Everest Base Camp that year in 2005 when she was thirty-one. The Himalayas were such a contrast to the landscape and fast pace of San Francisco. Here was a place without cars, with prayer flags and rickety bridges, yaks crossing, where everyone seemed so kind. "There was something about this country life that was so welcoming," Silvia told me. "There was no attitude."

Walking beside the Dudh Kosi river, she saw whitewater so turquoise and trees so green, she thought she was in a watercolor landscape. She watched the sun rise, illuminating the profile of Everest.

Silvia said she felt like she could walk forever. With her high-altitude Andean ancestry, and immense inner strength, she made it to base camp much faster than expected. In many ways, the Himalayas reminded her of home in Peru. All that nature made her soften and start to heal a bit. She felt smaller and more connected. She said the mountains gave her such a strong sense of belonging. In so many ways, she said, "the mountains showed me I wasn't alone." They were there to support and hold her. Afterward, Silvia started to speak more openly about her abuse.

Silvia knew she wanted to come back. But how? And when? It was a year later that she wondered if maybe she could become a mountaineer. She had zero experience climbing mountains and zero gear of her own, but she also had nothing to lose. That's when she decided to pursue climbing the Seven Summits. She would start with the easiest first, and possibly climb the mother of all mountains, Everest, last. She went up Kilimanjaro and Mount Elbrus. In 2013, she climbed Aconcagua, feeling deeply connected to all of the generations of Andean women that had come before her.

Silvia's journey also led into new terrain in her own life. She opened up and started talking so much more about her experience with trauma. In 2014, she started the nonprofit Courageous Girls, which helps other survivors of sexual abuse and trafficking find their voices.

In 2016, she was ready to climb Everest. But she didn't go alone. On the eighty-mile trek from Lukla to base camp, she guided five other Nepali and American women, all survivors of sexual abuse. Their trek was a whole other mountain to climb. One of the young women needed medical help, and they were lucky to run into a female doctor on the path (trail magic). At one point, Silvia wasn't sure if the girls would even open up about their story. She stepped back, surrendered, and let the trip, and the women's catharsis, unfold as it should.

Mind you, this was all before her own climb up to the 29,029-foot summit with a group of men, some of whom didn't make it to the top. Silvia did, and hers is the first story I've read about mountain climbing that talks more about the lessons that come from surrendering and yielding to a mountain rather than pushing and conquering one. Willing her way through life and up mountains wasn't easy, but it was possible. As Silvia says, we all have our own inner mountain to climb.

After her experience healing in the mountains, Silvia became more than a trail angel. She became a trailblazer. In sharing her story, she made so many other survivors feel less alone. Three of the young women she took to base camp, in fact, have become mountain guides themselves. When I checked in with her for this book, she'd received a grant to take hundreds more survivors of trauma into the mountains.

I think that's one of the best parts about wild ideas. We have no clue how our own singular journey will be an act of trailblazing for someone else. Your wild idea is an act of kindness, maybe even trail magic, for the world. You have no idea who you'll inspire. Even if it seems small, it will resonate with someone.

Being kind, paying it forward, becoming a trail angel—this is a huge part of living wildly. And it often feels more incredible than surfing any wave or climbing any mountain.

HOW TO BE A TRAIL ANGEL, EVEN OFF THE TRAIL

We have no idea what others are going through, and sometimes just an encouraging smile can go a long way. When I lived in Costa Rica, I had a friend, Lulu, an older surfer in her seventies who rode around on her beach cruiser passing out homemade banana muffins and cookies. It always made our day. Beyond food, you can always give someone a compliment, encouragement, a smile, or just be there to support others on their own adventures.

1. For those going to an actual trailhead known for having thru-hikers pass by, Barney Mann suggests bringing a cooler, some food, chairs to sit on (for other tired hikers, not just for you), maybe a table to put things on, and a something for shade, like an open-side pop-up tent. Have fun; just remember that trail organizations advise to never leave a cooler, food, or beverages unattended, as it could attract animals. Pack out what you carry in.

2. When it comes to food, keep it simple. Barney Mann will never forget the story of the Sierra Nevada hiker who hiked in dry ice and all ingredients to make fresh root-beer floats for hikers, but that's a big commitment. Boxed juices, sodas, or fresh fruit, also work well. You can't go wrong with homemade cookies. I will personally never turn down a fresh cold juice, fresh fruit, dark chocolate, or a cold kombucha!

3. If helping hikers on actual trails, think about your
    boundaries before starting. Do you want to give
    people rides? Are you comfortable just giving
    people food? It's best to do things only within
    your comfort level. Trust your gut when it comes
    to safety. If a situation feels dicey, it probably is.
    Always stay safe.

4. Many major trails with thru-hikers have web-
    sites or social media pages. If you have a question
    about how to be a trail angel on an actual thru-
    hiking trail like the PCT, or want to know the best
    trails to show up to and meet thru-hikers, ask
    questions of those in the know.

Here are some other ways to be a trail angel and share
trail magic with other adventurers:

1. Take a friend or someone else on a hike. Bring
    snacks, and yummy treats, and show them parts
    of nature they've never seen. Showing someone a
    trail or even a national park for the first time will
    likely be as rewarding for you as it is for them.

2. Be on the lookout for others. When on an adven-
    ture, if you see someone who looks like they are
    struggling on the trail, the slope, in the water, et
    cetera, be willing to help if you can, and don't be
    afraid to alert someone to a known danger.

3. Leave trails better than you find them. This goes
    without saying, but taking care of the places we
    love to play is a big part of adventure. Anytime I

go to the beach, I grab a few pieces of litter and pack out whatever I carry in.

4. If you are an adventurer, share your skills. Not everyone knows how to rock-climb, surf, or paddle, so if you can take someone along safely, do it. You can even take a friend or a newbie on a picnic or host an outdoor barbeque and share a delicious outdoor meal.

5. Volunteer to help build and maintain actual hiking and biking trails and support those doing so. I recently learned one of the biggest-growing bike trail communities is happening right now in Arkansas, courtesy of generous donors and activists.

6. It never hurts on an adventure to have extra water, snacks, and things specific to the adventure, such as surf wax and sunscreen when surfing, chalk when climbing, et cetera. I have hooked up countless people with surf wax and sunscreen at the beach. Doing so, I've met new friends.

7. While running, hiking, climbing, paddling, or whatever you are doing, share a smile and kindness. Sure, you're going to meet hermits who don't want to talk to you, but smiles and words of encouragement are free, and often go a long way.

CHAPTER 11

SCENIC ROUTES
AND SIDE TRAILS

Not all those who wander are lost.

—J. R. R. Tolkien
(The most cliché outdoor quote ever, but always true!)

When it comes to adventure, the parts that are often the most glorified are the starting and finish lines. These are the parts we spend the most time anticipating, planning for, telling people about, and the most time trying to get to. But what we remember the most are not only the starts and finishes, or those highs and lows, when stuff goes wrong or we experience trail magic. We also remember when we spontaneously take the side route to the epic view that's out of the way. Or when we take time to skinny-dip in an empty lake. Or when we say *yes* to an invitation from a kind stranger that leads us to one of the best nights of our lives.

Your adventure might involve speed—say, going for a record or an FKT (Fastest Known Time)—which is all fine and dandy if that's your wild idea. But for most of us, sometimes we just need to slow the heck down to experience the best parts of our adventures.

That's how it was for Noami and Dustin Grevemberg, who set out in a

216

1985 VW van in 2016. "We were zipping across the country to see and do it all," Noami told me. But after a while, that way of living became a bit too much. It was hard to establish a routine or find a sense of place. Every day, they'd have to load up the van, drive somewhere else, then locate a whole new place to park the van, to find food, a restroom, et cetera. It went on like that for months.

The couple had named their journey Irie to Aurora. *Irie* came from Noami's Trinidad heritage, meaning "pleasing or good." Irie is the name they gave to their van. Aurora was named for the aurora borealis, the northern lights that Noami had dreamed of visiting since she was a kid. Somewhere after actually seeing the aurora borealis in Alaska, the couple decided enough was enough.

First, Irie (the van) was old. She didn't go much faster than 55 or 60 miles an hour on a good day. Merging onto a freeway was challenging. Getting passed by cars going 70 was scary, let alone 85 miles per hour. Most of the time, because of the speed, they were forced to take the scenic route.

That allowed the couple to see so much more. From this, Noami and Dustin adopted a philosophy they called "slow van travel." Instead of going to a place for a few nights or less, they began staying for a month at a time. Sometimes they'd park for two weeks on one side of town and two weeks on another. A month might not seem like a long time, but it gave them a chance to experience local markets, restaurants, and businesses, to check out the town library, and to really get a feel for a community. It also gave them a chance to rejuvenate and restore.

"For me, slow travel is about taking the time literally to slow down," Noami says. "With that comes a certain type of empowerment. Even as you travel, you are really able to create a sense of place, build community, and immerse yourself in local culture."

Slow travel has also totally shifted the type of travelers she and Dustin became. "We often go where the road takes us," Noami told me when I asked about her favorite scenic route story. She notes that the Oregon Outback was a huge highlight for the couple. It's so remote, you have to take extra gas with you. Off one side road, she said, they came to a desert playa, an old lake bed of hard cemented clay with mountain ranges on either side and hot springs in the middle. "It looked like Martian landscape, and we felt like we were the only people in the whole world," she said.

It was a pretty magical feeling, and such a contrast to the city life they'd been living. That experience brought them to a new place. And that's the point of travel and adventure: to experience a total shift in place, sense of time, and how you feel. "The best part about scenic routes is they allow you to wander a bit, which is the point I suppose," Noami says.

Anytime we take a side trail just because, I call these entire moments scenic routes, and they are often some of the best parts of why we adventure in the first place. Of course, there are also literal scenic routes. For example, you can take the freeway or the coast road for much of the California coast, and in my opinion the coast road is always prettier, even though it usually takes much longer.

SOME PEOPLE'S whole wild ideas are defined by the scenic route. In the case of Tom Turcich, that route went around the entire planet. In 2015, the day before his twenty-sixth birthday, Tom walked out his door in Haddon Township, New Jersey, and proceeded to spend the next seven years walking across all sorts of roads all the way around the globe. He became the tenth person to ever complete such a feat, and his dog, Savannah, became the first dog to do so.

The idea of walking around the globe came to Tom after a classmate passed away unexpectedly when Tom was in high school. He learned right then that life is short, and he wanted to honor his friend by experiencing as much life as possible, testing himself and seeing as many countries as he could along the way. He had a very clear why.

All through college and afterward, Tom stayed focused on his goal. He still had fun and was in a fraternity, but he worked odd jobs and installed solar panels to pay off student loans and contribute to his trip. He landed a sponsor, a small company in his hometown called the Philadelphia Sign Company. The owner was so touched by Tom's story, he gave him about $14,000 each year to help pay for food and other costs.

Tom started in New Jersey and walked all the way down through Central and South America. Then he took a boat to Antarctica. From there, he crisscrossed his way around the UK, Europe, and North Africa. In 2020, five years into his journey, he was walking through Azerbaijan when COVID hit, and forced him to reroute, skipping Australia. In August 2021, he flew to Seattle. From there, he walked all the way back to New Jersey. After twenty-five thousand miles, he arrived back home in May 2022. I spoke with him about three weeks later.

Tom said that for the first year and a half of his trip he didn't stop walking. He walked about 24 miles a day, every single day, nonstop. Tom was so focused on his goal and also trying to prove to everyone else, and mostly to himself, that he could do what he set out to do, he felt like he had to keep going.

But somewhere in Peru, Tom realized maybe he should slow down. All the way down in Peru, accommodations were also a lot more affordable, and he realized he could stay in an actual hotel. After a full year and a half of sleeping in a tent, an actual bed in a hotel room with a shower was indeed glorious. By slowing down, and staying weekends in hotels, Tom learned he could rejuvenate. Like Noami and Dustin discovered, Tom could also take some time to get to know a place more intimately. Taking the weekend off was so enjoyable that after Peru, Tom decided to take weekends off whenever possible, and explore the sights wherever he was. The trip became so much richer after that. "I was able to dig into places on a deeper level. I also had something to look forward to each weekend," he said.

A seven-year wild idea, with planning and saving for many years before it, required intense stamina and focus. Tom had to say no to so many things: dinner invites, birthday parties, weddings, and more. Imagine everything you'd miss in seven years, but also how many invitations you might get walking as a stranger in a foreign land.

Tom declined a lot of offers. The times he did say yes, however, were especially memorable. Around twenty-two thousand miles and four and a half years into his journey, he was sitting in a tea shop in rural Turkey. It was his fourth day in the country, and a nice stranger struck up a conversation. They were having a great time talking, using Google Translate to understand each other, when the man invited Tom to join his family at a local villager's wedding.

"I was reluctant at first," Tom told me. The wedding had upwards of five hundred people—basically the whole town—and the party went on for hours, with a ceremony, praying, eating, drinking, and an ever-expanding circle of dancing, which started with the bride and groom and eventually included the entire party. Tom danced until 1:00 a.m., which was pretty late, considering he usually went to bed by 8:00 or 9:00 p.m. "It was such a cool opportunity, and I got incredible insight into a culture I had never been privy to," he told me.

"One of the greatest benefits of traveling is you're open to serendipity," Tom said. "It's easy to get so focused and so single-minded on an adventure that you close yourself off to serendipity, which is harder to find in your day-to-day life with your normal routines. With a trip, you want to achieve getting to your destination, but those random encounters are what makes travel (and wild ideas) so special."

> *ProTip:* If you are running a race or going for a record, then by all means, stay on the course. Go for gold. If you are not racing, take the scenic route when you get a chance to see something beautiful. If someone invites you to do something out of the ordinary and you feel safe doing so, and it gives you that jolt of good electricity, say yes! Slow down when you can. When you do, you'll see a lot more.

IF YOU GET A CHANCE to take a side trail to hike to a waterfall, a vista, or a jump rock, or someone invites you to do something that will make a lasting memory, say yes, even if it's kind of a pain in the butt. Even if you want to turn around. Even if you're tired and hungry. Because it often pays off and can change your life. Saying yes unexpectedly is actually how I met Johnny.

Early one Tuesday morning in December 2011, I was in Nosara, Costa Rica, to teach surfing lessons with Surf Diva. My co-instructor, Meli, who lived there full-time, invited me to surf with her the next day, before our lessons started. I didn't really sleep the night before, so I wanted to stay in bed, but I loved surfing with Meli. Even though I'd be in the water teaching for another four hours later that day, I just said yes.

At the time, Nosara wasn't that crowded, and not many people surfed at dawn.

The waves were amazing. Offshore, clean, and glassy—a surfer's heaven. I felt totally in my element. One, I was just excited to be in warm water, in one of my favorite places in the world, the place I'd been going since I was sixteen. Also, it was day two of a weeklong camp with a group of really fun women. Even Izzy, my best friend and boss, had come down to join us.

There were only two guys in the water when Meli and I paddled out. Both were great surfers—and extremely good-looking. Meli was in a serious relationship with a guy she's now married to and has kids with, but I was still very single. One of the guys had blond hair and was very attractive but sorta familiar looking at the same time. I couldn't figure out why, but for some reason I couldn't stop staring at him. The other was dark and handsome, and a little more talkative. I liked his wit instantly.

When I asked the blondie his name, however, I felt a rush shoot through my veins. I brushed the feeling aside as a result of my being a thirsty thirty-one-year-old who hadn't seen much action of late, and who had a long history of dating blonds. We talked a little more, and it turns out Johnny (the blond one) and Ben (the dark, handsome, and witty one) had both also been living in San Diego and we had mutual friends.

Meli and I kept sharing waves. A few times, we tried to out-paddle each other and take each other's waves. We loved egging each other on and goofing off. Ben and Johnny just laughed at us, and Ben asked us a few questions. We let him know we were teaching a lot of mostly single women to surf. Johnny, for his part, seemed a little more reserved. He talked less, but he was happy to share waves with us all. After a few minutes, a good wave came right toward me. Ben was clearly paddling for it, and in better position. I paddled for the wave, stood up, and looked back, quickly realizing Ben also took off. I'd cut him off, but it was too late to kick out.

"You owe me a beer!" Ben yelled. I did a quick take. That was the sort of line I regularly used on anyone I accidentally cut off surfing—or really on any guy I liked—and I was surprised to hear him say it to me. (Side note: Cutting someone off surfing is not okay, ever. *Maybe* if you are planning to date them and get their attention. But it's downright dangerous and not proper etiquette. In this one case, though . . .)

"Okay, meet us at La Iguana tonight," I told him, lighting up. I still couldn't believe they were from San Diego and he was using my line!

Every Tuesday night, La Iguana had a live cover band and you could dance outdoors on a grassy lawn, drink a fruity cocktail or ice-cold *michelada*, and still be home by 9:30 p.m. Dancing outdoors and still being in bed early was a dream to me. We planned to take our Surf Diva students there that night, and I imagined one of the single ladies might like talking to Ben or Johnny. "Okay, that's where we were planning to go anyway," Ben said when we all got out of the water. Johnny just smiled.

Sure enough, the guys showed up. I couldn't stop staring at Johnny. I wanted to know his story. Me being me, I wanted to ask him a million questions at once, but he seemed distant. I was also busy entertaining our surf students, so I wasn't fully focused. And so when Ben asked me out, I said yes. But in the back of my mind, I kept thinking about Johnny.

To make a long story very short, Ben and I went on one date back in San Diego and nothing happened. While he is a great guy, funny, and now married to an equally great woman, we had little chemistry. But whenever Johnny, who had just moved part-time to the East Coast, came back to visit San Diego, we all went surfing together.

Johnny was cute and mysterious, with a full head of blond flowing hair, bright blue eyes, and an amazing smile. I didn't totally understand what he did for work, aside from once being Ben's boss in finance. But he made me laugh, and had some interesting ideas on health, longevity, and how he wanted to live his life untraditionally. He didn't overtalk, but everything he did say seemed to have a point. It was a contrast to my family, where all of us talk all the time, sometimes just to hear ourselves talk, myself included.

Five months later, Johnny and I both ended up back in Nosara for a bit. He was commuting between Nosara and the East Coast, where he'd been helping take care of his mom, who I later learned had Alzheimer's. He could work remotely and was planning to move there full-time.

I'd come back from the Amazon and was settling down a little more. I wasn't sure what I wanted to do in terms of next life steps but did know what I didn't want to be. I didn't want to be such an Amazonian version of myself. I stopped dating and started focusing on myself. I found a job writing for a newspaper journalist who'd started a website that reported on the business of the outdoor industry. I loved being around other entrepreneurs who were passionate about the outdoors, and I was able to combine what I'd learned about business at Vans with what I knew about journalism. My job was to interview industry executives and write about them. I could get most of my interviews done at biyearly trade shows, where I'd conduct five to ten interviews a day for three days, randomly cold-pitching people at their booths. By the time each trade show was done, I'd have dozens of stories ready to go for the next few months.

At this point, I'd ruled Johnny out as any sort of romantic option. We did become good friends, though. When I wasn't teaching lessons, Johnny and I met in the water to surf, heading afterward to the local café for a fresh coconut cut open by a machete and a *café con leche* or banana smoothie.

We'd talk about his life and his family, and I'd ask him which woman in town he wanted to date. He would smile back at me and tell me, "Stanger, you're funny."

I usually had terrible game around guys I liked, but since I'd ruled Johnny out, I just acted like myself. Some days, since the Internet didn't always work and I didn't have a cell phone with an international plan, I'd walk over to his place and wake him up from his afternoon siesta to go surfing. He'd make me delicious smoothies with superfoods or wild jungle fruits he harvested from a neighbor's farm.

One evening, Johnny dropped by my place unexpectedly. When he came through the gate, an older friend who'd also dropped by took one look at him and one look back at me and said, "Have fun." As she gathered her stuff, she quickly grabbed me and whispered in my ear, "You better go for it!"

I did not expect to hear those words in that context. My plan wasn't to date Johnny, or anyone really. But everyone knew I had a crush on him. Everyone but me, that is.

Johnny came bearing ingredients to make raw chocolate bars, with superfoods like *maca* to add in. My hair was a disaster. I was wearing an old T-shirt and surf shorts. I am sure there were giant ants and bugs crawling through my place, which, by the way, had no furniture except an old couch and a mattress on the floor. Still, it was across from the beach, and it was amazing.

I was also on a work deadline and needed to finish a story. But *c'est la vie*. Sometimes you have to say yes to the adventure that walks through your door.

Johnny and I ate the chocolates and then tried watching a movie. My Internet wasn't working well, so we decided to try his place. We walked down the jungle path, and just when we walked inside his place it started to lightning and thunder, the first storm of the year. We laughed—clearly the universe was trying to tell us something.

We tried to watch the movie, but the Internet connection never really worked. Finally, I closed my computer, and Johnny turned to me. I looked up at him. We kissed. More than a decade later, he's still bringing me chocolate, and I am still chasing him in the ocean.

> *ProTip:* One of my favorite out-the-door adventures is to walk out down the beach at low tide for as long as possible, and then get a ride home. You can do this in many locations around the globe. Walk as far as you can to a safe spot, and catch a ride back with a friend or a rideshare. It's a great way to see a place. Always walk when you can or take side routes. Obviously, be safe and use your best judgment.

OKAY, maybe you didn't expect a love story in a book about adventure. But a big part of the spirit of adventure is saying yes to the one you don't expect. The one that takes you off the beaten path, up the dirt road to an amazing coffee shop. To the house of a new friend's cousin who makes you the most epic of meals. To a wave in Costa Rica where you meet your future mate.

I'm not the only person who met their future partner on their wild idea either—there is something about pursuing a wild idea that makes you open, vulnerable, and truly yourself, the perfect attitude to have when falling in love.

About a year before his trip ended, Tom Turcich stopped for a few days in Washington State. He checked into a hotel to work on a children's book he'd been thinking about on his walk, and his agent asked him to send a few chapters. That's when he met a woman who would become his girlfriend. They'd met online a few days prior, but once they connected in real life, he said he felt peaceful around her almost instantly. Normally, he would have just brushed off the feeling and kept going. He still had to walk from Seattle to New Jersey, after all. Instead, he stayed for a four-day weekend. "I wouldn't have built a connection with her if I hadn't," he said.

Something similar happened for Steph Jagger. A month into her ski journey in Argentina, a mutual friend set her up with a guy named Chris Rutgers, as they had a lot in common. They happened to be two Americans in Argentina, both skiing and renting different apartments from the same person in the mountain town of Bariloche.

Chris and Steph met right in the beginning of Steph's yearlong skiing adventure. They had dinner and skied a few times. But Steph didn't think anything of it. Meeting a mate wasn't on either of their minds. Steph was focused on skiing down the mountain as many times as she could. Chris was on sabbatical from Outdoor Outreach, the nonprofit he'd founded in 1999 to connect at-risk kids to the outdoors, the one I worked with and where I'd met Ryan Hudson. It was the first vacation Chris had taken in ten years.

The two kept crossing paths—traveling to the same place, seeing each other on the same flight to their next destination. When they both needed to drive to the airport in Santiago, Chile, they joined up, planning to stay at a crummy hotel in different rooms. But then Chris had an idea. He had a friend with a gorgeous lodge on a glacial lake. They could stay there and go to the airport early the next morning.

When they arrived, Steph was in awe of the lake. A double kayak sat onshore, and the two took it out for a spin. That's when Steph started to panic a bit about the whole situation. It wasn't like her to agree to go somewhere with someone she barely knew. But here they were together, in a kayak at a stranger's lodge, about to spend the night in a room with only one bed.

Steph was in the front of the kayak. Chris sat behind her. They paddled out to the middle of the lake. At one point, they stopped to soak in the scene. The Andes shot up in the background. Colorful lodges lined the shore.

Steph leaned back to stretch, and Chris grabbed her arms to help her deepen the stretch. It was a simple gesture, but it felt like lightning shot through her whole body. Steph knew there was something there. When they got back to shore—honest to God—golden retriever puppies came leaping up to them. The whole scene was right out of a movie, Steph told me, laughing. It was still only a month into her trip and the beginning of Chris's sabbatical, but the romance flame had sparked. Skipping ahead a few steps: the two have been happily married for over a decade. Steph told me that meeting Chris helped her bring out her very best self. In some ways, he pointed her toward a better trail.

The point isn't that you should slow down and take the side route so you can meet your soul mate, though I am a big fan of any adventure love story. The point is that when you stop to do the thing that brings you joy, sometimes the best moments just happen.

You might meet someone who changes you. Or an idea that changes your life. Or you might make your best memories ever—and memories, after all are what you take with you at the end. Maybe your scenic routes and side trails are just the passions you follow on the path to your wild idea that act as a guiding compass.

The common denominator is being able to say yes, to slow down, to wander a bit, perhaps not even knowing where you'll end up.

SOMETIMES THE SCENIC ROUTE can lead to a life's calling. My friend Eric Wolfinger is a food photographer, the co-creator of twenty-two cookbooks and counting; the *New York Times* has called him "the Annie Leibovitz of food photography." Eric and I grew up surfing together in the same town in San Diego. He always loved photography, travel, and especially cooking. But there is no set path to becoming the next Anthony Bourdain. So Eric created his dream job by taking the scenic route after college. The whole idea, he said, actually started when we were in high school.

When Eric took his PSATs at age fifteen, there was an accompanying questionnaire about what careers interested him. But when he read the careers listed—*accountant, lawyer, doctor*—he didn't see himself doing any of it. "It was like a full existential crisis," he said. He shaded in two bubbles that didn't feel like work: *Culinary Arts* and *Photography*.

Eric had always been entrepreneurial, selling mistletoe in fourth grade and detailing cars through high school, saving enough to convince his parents to let him take a gap year (which no one he knew did at the time). He lived in Germany and then Spain, which helped him get off the freight train of conforming to his parents' and others' expectations. Then he went to Pomona College, a four-year university, to get a good liberal arts degree. He majored in Spanish literature and political science. It wasn't until his senior year, when he started writing a food column for his college newspaper, that Eric started to get excited about working. It started simply enough—he interviewed the family who ran his favorite pho restaurant and spent an afternoon hanging out with the owner of a taco shop.

The thesis behind the column was to help his classmates eat better on the cheap, but Eric says it was always the people and the stories behind the food that lured him in. "It was the first time I found something that I was emotionally, intellectually, and spiritually engaged in, and was writing about things that mattered to me," he told me.

Before graduating from college in 2004, Eric went on a hike with his high-school English teacher, who also happened to be the women's cross-country coach. When Eric told Coach Dorman about his love of food and writing, Coach Dorman suggested he meet up with a fellow high-school alum and cross-country runner, Samin Nosrat, who was doing some great things in food in San Francisco. Two years ahead of Eric in school, Samin had also written a food column for the UC Berkeley newspaper. (If her name sounds familiar, that's because she would go on to write *Salt Fat Acid Heat*, the best-selling 2017 book and megahit food show on Netflix.) After college, she'd found her way into the kitchen at Chez Panisse, one of the most iconic restaurants in the Bay Area, and was then working for one of her mentors at an Italian restaurant. Eric took Samin out for dim sum, and she arranged for him to try out for an apprenticeship at the restaurant where she worked.

Eric had goose bumps even during the tryouts. They gave him a can of anchovies to fillet and debone, and a box of parsley to pick every single leaf off. It was the lowest of grunt work, but Eric loved the energy of the kitchen, and he loved the food and the people. He approached the most mundane duties with the same stoke he brought to catching a wave. He also realized that he wanted to be not just a food writer but one who deeply understood the craft of cooking. Now he was getting a master class.

A while later, a pastry chef told Eric about Chad Robertson, who had learned to bake bread in a tiny town in the French Alps and opened a small bakery in San Francisco's Mission District called Tartine. It sounded almost mythical. "It was less about the food, but I loved the story," Eric told me. He waited in the incredibly long line at Tartine, ate a delicious meal, and gave the kitchen manager his résumé to be considered for a *stagiaire*—a "stage," or brief unpaid internship.

Eric trimmed thirty pounds of bacon, squeezed two cases of lemons, and did it all with a smile. They kept asking him back, and soon he was making pastries and pie shells. He didn't want to become a pastry chef, but he figured he'd stay long enough to learn how to bake Tartine's incredible bread and maybe it would help him write better about food too.

Chad already had two apprentices, so Eric would stay after his shift and sweep floors and make himself useful, just so he could be around this incredible—and, at the time, quite secretive—bread-making process. In that time, Eric convinced Chad that his was the perfect surfing schedule and offered to be his mentor in an activity he knew a lot about. So, three days a week, before going in to bake, Eric and Chad would drive as far as an hour north up to Bolinas, in Marin County, or down to Santa Cruz to ride waves. Soon Chad was as obsessed with learning to surf as Eric was about baking bread. And with all that time in the car, Eric learned about the art of bread making.

After a year and a half at Tartine, in 2006 Eric was a proficient bread baker. However, there were still two people ahead of him at the bakery for an apprenticeship. That's when he decided to take the scenic route. He gave himself a year to create his own dream job. His brother was surfing in Chile, and Eric decided to travel through South America, to surf with his brother, and give himself his own dream job by writing a food blog, and taking his own photos with an early digital camera he'd also teach himself to use along the way.

He began making his way around the country. In Cusco, all the other people at his hostel were taking the train to Machu Picchu. But Eric realized he could just walk out the hostel door, hike up the mountain behind, get into the Sacred Valley, and follow the twenty-six-mile Inca Trail from there. He'd always been curious and adventurous. He spoke Spanish well. And he had a map he'd found at a pizza restaurant.

Eric camped along the way or stayed at the homes of locals. He'd teach them to bake pancakes with simple cornmeal, and they'd trade cooking lessons and drink a Peruvian corn beer called chicha. This was during the autumn harvest, and some farmers would bake potatoes right where they picked them, in ovens made from dirt clods. Eating a potato from the earth, cooked in that very same earth, on the Inca Trail made the potatoes—and the whole experience—even more delicious.

Eric stayed curious and open, and he was always helpful and kind. It was only after getting to know someone that he'd ask permission to take their photo and write about them on his blog. "Those were the stories I was looking for and the kinds of experiences I'd find when I was out just taking the scenic route rather than looking for a specific outcome," he told me.

"What I learned is that when you pursue what's interesting to you intrinsically, the valuable things will come from that, rather than pursuing a goal single-mindedly. My 'goal' at that time was to find food content for my blog, and I wasn't really finding it in the market or in the restaurants. My burning interest at that moment, however, was to take an adventurous self-guided hike to Machu Picchu and spend time with whoever crossed my path. That trip showed me that it's really when you take the slow and scenic route that the really good stuff reveals itself."

Eric traveled around South America for a year, chronicling it all on his blog, *Open Kitchen: Notes from a Wandering Cook*. At the time, he had no idea that he was creating the formula for an award-winning and gratifying career: To spend time with people. To cook with them slowly. To stay curious. And to tell their stories by sharing meals and taking photos.

When he got home, he had high hopes that *Gourmet* magazine or some other publication would see his blog and hire him on the spot. But there were no emails from magazines. He launched a business selling lasagna at the La Jolla Farmer's Market in San Diego to pay the bills.

Gourmet may not have been reading his blog, but Chad Robertson was. Not long after, Eric got a call from Tartine. One of the bread apprentices had left, and there was an open spot. Chad took Eric to dinner and told him that he wanted to do a book on making bread. And he realized that no one could bring a better storytelling and photography perspective to the bread-making process than someone who personally baked the bread. He wanted Eric to take the photos and help him tell his story. The result was *Tartine Bread*, a finalist for the 2010 James Beard Award and a classic on many bakers' shelves.

When Eric got that opportunity, of course he grabbed it. But he told me he's not sure he'd have the career he does today if he hadn't taken his time along the way.

I've always related to Eric deeply about that. To follow his dream, Eric had to have the courage to let go, and to have faith when he wasn't sure how it might turn out. "I spent eight years wondering what I was going to do with my life after college, but maybe I knew all along I just needed to let life point me in the right direction," he said.

"When you are young, dumb, and poor, but also ambitious, it's hard to stay the course," Eric said. "How does someone who is ambitious and driven learn to let go and let life unfold? That's the scenic route! That's where the real opportunities lie."

Follow Eric's lead. Take time to talk to people on your adventures, especially the ones where you don't think you have anything in common. Spend time with them; stay curious. Be kind and be helpful. Do the hard work with a smile. The people you meet on the trail will be your biggest teachers and guides. They will often also show you the best adventures—and, as Eric has demonstrated, some of the best meals—and may even lead you to the people, passion, or career you love the most.

WHEN PLAN B OUTSHINES PLAN A

Mountaineering guide Laurie Watt, from chapter 5, says that often on a mountaineering trip people are focused on reaching the summit. But because of weather and other factors, the probability of actually reaching the top of a major peak can be quite low. If you are focused on the summit, you will often come home disappointed, Laurie told me. But if you just focus on climbing, you will be a lot happier.

"If you can plan to summit just a part of the mountain and enjoy that experience, versus being disappointed that you didn't stand on this one spot on the planet that in the end is not that consequential, it makes for a better climb," she says. You may need to take a side route or a scenic route to get around the worst of the weather, or to avoid a potentially dangerous rockfall or avalanche. The great thing about side routes, Laurie says, is that they are often less crowded, less dangerous, and, because they aren't in the original plan, sometimes a better experience.

When Laurie attempted 20,310-foot Denali in Alaska, she was a customer on a guided trip. Her group made it up to 16,000 feet, but then the weather turned, and the group had used up most of their food and fuel. To keep going would have meant staying on the mountain for longer than their supplies would last. At first, they were disappointed they had to turn around, Plan B.

But her guide took them back to base camp through the night, and the experience of walking through the night was magical. There was no wind, so the visibility was incredible, and because they were in Alaska, they walked through an incredible purply twilight. "I saw some of the most beautiful things I have ever seen hiking back to base camp after we had to turn around," Laurie said. They made it back in time for celebratory beers. It was 5:30 a.m., but, Laurie said, "base-camp beers needed to be drunk. I let go of any disappointment about not touching the actual summit, and enjoyed the grand experience. That is the memory that sticks out for me."

CHAPTER 12

FINISH LINES

Finish lines are often the start of something else entirely.

—Unknown, but something my mom says all the time

When you reach the finish line of a race, or get to the end of the trail, your big moment goes by in a matter of seconds. Crossing the finish takes about the same time, whether your wild idea took a few hours or a few months. It's a blip on the radar of your entire existence. Finish lines are important for any adventure, and they can be awesome and full of joy. But what is not often talked about is the fact that reentry after a wild idea can take some time, and that finish lines aren't always as glorious as we imagined.

One year, flying home from my adventures in Costa Rica, I looked out the window, down at the earth below, as the plane took off. The landscape was lush with vibrant green jungle and the bluest ocean. Landing in Los Angeles at the LAX airport, I was overwhelmed by the twisting overpasses, crowded freeways, cars, traffic, and summer smog. It was jarring.

When you spend so much time in nature, reentering the urban world can be rough. I know one guy who vomited the minute he got back to the city after a long camping trip. The smell of the city was too much.

Aside from the sensory overload of reentry, life on an adventure tends to be simpler and more innate. Like only having to worry about waking up, packing your tent, the basic necessities of getting food and water, and setting up your shelter again that evening. You likely also had a strong sense of purpose on your adventure that made it very easy to get out of bed every day.

When Barney and Sandy Mann stepped across the Canadian border at the end of the Pacific Crest Trail in 2007, you'd think they would have had a giant party. But they felt relief rather than elation. Because of snowy conditions, only 103 hikers made it to Canada that year, according to the Pacific Crest Trail Association. More than half had to turn around, some just a few miles before the end.

Barney's parents met them with a bottle of champagne, which they shared with hiking friends, who felt like family by this point. But pretty soon afterward, the whole crew—these hikers who'd camped together for months on end—scurried out in a matter of hours to catch flights back home. It all felt anticlimactic.

The Manns finished the trail on a Friday. Sandy had to go back to teaching that Monday and quickly fell back into the rhythm of class. Barney, on the other hand, told me he flopped around for a month. He was deciding to retire or not (ultimately, he kept working part-time), but he grew so depressed, he couldn't even shave the beard he'd grown on the hike.

Barney missed the simplicity and excitement of seeing new things, spending every day outside under the stars, and only needing to put one foot in front of the other for four months. He missed all that awe and that concrete sense of purpose. Finally, after thirty days, he grabbed a pair of scissors, cut off his five-month-old whiskers, and went back to being a lawyer for three more years. Reentry, he said, wasn't easy, but the PCT had changed him in a big way. Not long after, he'd dedicate much of his time to being a trail angel.

Guidebooks don't always talk about this sort of thing. Whenever I come back from a big adventure, it takes me a while to adjust back at home. Trust me, it's a shocker.

Mountaineering guide Laurie Watt says she'll never forget coming home after three weeks on the John Muir Trail. Not only did the fifty-five-year-old mom have to catch herself from peeing behind a tree (which I laughed at, because I've done the same thing), but she had a hard time keeping up with cultural norms—things like having to shower and change clothes every day, and answering all those emails and text messages.

"Sure, when you are out there, all you want is a warm bed and a burger," she says. "But when you get back to your suburban life as a mom, there are things that are hard to adjust to—traffic, noise, people, the day-to-day, and the email list. Having expectations and giving yourself some cushion when you get back is really helpful."

Laurie says that you have to give yourself some grace. And to tell your partner and loved ones to give you a little grace as well. They may be so excited to see you, but helping them understand you are in a bit of transition will also help both them and you.

Another thing Laurie suggests is to plan some mini-adventures—even if it's just a trail run or a bike ride. In fact, of the adventurers I've spoken with, the ones who had another adventure planned, or at least something to look forward to, seemed to do better with reentry.

The Higginbothams had a celebration on the beach with beers. Casey also told me that he and Ryan had been celebrating the whole time in their own way. Each night when they made it to a beach unscathed, they felt grateful. And on the trip, they planned their next adventure: paddling another eleven hundred miles down the Baja peninsula, something they completed only two years later at the beginning of 2019. As with so many people, their finish was another start.

That's how it also was for climber Alex Honnold. After free soloing El Capitan, I asked Alex if he got the post-adventure blues. He didn't, he said, partly because he had other expeditions already lined up—to Alaska's Ruth Gorge, below Denali, and to Antarctica afterward. With something else to look forward to, he had approached free soloing El Cap as just another training climb.

"I knew it would be one of the most significant days of my life, but it needed to feel normal, so I didn't put that much pressure on myself," he said.

That's not to say you need to have another grand challenge lined up after your big wild idea is over. Most of us have jobs, families, and regular lives. But having purpose and a reason to get out of bed can transform our mental and physical states. Purpose is powerful.

As Laurie says, "I am trying not to get to the finish line. I hope there isn't one. I don't want to be done until I am dead. I want to keep finding the next challenge, the next adventure. The next out-of-comfort experience."

AFTER YOUR ADVENTURE, you may also be exhausted, both physically and mentally. This mental fatigue is a real feeling that many scientists are studying, especially among extreme adventurers who get a massive increase of dopamine pursuing extreme sports. The increase in dopamine is something many of them will keep chasing. And if you consistently partake in activities that amp your dopamine above baseline levels, your level of drive, energy, and motivation can take a hit.

With most people I interview for the podcast, the amount of time to decompress and process an adventure often correlates to its length. A weeklong trip might take less time to decompress from than a journey that took three years. Why? Well, you may have just completed the hardest thing you've done in your entire life, and there may not only be exhaustion but also grief. In the adventure world, people are starting to share their stories. One remedy is to not only get help but also be kinder to yourself and realize this is not abnormal. Just because you are struggling doesn't mean you are broken.

Steph Jagger learned this lesson firsthand after she broke the record for skiing the most vertical feet in a year. When she hit the 4-million-feet mark, she happened to be skiing back in Whistler. Her mom and nieces were there to greet her. But the celebration was quick, because to get the Guinness record she wanted to keep going. She skied for three more days, but it was spring and conditions were foggy and icy. Those last few days, she said, felt like a total slog. At the end of what she deemed would be a record, she decided to do one more lap down Whistler Mountain to really hammer it home. Afterward, she was emotionally and physically spent. There was no party. No fireworks. No Guinness trophy. She grabbed a hamburger all alone. The whole experience was deflating.

Like Barney, Steph felt a little lost. Sure, she'd completed a giant feat, but she had no idea what came next, and couldn't believe that the thought of figuring out her next step had even entered her mind after what she'd just accomplished.

After her grand adventure, Steph developed depression—an inky dark cloud, as she described it—that made her sleep a lot more than she was used to.

Part of it was pure exhaustion. She went to see a naturopathic doctor, who told her she had adrenal fatigue from all that skiing, as well as all the mental energy that went into planning her adventure. Her sheer lack of energy, and the emotions from finishing such a big adventure, led to situational depression, which many, including Olympians and adventurers, can experience after such a peak experience. Steph saw a therapist. She took medication. She wrote in a journal. She found her footing again, slowly.

It took a few years, but like anyone else who's chased a wild idea, Steph came out totally changed. She didn't fully realize just *how* she'd changed until years later, when she began writing a book about her journey. That was cathartic.

In 2016, six years after her big adventure, Steph was invited on a backcountry ski trip with a group of professional athletes. She was the only woman in the pack, which was fine; she was used to hanging with the guys, and she kept up with them easily. It was also joyful being out in nature in such a beautiful place, skiing again with great people, and staying overnight in huts along their skiing route. It wasn't an easy trip, but Steph had put in her time. She was a pretty accomplished skier by this point.

On one of the last days, the guys wanted to take another lap. Normally, Steph would have gone, not to be outdone and to prove to them—and to herself—that she could hang. But she was tired. She felt good, like she'd skied enough, and she wanted to end the trip on a high note.

"No, thanks," she told the guys. That was not like the old Steph. The old Steph, pre–skiing around the globe, pre–experiencing debilitating depression, would have said, "Hell, yes!" But Steph no longer felt the need to prove her worth.

After telling the guys to go ahead without her, Steph reached into her pocket and found some cold and slightly crusty, yet perfectly tasty, gummy bears that she'd stashed and forgotten about (emergency candy).

Steph bit into the gummies and savored the sweet, gooey taste. She knew she'd had a rich, meaningful experience, and that it would not feel any more complete with one more lap. She sat in the snow munching gummy bears and watched the guys come down the hill on their final lap and cheered them on. Finishing with joy and being able to pick her own finish line was exactly how Steph knew she'd grown. It didn't happen overnight. It happened over time, through the wisdom she'd gained on her adventure, and processing it afterward.

On her journey back to find her footing after her wild idea, Steph had realized that she had been using fear as a motivator: the scarier the undertaking, the bigger the fear, the more ego, the more that's on the line. Using fear to prove her "enoughness" had gotten her far in life. But it didn't help her find peace, and it just might get her hurt. And she knew firsthand from her own experience with depression that if you are motivated by fear you have to recruit a lot of adrenaline, which only creates a crash when you come down. On that ski trip with the guys six years after she chased a record, however, Steph no longer felt the fear or shame that would compel her to push beyond her limits to prove she could hang.

Over time, she learned she had to pick a new motivation to complete big goals and wild ideas, and to finish them.

"It sounds so clichéd, but I had to learn to love myself," Steph told me. "And to be tuned into myself. That day, when I was in the mountains with the guys, I was so happy with the skiing that I'd already done, I could use joy and love as motivation to stop."

Steph recognized that she could not only start using joy and love as her motivation to do wild things; she could also be softer on herself—that being softer was actually brave. That's when even more great things in her life started to unfold, like releasing her book *Unbound: A Story of Snow and Discovery* in 2017, and later led to an even bigger coaching business, more and deeper connections to others, and even another book.

Steph told me grace isn't something people will hand you like a medal at the finish line. Nor will most people throw you a party. That's something you will likely have to manifest entirely on your own. It doesn't have to be big. It just has to be meaningful to you.

WHEN PETE KOSTELNICK made it to New York on his run across America, it was a big deal. He'd broken a thirty-six-year standing record, and friends and family were there to greet him.

But to him the whole scene felt hectic. Running through the busy streets of New York City wasn't easy, and by that point Pete just wanted to be done. There were also a ton of media and fans wanting to take photos with him. Answering the same questions over and over and taking photos with people could have been fun, but when you're that exhausted it can be annoying.

Pete also had a numbers dilemma. Every day, he'd been counting *down* the miles rather than counting up. So when he got to mile zero, for him it felt anticlimactic. Pete said he experienced a bit of depression afterward. He took some time to recover. He went back to work, and pretty soon afterward he got the itch again. That's when he decided to run 5,300 miles from Alaska to Florida the next summer, averaging about 50 or more miles a day. This time, he made sure to count up along the way. That small change made a big difference in his personal mindset.

Pete also put a lot less pressure on himself this time around—he didn't have anything more to prove. Some days he invited strangers and friends to join him, but on the last day he decided to run on his own. This journey was just for him. Pete laughed telling me this; in some ways, he said, this was his recovery run from running across the USA. It was joyful and made him feel like a kid again to explore new places and meet new people along the way. He even poured champagne on himself at the finish.

Doing something just for himself became a big part of Pete's life. As one of the best ultrarunners of our time, he's continued to run amazing distances, setting records and trying new routes.

In 2022, Pete had more big projects scheduled, but since the pandemic canceled so many, he'd upped the ante on them. He had the wild idea to run 50 miles a day in 50 states in 50 consecutive days, and then take a very quick break before flying to Australia and running from Sydney to Perth in a month. To do so, he'd have to average about 80 miles a day for 30 days. Both running projects would be first-time records.

But one day that summer, on a sixty-six-mile training run in 90-degree heat, Pete found that he was drinking twelve ounces of water per mile and still had not peed once. He'd run in hotter conditions, and he'd run 65-plus miles in a day at least 250 times before. But around mile fifty-five, Pete suffered heat exhaustion and was pretty close to heatstroke. He was cramping so badly that he couldn't stand up. Pete had pushed too hard, and in some ways, he said, he'd also lost sight of running for himself in the process.

All this time running solo has made Pete pretty self-aware. So Pete did something bold. He canceled both his big race across America and the one across Australia. His life had become a series of such wild ideas that it felt wilder to just to chill out and hit the "reset" button.

Now, at thirty-five, having run more miles than most people do in a lifetime, Pete is acting as support crew for other ultrarunners going for their own major running feats. He wanted to help other people with their own wild ideas, as so many people had helped him. Running alongside these races also had the added bonus of getting him deeper into nature. Many of the runners he supported were competing in trail races. Pete would still run distances longer than most of us can fathom, but he would rediscover the pure love of running and help out some good friends along the way.

Pete is a good example that when you pursue wild ideas you can't pursue them just for the finish lines. Finish lines and records are cool. But they are often not as sexy as we think they'll be. Sometimes you have to give yourself some room at the end of an adventure to really decompress. And sometimes you will have to turn around before you even get to the end. As Pete himself told me, the journey is always so much cooler than the actual finish line.

DESTINATIONS ARE FUNNY. We spend so much time obsessing on getting to them, but we don't always know what we're going to get when we get there. And when we do arrive at the end, new adventures will often be foisted upon us, even those we don't want and never asked for.

As Marty and Chris Fagan skied across Antarctica, they saw nothing ahead but the vast whiteness of the snowy landscape and a little blue sky. But at day forty-eight, they saw an actual dot in the distance. Because the South Pole is a scientific base, there are a handful of man-made objects on it. For the last dozen or so miles, Chris and Marty were thrilled to focus on the dot, rather than just use their compass, which they'd relied on for the last month and a half.

Even with the destination in sight, that final day wasn't easy, though. "It was like Antarctica just decided to say, *We're going to test you to the limit, and you're not there. You still have a day to go,"* Chris told me. Temperatures hovered around -50, with howling winds. They decided to forgo any breaks and just ski those eleven miles until the end.

Once they were within a mile of the Pole, Chris got emotional. She had tears in her goggles. "I just had an overwhelming feeling of completion and satisfaction and pride," she said.

The celebration wasn't long, though. There were no eco-friendly balloons awaiting them. And no margarita machine (but someone should really think of that). They instead called their son back in Washington. "Keenan, we're at the Pole!" Chris and Marty screamed into the phone, crying the whole time.

Chris felt especially grateful for that moment. It was something they could all share together as a family, a memory they would have for the rest of their lives, something better than any trophy or party.

Because the South Pole is so remote, it took a few days and several flights to get all the way home. In many ways, that allowed them to decompress a bit after their grand expedition.

For a full year afterward, Chris said all she felt was immense gratitude that they'd been able to do something so amazing.

In 2016, about two years after their big expedition, Marty discovered he had Stage 4 squamous cell carcinoma, a form of skin cancer that had made its way into his lungs. He had learned through his life of adventure that he would have to take things day by day, but he and Chris decided to keep on adventuring. It was the only way through. So that year, Marty ran 94 miles around Mount Ranier and also completed a number of ultramarathons. He and Chris hiked with Keenan, then fifteen, to Everest Base Camp. A year later the family climbed Kilimanjaro, and every year since they have done a grand adventure—fast-packing around Mount St. Helens; sailing an outrigger canoe from Port Townsend, Washington, to Ketchikan, Alaska; hiking up Mauna Loa, on the Big Island of Hawaii; and fast-packing the Tour du Mont Blanc, about 105 miles through the Alps.

Chris told me that Marty had made a conscious decision when he got cancer. He was going to keep doing the things he loved, and he wasn't going to let cancer take away from his family or his happiness. He also managed to get lucky with his health.

He took a new immunotherapy drug that slowed the tumor growth, and also underwent radiation. After two years of treatments, he was asymptomatic for two years until, in 2020, small spots showed up on his sacrum and rib.

As of this writing, cancer is still a part of their lives, but they've decided that leaning into adventure and being grateful for every day will always be the bigger part.

Chris told me the South Pole was a defining moment for their marriage. It made them stronger and more grateful and created the desire to do even more adventures together. When I reconnected with them for this book, Chris and Marty were kayaking in the Exumas, in the Bahamas.

Chris told me one thing that's helped them in their life of adventure is that they've really focused on the whole enchilada—the planning and prep, the actual journey, and everything they could take from it afterward. I learned a lot in chatting with Chris.

"We are on this planet to live life fully," she told me. "Once you figure out what your thing is that makes you feel the most alive, I feel like that's what you need to go do. Ultimately, for our son it was to model for him what it feels like to live a full life that makes you feel most alive. That's how you're going to contribute most to the world, I believe."

THROUGH MY OWN wild ideas, and with adventurers like Chris and all the others mentioned in this book as my guides, I've also learned to celebrate a little more along the way. And to give myself grace as my wild ideas have evolved. This has all taken time, of course.

After I got back from the Amazon in 2011, I started to experience depression again. I was covered in bugbites, sick to my stomach, and facing a pile of work I probably should not have taken on. Life was feeling mundane and overwhelming.

I went back to Costa Rica to teach surfing—and this time I surfed every single day. I was usually picky about conditions, but I surfed whether the waves were big, small, scary, choppy, blown out, or glassy and smooth. It was a foggy period that made it hard to get out of bed. But surfing always made me feel better, even though my depression was looming anytime I wasn't in the water.

This came to a head a few weeks later, when I had a surf student who spoke no English, but fluent French and average Spanish. Considering I spoke zero French, we communicated through my below average Spanish, as well as with gestures and smiles. We laughed a lot. At first, she was terrified of paddling to the outside, out past the breaking waves, but she was a fast learner.

I began to do a practice with her where we let the waves explode in front of us and dived under the tumultuous whitewash. I told her in my broken Spanish that, instead of fearing the waves, she should try to relax and imagine the pounding water was giving her a powerful massage. The water was warm, and the bottom was sand. This was one of the most forgiving surf breaks around. Reframing our mindset and surrendering to the ocean worked. She started riding outside waves to shore.

As my French student got over her fears of bigger waves, I got over my fears around dealing with depression. I started to acknowledge it, to write about it, and while people didn't talk as openly about mental health back then as they do now, I started to share my story with others. That alone helped the cloud lift. In many ways, sharing was its own surrender.

I also chilled out. It wasn't long after I taught my French student that Johnny came over with chocolates. Eventually, I surrendered to the idea of being more than friends with Johnny too. I decided to say yes to the adventure of love. Of course, we did it our way. After only two and a half months, we moved to New Zealand, to the small surfing and farm town of Raglan.

We'd planned to go for just two months. One of the reasons we'd fallen in love with each other was our shared values of wanting a life with more adventure. We both wanted to try out another place besides Costa Rica before setting up a permanent nest. But also, I kind of knew that going on a big trip with a guy I'd just met was a great way to test if it was going to work out. Usually on an adventure, the best and the worst of someone comes out. You get to know them really well quickly.

We'd originally planned to go to Nicaragua, but our accommodations, plane tickets, car situation, and just everything about it wasn't lining up so easily. On a whim, I looked at tickets to New Zealand. Serendipitously, it was the same amount of money to travel there at the time. The country was also a place I'd fallen in love with after visiting in college, and had always vowed to return to. Once we bought the plane tickets, the whole trip lined up so flawlessly, I knew I'd made the right decision.

At the time, I was still freelance writing, but I started to listen more to my own intuition about the stories I wanted to tell and was trying to live with more grace rather than continuously proving myself as an adventure journalist.

My wild ideas had also evolved. In New Zealand, I met incredible people—many who seemed so connected to the land and had a sense of humor and honesty I admired. When I went to the pharmacy to buy cotton balls, the cashier told me to go next door to the grocery store, where they were less expensive. When I left my sandals on the beach, someone drove them to my house, along with a pie! The local real estate agent took us caving to find glowworms, never bothering us to actually buy a house from him.

While there, I learned a Maori word, *aroha*. It's similar to the Hawaiian word *aloha*, which means "love," yet so much more. Over the years, I've learned that many cultures, especially indigenous cultures with strong ties to the land, have so many more words that explain things better than English can, especially when it comes to intangible concepts like love and how we view nature.

Aroha is a love for each other. A love for ourselves. A love and also a deep respect for the land and for Mother Nature and our existence. A deeper love than just love.

And love is a big part of living wildly. Love for our land, our bodies, one another, and for what we are capable of when we live with grace, with respect, and especially with kindness. That love extends out from us in rippling waves, not just to the people we meet on our adventures, but to the cultures we experience and, more than anything, to the planet.

In New Zealand, I hiked and surfed a lot. We were regularly stopped by cows and sheep in the road, and around every bend was a vista that evoked awe: a green pasture next to a vibrant blue ocean or a waterfall with a cave underneath and real live glow worms.

WHEN I RETURNED from New Zealand, I took a few marketing jobs and continued to hustle and pitch magazines. I was eventually motivated to start the podcast that became REI Co-op Studios' *Wild Ideas Worth Living*, which led me to this book. While I was living the dream, I have never worked so hard in my life. Being your own boss is not always easy. But I love the flexibility working for myself has given me, and it's an absolute gift to do something I love, with people I adore and enjoy working with.

I've also learned. I don't crash and burn as radically as I used to. I've realized the Will to Wild isn't just about going on adventures: it's about choosing to live with intention, and that intention evolves over time. Don't get me wrong: adventure hasn't cured every single problem, but it has helped me live in a way that makes me feel less alone and more connected to others and the greater world.

One thing adventure has also taught me is to surrender. To control what I can and to let go of what I can't. For example, at age thirty-five, after I got back from New Zealand, I noticed my lips were turning white. At first, I thought it was just sunburn, but turns out to be an autoimmune condition called vitiligo that causes patches of my skin to depigment. Most people don't notice it, but I can if I have a tan (and as someone who surfs a lot, I'm often tan). No one really understands what causes it, and believe me I have spent a good chunk of my hard-earned money on the best natural and Western docs in the world, and all sorts of remedies, potions, lotions, and diets to cure it. It tends to get aggravated by stress, which is challenging because seeing small patches depigment is stressful in itself.

I meditate, I've gone back to that Buddhist monastery in San Diego (a few of the monks now surf!), and I have a lot of wonderful tools I use to cope. Time in nature is still one of my favorite tools. So are the lessons I've learned from my time outside, like the fact that nature doesn't judge you by your skin, and also that nature can withstand a lot of adversity. Most trees just get better with age. Most of all, through my own adventures and time outside, I've come to appreciate the stronger, deeper parts of my own self.

I remind myself often of the lessons from Edith Eger, that I can let my worries imprison me, or choose curiosity over fear. Also, that consciously putting good thoughts in my mind is as important as nourishing my body. For me, time outside is soul food.

One thing that's also changed is as I've grown older, I spend more time in nature with kids—mostly my niece and nephews. I take them on hikes where we sometimes only make it a mile, and spend an inordinate amount of time walking on logs and playing, pretending the earth below is hot lava. The kids have shown me the best parts of adventure: that playful feeling I

had as a kid at camp. Adventure makes us all feel like kids. Best of all, they
have recently learned to surf. For so many years I was the only one in my
family to paddle out in the ocean or even go to the beach, and now that
I've helped teach my niece and nephews to ride waves my entire family
frequents the beach more. It's awesome.

Another thing that's changed is I've been able to connect to so many
listeners and amazing guests pursuing their own wild ideas that their stories have continued to push me to explore new ways to interact outside
and also to help encourage others to go after their own wild ideas. Just to
throw it out there, I'd love to try ice climbing, and there are so many more
places I'd like to explore.

WHEN I GOT TO this part of the book you're now reading, I was having
a hard time with the ending. It felt comically ironic that finishing the part
about finish lines was so hard. Every day for a year and a half, whether I
procrastinated or dived right in, I knew I had a book to write. That wild
idea gave me a big something on my to-do list to look forward to.

Through the writing, I went through all of the emotions of an adventure. I had self-doubt, fear, imposter syndrome. I convinced myself that,
because I'd been podcasting for the last six years, I could no longer craft a
sentence. I went out and bought three different brand-new computers and
an office chair only to return them all and write this whole thing from my
old laptop that I took with me to different places to write, rarely sitting
down. And of course, life threw some serious curveballs. One editor quit.
Another got fired. Two friends passed away from cancer. My stepdad had
an emergency heart procedure. We had some unexpected challenges within
our extended family. Like many of us, I also got COVID and wondered
if it would last forever. Some parts of writing felt especially challenging,
many moments were joyful (especially where I could use the word "penis"),
and some were just like a day at the office. I felt like I was going to puke
writing the parts where I felt most vulnerable—especially about my experience with depression in 2009.

I did my best to follow the steps here and practice what I just wrote. I
listened and looked for signs. I went outside a lot. I used as much courage
as possible to be vulnerable. And I invested in myself by hiring an outside

editor (thank you, Elizabeth!). Eventually, I just sat down to write, and dealt with things when they went haywire (which they did many times). One thing that was challenging is that writing can be such a solo activity, I'm really looking forward to connecting with a wider community after this book actually arrives in bookstores.

In many ways, it's been the perfect adventure. I've come to realize that adventure is often just life magnified. There are parts that are wickedly fun and others that are sometimes mundane. The magic is found along the way, and at the viewpoints.

Before turning in the manuscript, I decided to paddle out at my local break. The surf wasn't great, but I wanted to celebrate, and eventually everyone else went in. I was all alone in the water, so I sat and stared at the bottom of the ocean, looking for a sign, something amazing to tie this book up with a bow.

I was hoping to see a dolphin, a fish, or at least a stingray. For the last few months, I'd been cooped up inside trying to finish this book and recording dozens of podcast episodes. I was working long hours and I felt worn out.

I was desperate for an adventure. I wanted to push myself, and also soak in a change of scenery. I had an idea: I wanted to go back to Rockpile, across from my old apartment in Laguna Beach. I took a wave in, and ran to look at the tide chart posted on the lifeguard tower. High tide was at 2:00 p.m.

I grabbed a towel, put my surfboard in a bag, filled up a water bottle, and drove an hour and half north. As I pulled into Laguna Beach, there was a perfect parking space open, and when I got out of my car to check the surf, Rockpile looked like a postcard. The water was turquoise blue, glassy, with almost zero wind, and absolutely gorgeous. But it was totally flat.

Go figure! I kept watching, and eventually saw a few waves come through. I grabbed my board and decided to give it a go. As I was walking to the break, so many memories came flooding in. I remembered how much angst I'd had about paddling out at Rockpile. About how unsure I was about my life. How uncomfortable I was in my skin, and how awkward I was on my surfboard.

Today, as before, there were three guys in the water. One recognized me from a decade ago, and we had a good laugh.

It was shallower than I remembered, mostly because the waves were so small, so you had to get as close to the rocks as possible. I could feel my feet and then my fins touching them. Then a wave came. As I paddled for it, I felt that same nervous energy go through my body as I used to feel. I looked down and saw only rocks again. No one asked, "Are you gonna go?"

I just paddled hard, then *whoosh*. I made it.

When I paddled back out, one of the guys was taking off on the left. In all my years of surfing Rockpile, I'd never once gone left. Doing so required getting even closer to the rocks. The takeoff was so much closer to the Cheesegrater, you had to time it perfectly to miss it, and it had just seemed silly.

But that day the surf was really small, and by this time I had a lot more years surfing reef breaks under my belt. I was ready. The local told me where to line up. The wave came, I looked down, but my board was headed right for the Cheesegrater. There was no way this was makeable on my small board. He told me to go anyway, but it looked like I was headed straight for the rocks, so I bailed. I paddled back out to try again.

A few minutes later, another wave came. As the rock stared me in the face, I decided to paddle anyway. *Whoosh.* This time, I flew right past it. I didn't even have time to say, "Make it, make it, make it." The mantra is now just embedded in my head. I know I will make it.

I caught a few more waves and then ran back up the stairs and headed home, crusted with salt water. I could feel my energy shift. I'd been in a crappy mood before, but it felt good to have my heart race again, to experience a small thrill in the most beautiful setting. It was another reminder that a little adventure *always* goes a long way. That itself felt like the biggest celebration.

Finish lines are fun. I know I am going to be pretty excited when this book is actually published, but I also know this end is just the start of something entirely new. One thing I am trying to learn is to take the pressure off the outcome. Because the truth is, we have no idea what the finish line will look like most days—if it will rain or be sunny or people will even be there to greet us.

I hope that, if you take anything from this book, you will go outside, get out of your comfort zone, meet new people, pack your own kind of emergency candy, have some fun, and that you'll be kind to others and yourself along the way. I hope you will dive in and get a little dirty. I hope you will take the scenic route if you can, say yes to a kind stranger's request, be a trail angel to someone else, and somehow find your own Will to Wild or your next wild idea. Even if you are starting small, like watching the sunset wherever you are or having your coffee or tea by a tree or a stream, I truly believe a little adventure goes a long way. As I say at the end of every single one of REI Co-op Studios' *Wild Ideas Worth Living* podcasts, some of the best adventures happen when you follow your wildest ideas.

 ProTip: Plan your next adventure before the one you're on is over. Celebrate during it!

APPENDIX 1

REI Co-op's *Wild Ideas Worth Living* Episode List

If you're looking for even more inspiration for your own wild idea, check out my podcast *Wild Ideas Worth Living* at www.Rei.com/WildIdeas WorthLiving or anywhere you can listen to podcasts. A list of guests and episodes through 2022 follows:

2016/2017 Shows
"Steph Jagger—Lift Your Restraining Device"
"Pete Kostelnick—Running across the Country Faster Than Anyone"
"Cindy Whitehead—Stories from a Female Skateboarding Pioneer"
"Joel Van Der Loon—Survival Skills for the Wild and Living Closer to Nature"
"Ryan and Nicole Levinson—TwoAfloat's Nicole and Ryan Levinson on Sailing to French Polynesia to Chase Their Dreams despite Any Limits"
"Alison Teal—How to Thrive on *Naked and Afraid*, Travel the World with a Pink Bikini and Make a Difference in the World"
"James Nestor—The Art of Freediving and Writing an Award-Winning Book"

"Dean Karnazes—Becoming the Ultramarathon Man"

"Bethany Hamilton—How to be Unstoppable and Live Life Fully"

"Jaimal Yogis—Facing Fear with Mindfulness and Love"

"Alana Nichols—Three-Time Paralympic Gold Medalist on Being a Champion No Matter What"

"GracedByGrit—Creating a Business by Women for Women with Kate Nowlan and Kimberly Caccavo"

"Chris Burkard—Becoming a World-Class Adventure Photographer"

"Caroline Paul—How to Cultivate Bravery"

"Brendan Brazier—Creating Plant-Based Nutrition Culture"

"David Goldman—Using Intermittent Fasting and a Whole Food Plant-Based Diet to Produce Optimal Performance"

"Amy Ippoliti—Saving the World with Yoga and Activism"

"Chris Sharma—Tackling Walls and Life with a World Class Climber"

"Sarah Robb O'Hagan—Bringing Your Most Extreme Self to All That You Do"

"Eric Wolfinger—How to Be a World-Class Traveling Food Photographer"

"Becky Mendoza & Emi Koch—How to Protect the Environment, Travel the World, and Give Back to Local Communities"

"Norah Eddy—How to Use Business to Improve the Health of the Oceans"

"Mark Lukach—Writing about a Taboo Topic to Help Others"

"Brogan Graham—Empowering People to Get Fit and Talk to Strangers around the World"

"Devyn Bisson—Creating Documentary Films That Impact Change"

"Gretchen Bayless & Taylor Hood—Living the Van Life and Traveling the World with Roamerica Rentals"

"Izzy Tihanyi—Business in a Bikini: Sharing the Stoke of Surfing"

"Angela Davis—Motivating the Masses and Taking Fitness Seekers to Church on a Bike"

"Rebecca Rusch—Biking the 1.200-Mile Ho Chi Minh Trail in Search of Her Father and Finding Magic"

"Grant Trebilco—Breaking Stereotypes of Mental Health Issues through Surfing"

"Cyrus Sutton—Making Films That Explore How We Interact with Our Planet and Our Passions"

"Damien LeRoy—How to Survive a Paragliding Crash, Be a Professional Adventure Athlete, and Live with Positivity"

"Shanti Hodges—Building Communities by Getting Parents and Kids Outside"

"Steve Casimiro—How to Create an Adventure Media Company and Share Deeper Stories"

"Chris Cote—How to Be a Professional Action Sports Personality"

"Gale Straub—Inspiring Women to Get Outside with a Podcast"

"Zeppelin Zeerip—How to Go Far as a Snowboarder, Activist, and Filmmaker"

"Todd Glaser—How to Become a World-Renowned Surf Photographer"

"Caroline Gleich—Climbing Mountains, Conquering Fears, and Speaking Up to Protect Where We Play Outside"

"Chris Guillebeau—Taking Your Side Hustle from Idea to Income"

"Courtney Conlogue—How to Be a Pro Surfer and Achieve Tough Goals"

"Ari DeLashmutt—Confronting Fear Hundreds of Feet in the Air on a Highline"
"Karen Rinaldi—Why Sucking at Something Can Turn Out Great and How to Publish Stories"
"JP Sears—How to Live an Ultra Spiritual Life and Have a Sense of Humor"
"Kimi Werner—Slowing Down to Have Magical Encounters Underwater"
"Chris McDougall—Writing Untold Stories about Running and Amazing Human Performance"
"Rob Greenfield—Inspiring Others to Live a Low Impact, Sustainable Lifestyle"
"Liz Clark—Learning about Yourself While Living on a Boat and Sailing over 20,000 Miles"
"Willow Belden—Sharing Intimate, Inspiring, and Thoughtful Stories from the Outdoors"
"Cliff Kapono—How We Are Physically and Emotionally Connected to the Ocean"
"Sal Masekela—The Voice of Action Sports on Telling Better Stories"
"Diana Nyad—How to Achieve Impossible Goals like Swimming from Cuba to Florida"
"Dr. Alan Goldhamer—The Crazy Benefits of Water Fasting and Living a Plant-Based SOS-Free Lifestyle"
"Kelly Clark—How to Be the Most Winning Half-Pipe Snowboarder Ever"
"2017 Recap"

2018 Shows
"Mike Coots—How to Be a World-Class Adaptive Surfer, Shark-Attack Survivor, Photographer, and Marine Life Advocate"
"Dr. Rhonda Patrick—Health Hacks for Performance and Longevity"
"Ami Vitale—Traveling the World, Telling Stories, and Creating Awareness through Photography"
"Mirna Valerio—Running Ultramarathons and Being a Beautiful Work in Progress"
"Andy Davis—Making a Living with Enthusiastic, Amazing Art, Inspired by Surf Culture"
"Donna Carpenter—Burton's CEO on Creating an Awesome Company Culture and Resisting the New Normal"
"Outdoor Outreach—Transforming Young Lives through the Outdoors"
"Brendan Leonard—How to Run 100 Miles, Get Paid to Write Books and Blogs, and Make Movies and Cartoons about Adventure"
"Kimmy Fasani—How to Be a Professional Backcountry Snowboarder and Cookie Tester"
"Stacy Bare—Using Adventure to Help Veterans, Yourself, and Others"
"Florence Williams—Proof Being in Nature Can Make You a Healthier, Happier Person"
"Liz Frugalwoods—Retire in Your 30s by Being Financially Frugal"
"Nick Mott and Shelby Stanger—Adventure and Podcasting with REI Co-op's Two New Shows"
"Andrea Bemis—How to Be an Organic Farmer, Feed Your Community, and Publish a Gorgeous Cookbook"

"Jen Sincero—How to Be a Badass at Making Money and Go after What You Want"

"Lacey England—Challenging Stereotypes and Protecting the Outdoors as a Wildland Firefighter"

"Diane Van Deren—How to Run Ultramarathons and Set Records at 58 Despite Brain Surgery"

"Mark McInnis—Turning His Love of the Outdoors into a Photography Career"

"Karen Ramos & Adriana Garcia—Starting a Movement to Encourage Diversity in the Outdoors"

"Catra Corbett—How to Get Sober, Transform Your Life and Become a Record-Breaking Ultramarathon Runner and Author"

"Cheryl Strayed—On Hiking, Getting Outside, Being Kind, and Writing like a MOFO"

"Rebecca Rusch—How to Take Risks and Carve Your Own Trail"

"Michael Finkel—Writing about the Last True Hermit and Other Adventurous Stories"

"Beth Rodden—On Rock Climbing, Living in Yosemite, and Reframing the Perfectionist Mindset"

"Aspen Matis—Finding Emotional and Physical Strength on the Pacific Crest Trail"

"Wim Hof—Using Nature to Rediscover Our Inner Power"

"Scott Carney—Biohacking Your Body Using the Environment, Writing, and Debunking Gurus"

"Scott Jurek—How to Revitalize Your Purpose, Tackle the Longest Trails, Set Records, and Write Best-Selling Books"

"Andy Ruben—Changing the Way Consumerism Works and Saving the Planet with Re-Commerce"

| "Jamie Mitchell—World Champ Paddleboarder and Big Wave Surfer on How to Win Multiple Titles and Care for the Ocean" |
| "Alex Honnold—The World's Best Climber on Free Soloing El Capitan and Putting Yourself Out There" |
| "Courtney Carver—Tackling Autoimmune Disease with Minimalism and Embracing JOMO (the Joy of Missing Out)" |
| "Peter Mel—Balancing Life as a Big Wave Surfer, WSL Commentator, and Family Man" |
| "Rue Mapp—Starting a Movement to Celebrate Diversity and Get more People Outside" |
| "Tate MacDowell—Summiting Grand Teton on Chemotherapy" |
| "Shannon Walker—How to Become an Astronaut and Get a New Perspective on Earth from Space" |
| "Gabby Reece—Advice on Life, Finding Balance, and Optimizing Fitness and Health" |
| "Samin Nosrat—The Adventure of Good Cooking" |
| "Elizabeth Weil—Writing and Publishing Stories about People Who Live Their Wild Ideas" |
| "Eric Goodman—Helping People Optimize Performance and Relieve Pain through Foundation Training" |
| "Jesse Itzler—How to Build Your Life Resume" |
| "2018 Recap" |

2019 Shows
2019 Trailer
"Mindfulness with John Allcock"
"How to Unplug with Danny Kim"
"Creating Art as a Couple with Jimmy Chin and Chai Vasarhelyi"
"Facing Fear with Kim Chambers"
"Design to Empower with Sally Bergesen and Sensi Graves"
"Lessons from a Hawaiian Waterman with Brian Keaulana"
"Adventure Storytelling with Steve Bramucci"
"Earth Day Plastic Pollution with Rob Machado, Alison Teal, and More"
"Making It as a Musician with G. Love"
"The Stuff That Matters with Karen Rinaldi and David Romanelli"
"The Power of Choice with Dr. Edith Eger"
"Be Wildly You with Pattie Gonia"
"Living off the Land with Rob Greenfield"
"What to Cook While Camping with Brad Leone, Anna Brones, and Brendan Leonard"
"The Making of Bethany Hamilton: Unstoppable with Director Aaron Lieber"
"Making It as an Artist with Loveis Wise and Lisa Congdon"
"Lessons from Extreme Adventurers with Jerry Holl, Julie Hotz, and Ryan Higginbotham"
"The Importance of Doing Nothing with Bonnie Tsui"
"The Adventure of Self-Love with Sarah Herron"

"Climbing Mountains with Caroline Gleich"
"Finding Your True North with Emily Miller"
"Running with Donkeys with Chris McDougall"
"Recycling with Helen Lowman"
"Not Impossible with Mick Ebeling"
"Whole Health with Melissa Hartwig Urban"
"2019 Recap"

2020 Shows
"Chris Fagan: South Pole Quest"
"Jeremy Jones: Protect Our Winters"
"Latoya Shauntay Snell: Running Fat Chef"
"Shanti Hodges: Getting Kids Outside"
"Ben Finley & Art Clay: Brotherhood of Skiing"
"Mike Posner: Becoming Someone You're Proud Of"
"Changing Course"
"Breathwork with James Nestor"
"Redefining Routine with Latoya Shauntay Snell"
"Baking Bread with Eric Wolfinger"
"Finding Humor with Brendan Leonard"
"Bonus Episode: Favorite Outdoor Memories with Selema Masekela, Chris McDougall, and Bonnie Tsui"
"The Greatness of Dogs with Ben Moon"
"Wildlife at Yosemite with Park Ranger Jamie Richards"
"Challenging the Status Quo with Joe Gray"
"GirlTrek: Black History Bootcamp—Nina Simone"
"Amber Pierce—Reframing Competition for Women"
"Meagan Martin: Climbing Warrior"
"Holistic Lifestyle and Business with Joe Kudla"
"Gambling in the Winds with Jesse Huey"
"Cycling through Changes with Laura King"
"Diversifying Surfing with Textured Waves"

"Cycling Is for Every Body with Kailey Kornhauser"
"Designing Gear for Women with Edita Hadravska"
"Building Products to Last with Christiane Dolva"
"Ally Coucke: A Girl and Her Dog"
"Running for a Cause with Clare Gallagher"
"The Dark Divide with Tom Putnam"
"Backcountry Skiing with Noah Howell"
"A Look Back at 2020"

2021 Shows
"Learning Something New with Dylan Efron"
"For the Love of Birding with Corina Newsome"
"Running the AT and PCT with Karel Sabbe"
"Connected by Speed with David Brown and Jerome Avery"
"Freeskiing with Michelle Parker"
"Healing in the Outdoors with Adam Campbell"
"A Good Day with Brett Eldredge"
"Preserving Our Parks with Keith Eshelman and Sevag Kazanci"
"Climbing Mountains with Tyrhee Moore"
"Grow Cycling with Eliot Jackson"
"Running Slow with Susan Lacke"
"The Trees Remember with Angela Tucker"
"Mental Health, Music, and the Wild with Joseph Mulherin"
"A Triumphant Return to Triathlon with Sika Henry"
"Road-Tripping with Mikah Meyer"
"Bonus Episode: The KEEN Effect"
"Being a Trail Angel with Barney and Sandy Mann"
"Outdoor Defense with Nicole Snell"
"Exploring National Parks with Misha Euceph"
"The Power of Nature with Florence Williams"
"Climbing on the Global Stage with Alannah Yip"
"Cold Water Surfing with Pete Devries"
"Finding Bigfoot with Cliff Barackman"

"Making Room to Dream with Ryan Kinder"
"Outdoor Outreach with Lesford Duncan"
"Connecting with Indigenous Roots with Christian Gering"
"Trail Sisters with Gina Lucrezi"
"Bonus Episode: Nutrition with On Running and Alicia Monson"
"Bonus Episode: Training with On Running and Allie McLoughlin"
"Bonus Episode: Recovery with On Running and Leah Falland"
"A Look Back at 2021"

2022 Shows
"Welcome to Wild Ideas Worth Living"
"Spirit of the Peaks with Connor Ryan"
"Deeply Moving with Elena Cheung"
"Embracing the Unexpected with Tim Brown"
"Growing a Garden with Marcus Bridgewater"
"Climbing Everest with Eddie Taylor"
"Diversifying Design with Angela Medlin"
"Unity Runners with Nicol Hodges"
Celebrating Women's History Month Trailer
"Cook Out with Chef Maria Hines"
"How to Suffer Outside with Diana Helmuth"
"Seven Summits with Erin Parisi"
"Heartbreak with Florence Williams"
"An Inclusive Outdoors with Lucienne Nicholson"
"Torn with Max Lowe"
"Running for Change with Nicole Ver Kuilen"
"Making Gear for Good with Davis Smith"
"Remembering Our Mothers with Steph Jagger"
"Creating Thousand with Gloria Hwang"
"Cave Diving with Rick Stanton"
"Getting Kids Outside with Raquel Gomez"
"Wayward with Chris Burkard"
"Embracing Adventure with Brittany Washington"

"Adventure and Business with David Sacher"

"Life on the Road with Noami Grevemberg"

"Photographing Home with Mylo Fowler"

"Adventuring Outside with Miranda Webster"

"Building a Running Community with Iman Wilkerson"

"Healing in the Mountains with Silvia Vasquez-Lavado"

"Adventuring at Any Age with Laurie Watt"

"Finding Yourself in Climbing with Mario Stanley"

"Making Art Outside with David Zinn"

"Unconventional Ultra Running with Katie Arnold"

"Riding Waves with the Boogie Board Wave Chasers"

"Wildfires and Imperfect Activism with Graham Zimmerman"

"Walking Around the World with Tom Turcich"

"All Bodies on Bikes with Marley Blonsky"

"We Are Nature with Rue Mapp"

"Equity and Climate Justice with Leah Thomas"

"Indigenous Brewing with Missy Begay and Shyla Sheppard"

"Making Indigenous Art with Louie Gong"

"Winter Treks with Emily Ford"

"Building Green Space with Stacy Bare"

"Motorcycles and Mindfulness with Monica Ramos"

"Hike Clerb with Evelyn Escobar"

"Rafting for Peace with Mauricio Artinano"

"Streets to Peaks with Ryan Hudson"

"Paracycling with Meg Fisher"
"Movement Diet with Katy Bowman"
"Looking Back at 2022"

There are fifty new shows releasing in 2023, so you can find and listen to them by typing in *Wild Ideas Worth Living* wherever you listen to podcasts.

APPENDIX 2

Awesome Outdoor Organizations

There are hundreds of outdoor organizations and groups doing great things outdoors—even one where you can find a job in the outdoor industry. Here are some of the outdoor organizations and groups I've come across while interviewing guests for *Wild Ideas Worth Living*, and their mission at the time of writing this book.

Organization Name	Website	Mission
All Bodies on Bikes	https://allbodies onbikes.com/	Creating and fostering a size-inclusive bike community
American Alpine Club	https:// americanalpine club.org/	Sharing and supporting our passion for climbing and respect for the places we climb
Basecamp Outdoor	https://wearethe outdoorindustry .com/	The place to find careers in the outdoors and more
Black Girls RUN!	https:// blackgirlsrun.com/	Encouraging and promoting Black women to practice a healthy lifestyle

Challenged Athletes Foundation	https://challenged athletes.org/	Providing support to athletes with physical disadvantages
Changing Tides Foundation	https://changing tidesfoundation .org/	"Empowering women to protect the planet"
City Kids Wilderness Project	https://citykidsdc .org	"A non-profit organization founded on the belief that providing enriching life experiences for DC children can enhance their lives, the lives of their families, and the greater community"
Continental Divide Trail Association	https://continental dividetrail.org/	Working to complete, promote, and protect the Continental Divide National Scenic Trail
Courageous Girls	https://courageous girls.org/	Healing and empowering survivors of violence and abuse through adventures in nature
First Decents	https://first descents.org/	Providing life-changing outdoor adventures for young adults (ages 18–39) impacted by cancer and other serious health conditions
Get Out, Stay Out/ Vamos Afuera	http://vamosafuera .org/	"Grassroots, Central Coast nonprofit that invites Indigenous Migrant youth to run, play, and discover themselves in the natural environment"

GirlVentures	https://girl ventures.org/	Inspiring girls to lead through outdoor adventure, inner discovery, and collective action
Greening Youth Foundation	https://gy foundation.org/	Engaging "under-represented youth and young adults, while connecting them to the outdoors and careers in conservation"
Grow Cycling Foundation	http://growcycling foundation.org	Promoting "education, access, and opportunities that increase participation and diversity in cycling"
High Fives Foundation	https://highfives foundation.org/	An Adaptive Sports foundation to help athletes achieve their goals
Hike It Baby	https://hikeitbaby .com/	Connecting families with babies and young children to the outdoors and to one another
Latino Outdoors	https://latino outdoors.org/	Inspiring, connecting, and engaging Latino communities in the outdoors
Native Women's Wilderness	https://native womenswilderness .org/	Inspiring and raising "the voices of Native Women in the Outdoor Realm," encouraging "a healthy lifestyle within the Wilderness," and providing "education of the Ancestral Lands and its People"

OneWave	https://onewave isallittakes.com/	"Raising awareness of mental health through" a simple recipe: "saltwater therapy, surfing and fluro"
Out There Adventures	http://outthere adventures.org/	"Fostering positive identity development, individual empowerment and improved quality of life for queer young people through professionally facilitated experiential education activities"
Outdoor Afro	https://outdoorafro .org/	Celebrating and inspiring Black connections and leadership in nature
Outdoor Outreach	https://outdoor outreach.org/	Connecting youth to the power of the outdoors
Outdoorist Oath	https://outdoor istoath.org	Encouraging people to make a commitment to the planet, inclusion, and adventure
Pacific Crest Trail Association	https://www.pcta .org/	Protecting preserving, and promoting "the Pacific Crest National Scenic Trail as a world-class experience for hikers and equestrians, and for all the values provided by wild and scenic lands"
Run Down app	https:// therundown .run/	Connecting runners to their local running community in major cities such as LA, San Diego, and more to come

SheJumps	https://shejumps.org/	Inspiring people to jump beyond their limitations, helping women and girls take risks in the outdoors to enable them to break through fears and internal/external barriers in life so they can grow to their full potential
SOS Outreach	https://sosoutreach.org	Working to change young lives by "building character and leadership in underserved kids through mentoring outdoors"
Stoked Mentoring	https://stoked.org/	Empowering "underserved youth to reach their fullest potential, instilling passion, resilience and determination" through mentoring and board sports culture
Textured Waves	https://www.texturedwaves.com/	Propagating "the culture and sport of women's surfing towards women of color and underrepresented demographics through representation, community and sisterly camaraderie"

ACKNOWLEDGMENTS

Writing this book was its own will to wild, but without as much time in the elements.

I wrote this book in many places, in different spurts, and at different points in my life. Some of my own personal stories came from diary entries years ago, including the story about my dad that was first written when I was eleven, and the story about my depression written when I was twenty-nine. It wasn't easy, and as with all my adventures, there were a lot of people who helped get me to the finish line.

First, my love, Johnny, who encouraged me to start a podcast many years ago, and who is my favorite person to pursue and enjoy wild ideas with. Thank you for also being a great editor. Blame Johnny for any mistakes, please.

To the entire team at REI, who took on my podcast when podcasts were still new and proving themselves, thank you. Paolo Mottola and Joe Crosby, for your leadership and vision. Chelsea Davis for taking *Wild Ideas Worth Living* to another level, and Jenny Barber, who is carrying the torch. To all of the folks at REI Co-op who outfit and advocate for all to enjoy the outdoors, it's an honor to work with such a great company doing so much good!

To the rest of the *Wild Ideas* podcast team: Annie Fassler, who has been with me since the first few shows; Sylvia Thomas, who has been an incredible addition to the team; and to the entire Puddle Creative Podcast team, the podcast is richer because of you. Thank you also to Sylvia

Mah, who helped me with my original podcast business plan, and to Harry Duran, who helped me get the first few episodes off the ground.

When it came to actually writing this book, there was one person who metaphorically held my hand during the whole process: Elizabeth Hightower Allen. You served as an all-purpose editor and book therapist who helped me get unstuck and craft words into pages. I really hope we hug in-person soon. Florence Williams, you are a genius for recommending her!

My writing and editorial friends: Steph Jagger, Kimberly Johnson, Chris McDougall, Silvia Vasquez-Lavado, Florence Williams, Scooter Leonard, Steve Bramucci, Gretchen Stelter, Kai Sotto, Caroline Paul, Shanti Hodges, Gale Straub, Karen Rinaldi, Bonnie Tsui, Gillian Flynn, Lora Bodmer, Sunshine Makarow, Alison Guidry Gates, Jaimal Yogis, Douglas Evans Weiss, Jim House, and James Nestor—you gave me wonderful editorial insight early on, and I so appreciate you!

Thank you to everyone I wrote about in this book. Because I had to re-interview almost all fifty of you, most of you received multiple calls and emails from me. Some of you were even on adventures when I reached out. Alex Honnold once answered my email from a satellite phone on a glacier! If you are inside this book, thank you for being you, for pursuing your wild idea, for inspiring me, and letting me share some of your story. To those inside who are also authors—thank you for your invaluable wisdom on the adventures of book writing.

There were many more stories from podcast guests I wanted to tell, but books have page limits. Thank you to those who agreed to appear in this book, and to everyone I've ever interviewed for the podcast or an adventure story.

I only talked about the specifics of this book to a few people, mostly my Saturday surf crew: Yassi Mesbahzadeh, Izzy Tihanyi, and Alisa Valderrama; thank you for making me laugh at myself and for letting me drop in on you. Izzy Tihanyi, Amy Sabreen, Chelsea Davis, and Laurie Watt were the first to read any pages of this book. Laurie Watt also advised on adventure technical details.

To the rest of my surfing, coffee-ing, walking, and running buddies and neighbors who cheered me on during this adventure, and even those inside this book, thank you for checking in about my writing. I'm looking forward to in-person hugs and parties!

Todd Glaser, Jenna Glaser and Sarah Lee—you are absolute photo pros. Thank you for the photos that I'm using to promote this book and the adventurous photoshoots!

Thank you also to every journalism and writing teacher I've ever had. I agree with you: reading is helpful for writing. I'll try to read more before I write the next one!

To the Harmony Hotel in Nosara, Costa Rica, especially to Monica Ramos, Lee Bailly, and crew—you provided the best place in the world to finish this book, and I'm grateful for the sanctuary and community you've fostered, especially the howler monkeys above your property that never let me sleep in past 6 a.m.

To my favorite coffee shops around the world (you know who you are)—thank you for letting me overstay my hour of internet usage, refills of long blacks with steamed almond milk and mocha, and summertime cups of cold brew. Thanks especially for indulging my humor, and for ignoring me when I told you I was giving up caffeine.

To my family—my mom, Louise Stanger, for always encouraging my wild ideas, and for leading by example. You are the biggest badass I know. I love you! My stepdad, John Wadas, who always answers my calls when I need him, you are such a rock in our lives. My sisters, Felicia and Sydney, who also embrace a life of wild ideas, thank you for paving the path. I love our 6:30 a.m. phone calls and am so grateful for your unconditional love and support, and also for having kids because niece-and-nephew time is the best! And thank you for letting me write about you . . . or not about you.

To my agent, Danielle Svetcov—you are a wizard. Thank you for your hustle, for getting me a book deal, and for always being willing to pick up your phone, lend an ear, and give sound advice. There are more great things to come from this. My attorney, Jim Kiick, you rock!

Simon & Schuster—my first choice in publisher for so many reasons beyond that we have the same initials. Thank you for taking a chance on a first-time author with a lot of energy. Ronnie Alvarado, thank you for your guidance, experience, and editorial wisdom. To the rest of the team at Simon & Schuster, I know it takes a village to get a book into the world. Thank you to Richard Rhorer, Emma Taussig, Elizabeth Breeden, Nan Rittenhouse, Suzanne Donahue, Jessie McNeil, Laura Jarrett, Greta

Skagerlind, and Laura Levatino. A spine on a shelf looks and feels pretty sweet.

If I accidentally overlooked you, sorry. If you found a typo, you're not alone!

To everyone who has ever listened to one of my podcasts, written a review, shared your own wild idea with me, thank you.

The adventure continues . . .

Wildly with love,
Shelby

ABOUT THE AUTHOR

Shelby Stanger is a journalist and the host and creator of the award-winning podcast, *Wild Ideas Worth Living,* an REI Co-op Studios Production. Over the years, Shelby has surfed from Canada to Costa Rica; sandboarded down desolate dunes in Cape Town; paddled down a remote portion of the Amazon River (so many bug bites); and interviewed countless CEOs, athletes, and activists. Her journalism work has appeared in publications like *Outside Magazine,* ESPN, CNN, *The San Diego Tribune,* and *Surfer Magazine.* In between adventures and podcasts, Shelby consults with highly motivated individuals and brands to tell better stories, and to even launch their own podcasts and wild ideas. She continues to be passionate about how we can use the power of adventure to improve our mental wellbeing. Catch Shelby live at a speaking event, sign up for her newsletter, and find more at www.shelbystanger.com.